POSITIVE YOUTH JUSTICE

Children First, Offenders Second

Kevin Haines and Stephen Case

First published in Great Britain in 2015 by

Policy Press
University of Bristol
1-9 Old Park Hill
Bristol BS2 8BB
UK
t: +44 (0)117 954 5940
pp-info@bristol.ac.uk
www.policypress.co.uk

North America office:
Policy Press
c/o The University of Chicago Press
1427 East 60th Street
Chicago, IL 60637, USA
t: +1 773 702 7700
f: +1 773 702 9756
sales@press.uchicago.edu
www.press.uchicago.edu

British Library Cataloguing in Publication Data
A catalogue record for this book is available from the British Library.

Library of Congress Cataloging-in-Publication Data
A catalog record for this book has been requested.

ISBN 978 1 44732 171 2 paperback
ISBN 978 1 44732 173 6 ePub
ISBN 978 1 44732 174 3 Kindle

Cover design by Qube Design Associates, Bristol
Front cover: image kindly supplied by Getty Images

Contents

List of tables and figures

Tables

Figures

About the authors

Kevin Haines is Professor of Youth Justice in the Department of Criminology at Swansea University. Kevin has published extensively on youth justice and children's rights issues. He co-authored the seminal texts *Young people and youth justice* and *Understanding youth offending: Risk factor research, policy and practice.*

Stephen Case is Associate Professor in Criminal Justice and Criminology in the Department of Criminology at Swansea University. He has published in a range of international journals and conducted research for the Youth Justice Board, Home Office and Welsh Government.

Acknowledgements

This book is the product of a long-standing reflective research partnership between the authors, research colleagues at Swansea University Centre for Criminal Justice and Criminology and policy makers and practitioners primarily within and associated with Swansea youth offending team. Over a near 20-year period, the youth offending team has opened its doors and minds to researchers, offering unrivalled access to its steering group, senior management team, front-line practitioners, operational and strategic meetings, policy and practice documentation, statistical databases and, perhaps most importantly, to the children and families who have come into contact with the youth justice system. A series of long-term, reflective research and evaluation projects have resulted, with children, families, practitioners, policy makers and researchers working collaboratively to identify issues, strengthen relationships, improve practice and enhance outcomes for local children within and outwith the youth justice system. As researchers, we are acutely aware of the privileged position in which we find ourselves, thanks to the openness, honesty, integrity and insight of the staff at Swansea youth offending team and its partner agencies across the local authority area and further afield in Wales, along with those children and families who have offered their crucial perspectives and experiences. We offer profound thanks to those individuals and organisations for their dedicated and continued support, professionalism and contributions as our research partners.

INTRODUCTION

A Children First, Offenders Second philosophy of positive youth justice

It is absolutely essential that all professionals in the youth justice system (YJS) have a guiding philosophy of practice for their work with children; a sense of objective and purpose to frame and animate their knowledge and skills bases. Without a coherent and explicit philosophy, policies and practitioner knowledge are simply information and understanding; practitioner skills are simply abilities, expertise and techniques; lacking in foundation and application. A youth justice philosophy 'gives purpose to action … [and]… shapes the way in which we use knowledge and skills to achieve certain outcomes' (Haines and Drakeford 1998: 69). Since the inception of a YJS in the UK and latterly in the constituent countries of the UK (England and Wales together, Scotland, Northern Ireland), youth justice policy and practice has been characterised by tensions between *welfare* principles and *justice*-based approaches to dealing with children in conflict with the law and the youth justice system (for a detailed historical account of the development of youth justice in England and Wales, see Muncie, Hughes and McLaughlin 2002; Newburn and Morgan 2007). These overarching philosophies have fluctuated between dominating youth justice priorities and each has been marginalised at the expense of the other, although elements of both have persisted in successive manifestations of policy and practice targeting children in conflict with the law and the youth justice system, rendering youth justice a messy, complex and contested domain (see Smith 2006).

The ambiguity and ambivalence that has pervaded youth justice in England and Wales was compounded from the late 1980s onwards by the emergence, on the one hand, of a corporatist philosophy that sought to engender multi-agency partnership working between youth justice stakeholders and to manage the YJS effectively and efficiently (see, for example, Pratt 1989) and 'New Orthodoxy' (see, for example, Haines and Drakeford 1998) practice, on the other. A so-called 'third way' approach (not welfare, not justice) to the delivery of youth justice emerged following the *Misspent Youth* report (Audit Commission 1996) and New Labour's commitment to a managerialist,[1] actuarialist risk agenda manifested in risk assessment and risk-led intervention (see Smith 2006; Case and Haines 2009). This book offers an extensive critique of the contemporary managerialist, risk-based model of youth justice that dominate and shape practice; making a detailed, evidence-informed case for a new model of youth justice founded on a Children First, Offenders Second (CFOS) philosophy. The proposed model of positive youth justice, CFOS, is driven by systems management and child-friendly and child-appropriate techniques and is committed to the principles of enabling children to access and actualise their rights and entitlements, to achieve social inclusion through participation and engagement – principles that have informed and guided elements of (inter)national policies and practices for working with children since the 1980s – and to enhance positive outcomes for children.

A brief history of progressive-regressive youth justice agendas

In order to understand the genesis and development of CFOS, it is helpful to briefly review some of the major themes and developments in youth justice that preceded it. In the 1980s, a diverse group of academic critics, senior civil servants and innovative youth justice practitioners began to gain a foothold by consistently warning against the damaging effects of formal

---

[1] A set of techniques to reorganise youth justice structures and processes in order to prioritise effectiveness, efficiency and economy (Muncie, in Goldson 2008a).

state intervention on the lives of children, while proffering strong support for changes to youth justice practice, based on:

- **diversion** – using cautioning as a way of diverting children from the YJS;
- **alternatives to custody** – using community-based interventions instead of custody for children.

Throughout the 1980s, the use of cautioning measures expanded rapidly within the YJS and alternatives to custody became a (near) universal provision (Bottoms et al 1990), with levels of both custody and recorded juvenile crime decreasing across the decade: a phenomenon which Allen (1991) has characterised as 'the successful revolution'. The strongly pro-diversion and anti-custody ethos of 1980s' youth justice policy was labelled 'new orthodoxy' thinking (see Haines and Drakeford 1998) and gave a guiding philosophy to a body of practice that was underpinned by an emerging research/evidence base, which suggested that much formal intervention with children was potentially unnecessary and could be extremely damaging because:

- **offending by children had become an exaggerated phenomenon** – most offending by children was trivial in nature and the majority of offenders would mature out of crime naturally without intervention (compare Rutherford 2002; see also Glueck and Glueck 1930);
- **formal intervention was detrimental and counter-productive –** involvement with the YJS served to label children as 'offenders', such that they grew to live up to this label (that is Labelling Theory – see Becker 1963; Lemert 1967); a self fulfilling prophecy which accelerated the severity of future sanctions applied to children ('up-tariffing' – Barry and McNeill 2009) and led to certain services (especially welfare-based interventions) bringing increasing numbers of children into contact with formal systems of control ('net-widening' – Cohen 1985).

Alongside the new orthodoxy's research-based and theoretical/ philosophical objections to formal intervention and the consequent promotion of diversionary approaches, new orthodoxy thinking was animated and directed by the application of a technical systems management model (see Tutt and Giller 1987), which conceived of the YJS an interconnected and mutually reinforcing series of decision-making points. In this perspective, the criminal justice process and diversionary goals could be positively 'influenced by targeting specific decision-making points in the process whereby the outcome for particular individuals may be changed' (Bell and Haines 1991: 121).

The punitive turn to regressive youth justice

By the early 1990s, diversion had become widely accepted as a 'hugely beneficial way of dealing with the mass of young people who become peripherally involved in crime' (Haines and Drakeford 1998: 105). However, despite the continuing acknowledgement of the success of pre-court diversionary practices and cautioning into the early 1990s (see Department of Health 1994), diversionary practices began to come under attack in the early 1990s from official sources such as the then Home Secretary Michael Howard, who accused local authorities of 'bringing cautioning into disrepute' (Home Office 1994: paragraph 7). These attacks were politically motivated, rhetorical and rarely grounded in empiricism, an approach that became an ironic theme of policy generation and critique emerging from successive governments otherwise committed to 'evidence-based' policy and practice (see also Goldson and Hughes 2010).

The new decade witnessed a sea change in youth justice, away from more welfare-oriented diversionary principles and towards a sentencing philosophy and policy grounded in the *justice*-based 'just deserts' approach outlined in the Criminal Justice Act 1991. The just deserts model required courts to undertake a balanced consideration of the severity of an offence alongside offender information such as age, attitude, maturity, culpability and reasons for offending, then to select an appropriate sentence from a 'tariff' of sentencing options (see Haines and Drakeford 1998). The move to a just deserts philosophy heralded a 'punitive turn' within the YJS of England and Wales and, indeed, across Westernised juvenile justice systems more generally (Muncie

200b), characterised by neoconservative correctionalism (striving to punish and correct perceived deficiencies in the individual) and neoliberal responsibilisation (holding children and parents responsible for offending behaviour due to a contradictory combination of agency/choice and an inability to resist or negotiate risks). The punitive turn led to an increased governmental authoritarianism, precipitating youth justice policies and practices that, to a large extent, either breached or ignored the guidelines for the treatment of children enshrined in a growing body of children's rights conventions, most notably the United Nations Convention on the Rights of the Child 1989 (UNICEF 1989; see also Muncie 2008b).

Managerialism and risk: New Labour and the 'new youth justice'

The welfare versus justice debate that had driven policy and practice development since a formalised YJS was legislated into existence in the UK was rendered obsolete by the incumbent 'New' Labour administration in 1997. The Labour government came to power in the context of rapid globalisation and the emergence of a 'risk society' (Beck 1992), alongside the Tory legacy of increasing public concern over crime levels and the (in)ability of the YJS to deal effectively with the perceived youth crime problem (Case and Haines 2009). Their response was a clinical and (some would argue) cynical root and branch reform of the YJS. Reflecting the punitive turn in international youth justice and channelling the recommendations of the *Misspent Youth* report (Audit Commission 1996) and the White Paper *No More Excuses* (Home Office 1997), the government pushed through the groundbreaking Crime and Disorder Act 1998, which mercilessly swept aside welfare and justice concerns in favour of a bold refocusing of youth justice priorities on the (predominantly risk-focused) prevention[2] of offending by

[2] As we go on to discuss at length in Chapter Six, the concept of crime *prevention* used in the Crime and Disorder Act 1998 can be more accurately understood as the prevention of 'risk factors' influencing the lives of children and the consequent *reduction* of offending by 'at risk' children and those convicted of an offence.

children and improving the functioning and operation of the YJS (Case and Haines 2009). The Crime and Disorder Act 1998 emphasised the need to ground youth justice practice, particularly crime reduction interventions, in a thorough (risk) assessment of the likelihood that children who came to the attention of the YJS would reoffend. The prioritisation of risk as the dominant (although not exclusive) driver of youth justice policy and practice and the sweeping, contested conclusions of risk factor research (see Case and Haines 2009 for a detailed critique) underpinned the application of the risk factor prevention paradigm across youth justice practice (simply put, the identification of risk through assessment and the targeting of this risk through intervention). The risk movement that swept across youth justice in England and Wales enabled the Labour government to 'other' children – to individualise the blame for offending and thus to responsibilise children (their families and, to a lesser extent, local communities) for their behaviour – to the neglect of wider social or government responsibility. This manifesto was shaped and directed centrally by the creation of a government 'quango' (quasi-autonomous non-government agency), the Youth Justice Board for England and Wales, whose function was to manage and monitor the performance of newly created multi-agency youth offending teams (YOTs) in every local authority area. In this way, the government was able to perpetuate a dichotomy of centralised–localised youth justice through a managerialist agenda. Privileging risk allowed the government to utilise managerialism to simultaneously demonise children in conflict with the law and the youth justice system and to control the central–local relationship and the practice of YOT staff.

Notwithstanding the risk-led, punitive, controlling and managerialist youth justice agenda emerging from Westminster (the English base of the UK government) in the late 1990s,[3] a distinct form of youth justice policy has emerged in Wales since its partial devolution in 1999; all the more notable because youth justice remains a non-devolved policy area to this day. A 'dragonised' model of youth justice (so-called because the Welsh flag contains a dragon as its national symbol – see Haines 2009b; Edwards and Hughes 2009) has been manifested in policy terms by a CFOS philosophy of positive youth justice: through adult practitioners taking responsibility for enabling children's access to a series of universal 'entitlements' to support, guidance, information and services (National Assembly Policy Unit 2002), by addressing social needs and by treating children in the YJS as 'children first and offenders second' (Welsh Assembly Government (WAG) and Youth Justice Board (YJB) 2004: 3). The notion of a CFOS positive youth justice arguably remains aspirational and, to some extent, rhetorical across Wales, yet we will argue that it has been animated and evidenced over a number of years within youth justice practice in Swansea, producing significant reductions in first-time entrants into the YJS and reconviction rates among those children who have received youth justice disposals, alongside significant improvements in children's self-perceived levels of participation and engagement in services and in practitioners' perceptions of the quality of local multi-agency practice.

This book seeks to identify, explain and evaluate the bases, processes and outcomes of CFOS positive youth justice policy and practice, to contrast them with the dominant risk-based practices of the contemporary YJS and to situate them in the broader youth justice context. We will endeavour throughout

[3] We are mindful throughout of the dangers of over-simplifying, caricaturing and homogenising youth justice policy and practice in England and Wales and acknowledge that there is significant local mediation of policy and variation in philosophy and practice within – and between – countries (compare the Scaled Approach discussion of Haines and Case 2012 and the diversion discussion of Smith 2014). However, our intention is to characterise and contrast the *dominance* of risk-led policy and practice in England with the Children First social policy of Wales. Our recommended CFOS model of positive youth justice emerges from an interrogation of these policy and practice influences and the model's transferability internationally is evaluated in this context (see, for example, Chapter Seven).

to be attendant to the inherent complexities, dynamism and vicissitudes of youth justice. It is crucial to be sensitive to issues such as the structurally, politically and culturally contingent differences between and within youth justice and related (multi) agencies across countries, the potential disparities between political rhetoric and practical realities (for example influenced by the local mediation of centralised policy requirements) and the varying quality, range and influence of the empirical evidence used to underpin policies and practices. Our primary focus will be England and Wales because this is the context within which the principles and practices of CFOS positive youth justice have emerged and evolved as a direct challenge to the existing order, although we believe a CFOS-based approach has much to offer youth justice systems across the world.

Chapter synopses

In the opening chapter, 'Positive youth justice: introducing Children First, Offenders Second', we set out the philosophies and principles of CFOS and its objective to deliver special treatment to children. The model is outlined as reactionary against the punitive, controlling, stigmatising risk-based 'new youth justice' that dominates in England and Wales, while simultaneously offering a progressive and principled model of positive youth justice; a modern and distinctive economic-normative paradigm with its foundations in children's rights conventions. We then discuss the necessary complexity within CFOS and how this informs its approach to dealing with socio-structural inequalities and the prevention and intervention agendas. The chapter concludes having set out the terrain and principles for the CFOS model of positive youth justice, which we expand upon in subsequent chapters.

The following chapter, 'What is Children First, Offenders Second?', outlines and explores the central tenets of CFOS as a positive form of youth justice, contrasting each tenet with the guiding features of traditional and contemporary approaches to youth justice. CFOS positive youth justice is discussed as: child friendly and child appropriate (not adulterised), diversionary (not punishment, justice or welfare based), based on prevention as inclusionary (not exclusionary), evidence-based partnership (not programme fetishism), legitimate (not labelling and stigmatising), driven by systems management (not unprincipled net widening), a partnership with the state (not distrustful of the state) and responsibilising adults (not children). The purpose of this chapter is to set out clearly what CFOS looks like – what it *is* and what it most definitely *is not*.

Chapter Three explores 'The context of Children First, Offenders Second positive youth justice: evolution through devolution', with an overarching focus on *policy*. It charts the legislative 'evolution' of a managerialist, individualising and responsibilising form of youth justice (and arguably social policy) in England and Wales since the Crime and Disorder Act 1998 – a decidedly *offender first* and *offence first* response to working with children in conflict with the law and the youth justice system. This 'new youth justice' is contrasted with the geo-political context for a CFOS positive youth justice policy and practice in Wales, which has been driven by an evolving, distinctive identity of Welsh social policy since partial devolution in 1999 – characterised by universalism, participation, engagement and the pursuit of children's rights and entitlements. The relationship between Welsh social policy and an emerging national identity for youth justice policy is explored, as is the developing devolution of the youth justice agenda in Wales, which has been animated by a series of governmental reviews and bespoke national structures. We conclude by re-emphasising that government policy rhetoric is not necessarily realised (in whole or part) in practical realities at the local and national level for a variety of reasons, discussed in the subsequent chapters.

Chapter Four, 'Putting children first in the youth justice system', discusses and evaluates the managerialism that pervades the YJS in England and Wales – the management of the risk of reoffending presented by children through management of the performance, practice methods and foci of YOT staff. Particular critique is aimed at the reductionist, individualising and responsibilising Scaled Approach to risk-based assessment and intervention and at the disengaging nature of contemporary youth justice practice, which neglects the important voices of children and practitioners. We then explore the potential of the proposed revised assessment and intervention framework, AssetPlus, scrutinising its claims to reforming youth justice processes away from a risk focus and towards more positive and inclusionary practice, including more engagement with children's perspectives (through self-assessment) and practitioner discretion. We move on to a detailed examination of the role of children's *engagement* in the YJS and how this can be facilitated by their meaningful *participation* and practitioner discretion. The chapter concludes by advocating for the CFOS treatment of children in conflict with the law and the youth justice system – a model underpinned by systems management, guided by evidence-based partnership and driven by the participation and engagement of children, families and practitioners to generate meaningful, valid, promotional and future-focused practice.

Chapter Five examines 'Progressive diversion', moving beyond statutory responses within the YJS to consider a CFOS approach to diverting children away from the iatrogenic influence of formal intervention and contact with the YJS. We review the 1980s 'decade of diversion', animated by the successful use of cautioning, intermediate treatment programmes and juvenile liaison bureaux, and how diversion fell out of political favour in the 1990s in England and Wales as government pursued tougher, more responsibilising approaches to offending by children. The resultant movement of interventionist diversion through antisocial behaviour management and the reduction of first-time entrants into the YJS is explored; the former as a form of net widening and criminalising, labelling treatment of children; the latter as indicative of practice changes across youth justice organisations, particularly the police. The chapter concludes by discussing progressive diversion, using empirically supported local examples of evidence-based partnership and engagement in antisocial behaviour management and bureau diversion schemes, which demonstrate the potential for animating CFOS principles in a diversionary context to realise positive outcomes for children and their families.

The penultimate chapter, 'Progressive prevention-promotion', scrutinises the way in which successive governments have conceptualised and animated 'prevention' in the youth justice field as a targeted form of *early intervention* and the *reduction* of existing negative behaviours and outcomes (for example offending, exposure to risk factors), as opposed to the universal *promotion* of positive behaviours and outcomes for children. We progress from a detailed critique of the managerialism and negative foci of the risk factor prevention paradigm into a discussion of the *progressive prevention* approach adopted in Welsh policy documents. From there, the chapter moves into an examination of models of progressive prevention-promotion that prioritise protective factors (for example Positive Youth Development), enabling factors (for example Extending Entitlement evaluation) and the pursuit of positive outcomes for children (for example local Swansea programmes) and, as such, offer tentative evidence for the potential of a CFOS approach to prevention-promotion for use with all children, within and outside the YJS.

In the Conclusion, we revisit the guiding principles of CFOS and the central aims of the book in the light of the revised All Wales Youth Offending Strategy, entitled *Children and Young People First*. We discuss the new strategy's priorities, objectives and principles and how these cohere with the key features of the CFOS model, concluding by re-emphasising our advocacy of the principled, progressive and positive nature of CFOS.

ONE

Positive youth justice: introducing Children First, Offenders Second

This book is about society and the way it treats its children – particularly those who come into conflict with the law and the youth justice system. We intend to use the term 'children in conflict with the law and the youth justice system' throughout the book, for a number of reasons. Crucially, we have chosen to privilege the terms 'child' and 'children' over 'youth' and 'young people', in accordance with the United Nations Convention on the Rights of the Child 1989 (UNCRC) designation of a child as anyone under the age of 18 years (fitting with the 10–17-years-age of criminal responsibility in England and Wales) and its requirements for adults to offer children protection, provision and participation in accordance with their status as a 'child'. We see the law and the youth justice system (in both their shared and distinctive manifestations) as social constructs that reflect the (unequal) distribution of power in society. We see the term 'offender' as an expression of that unequal power distribution and as a label used to *other* children in justification of state intervention in their lives (see Kelly 2012). We see this intervention as all too frequently negative, repressive and punitive, and as frequently having (as evidence shows) negative consequences (albeit sometimes unintended) for the current and future lives of children.

Already, this argument raises a problematic issue – one that is central to this book and to the arguments that we will be making. While we do not see children as being separate from society, we also wish to argue that children have a special place in society and are deserving of special treatment befitting their lack of maturity, their relative powerlessness in society (compared to adults) and their need for adults to provide them with support and protection (see also Harding and Becroft 2013). Special treatment should apply to all children, including those who come into conflict with the law and the youth justice system. The nature of this special treatment, however, is absolutely crucial. Children have been subject to a process of 'othering' by youth justice policy and practice in successive decades (see Howe and Strauss 1992), whereby as a relatively powerless sub-group within society, they have been marked out and identified for special treatment by more powerful and dominant social groups, such as adult politicians, officials, professionals in and around the youth justice system (JYS). Othering within the youth justice system YJS has resulted in individual children losing their identity and becoming treated simply as members of a broader group labelled 'young offenders' and the nature of their special treatment has been largely discriminatory, negative, controlling and punitive (Haines and Drakeford 1998; Muncie 2008b; Creaney 2012). As Goldson (2010: 162) argues: 'By creating "outsiders"… labelling invariably gives rise to repeat interventions of increasing intensity that … ultimately establish, consolidate, and/or confirm offender "identities". Such "identities" attract further intervention and/or negative reaction and so the process continues.'

Youth justice policy and practice has been dominated by a process of neoliberal *responsibilisation* (Muncie 2008b), whereby children (primarily), parents, local communities and local multi-agency organisations have been held responsible for the perceived psychological and social 'failings' and 'deficits' associated with offending behaviour and the failure of formal interventions to prevent offending. There is a successive history of the YJS (in various guises or manifestations) failing children (see Thorpe et al 1980; Gelsthorpe and Morris 1994; Muncie 2008**b**; Sharpe and Gelsthorpe 2009; Bateman 2011). The negative and deleterious nature of the special treatment of children by the YJS will be contrasted, in this book, with our central argument for a Children First, Offenders Second (CFOS) approach to delivering youth justice policy and practice. Throughout this book we will argue that CFOS is a viable and principled alternative to established youth justice responses: a genuinely fresh philosophy that is distinct from welfare-, justice- or risk-based approaches, that is flexible yet principled, fit for our times and, moreover, holds the prospect of being genuinely effective – not just in reducing the amount of offending by children and the sentencing of children, but in promoting positive outcomes for children.

One of the central challenges for CFOS is to address the insidious responsibilisation of children in society. CFOS recognises that children are on a developmental trajectory. Adults from different agencies and working in different systems intervene in these trajectories all of the time: a YJS is not needed to justify intervention in a child's life. Our job is to help children to become responsible for their behaviour as adults, rather than making them (fully) responsible for their behaviour as children. The aim is not to see children as 'trainee adults' (WAG 2004: 3) or to make children (fully) responsible as mini-adults in a mini-adult criminal justice system. As such, responses to children's behaviour should be child friendly, child appropriate and meaningful to children – in full recognition of each child's place on their developmental trajectory. These responses must recognise the huge differences between – and within – age groups in what constitutes 'meaningful': different interventions and activities may be (more or less) meaningful for 10-year-olds compared with 16-year-olds, for example, or for some 10-year-olds compared with other 10-year-olds. Therefore, responses to children's personal and social circumstances and behaviours should be tailored accordingly in a child-friendly, child-appropriate and children-first way. While victims are assuredly deserving of sympathy and positive, constructive responses, this should not be on the back of, or at the expense of, the child. Too many children in conflict with the law and the youth justice system are victims themselves (for example of abuse, neglect, crime, socio-structural disadvantage). Punitive and responsibilising approaches only serve to further victimise children and, as we will later demonstrate, are ineffective in reducing crime and meeting the needs of victims. Responses to victimisation (of children and adults) should, therefore, be made by society, not by the child.

In Focus • CFOS and the vexed question of causality

Any attempt to respond to offending behaviour by children inevitably raises questions as to the causes of the behaviour being addressed. Offending is a quality of the label given to the behaviour, rather than the behaviour itself (Becker 1963), thus reflecting the power of certain social groups (for example adults) to socially construct and influence law making and the application of legal sanctions by the criminal justice system. We have used the term 'children in conflict with the law and the youth justice system' deliberately throughout to reflect our belief in the socially constructed nature of offending by children and to reflect that bringing children into conflict with the law and the youth justice system is more a product of system behaviour than the behaviour of children themselves. Any attempts to explain the causes of offending behaviour by children, particularly those that individualise explanation, need to be made very tentatively in the light of this.

The corpus of criminological research regarding causality is thin. We have a very limited understanding (from existing research) of the causes of offending in general and offending by children specifically. Our theoretical models remain significantly underdeveloped and untested and we have an even poorer (theory- and research-informed) understanding of what works in preventing offending and reoffending. Any claims that we can, with any precision or confidence, identify the causes of offending/reoffending and what works in preventing these must be very circumspect, particularly if the intended argument is 'one size fits all'. One would probably find broad agreement among criminologists and practitioners that influences relating to offending behaviour are typically to be found in the individualised domain of the psycho-emotional and the immediate social domains of family, school, community, housing, employment and social inclusion/exclusion processes.[4] As a result, in theoretical terms, self-contained and restricted (meso-level) social theories have achieved prominence, including Strain Theory (Merton 1938), Sub-Cultural Theory (Cohen 1955; Cloward and Ohlin 1960) and Social Control Theory (Hirschi

[4] In making this statement, we should make it very clear that empirical efforts to demonstrate these linkages, particularly those that have been artefactual in nature and those that fall within the remit of risk factor research, have been shown to be deeply flawed (methodologically and conceptually) and have actually added little or nothing to our understanding of the causes or effective responses to offending by children (see Case and Haines 2009).

1969); each could have legitimate claims to relevance in understanding offending behaviour, at least partially, by some children, some of the time. However, two essential problems remain: (1) lack of a coherent narrative – there is no single theoretical perspective that explains offending behaviour by children; and (2) evidential insufficiency – there is an absence of robust empirical evidence regarding the causes of, or influences on, offending behaviour by children.

To a certain extent, CFOS elides the vexed question of causality by focusing on (future-oriented) positive outcomes for children and in arguing that the work of youth offending teams (YOTs) and others should be focused on working with individual children to maximise the achievement of positive outcomes. It would be naïve to suggest that in making this elision, there are no implicit theoretical or empirical foundations to the approach we are advocating, whether this applies to the prevention of offending, the prevention of reoffending, the promotion of positive outcomes or however the debate is framed. In broad theoretical and empirical terms, CFOS draws primarily on two main theoretical perspectives: Strain Theory (that opportunities for many children are blocked and the aim of intervention is to unblock these opportunities) and Control Theory (reinforcing the importance of a dynamic social bond), but we do not subscribe to the notion of a unitary theory that explains why some children are brought into conflict with the law and the youth justice system or that is sufficient to guide all interventions designed to reduce what is framed as antisocial behaviour or offending.

Likewise, empirical evidence is used conditionally. That crime is a social construct and product of such processes as local policing we take as axiomatic. The first principle in any attempt to understand offending and why (and how) some children are brought into conflict with the law and the youth justice system must be to locate it within its social context. That this perspective is all too often overlooked, particularly in empirical approaches, is to the detriment of children. Secondly, the importance of local context is paramount, both in understanding the behaviour of the children and in evaluating responses to it. What works in one local context may not work in another. Thirdly, CFOS approaches questions of causality and 'treatment' from the perspective of the individual child. Actuarialism, group-based empirical research and crude de-individualised statistical analyses tell us little or nothing about the specific circumstances of any individual child. The search for (and claims to) universal empirical causes or solutions is a chimera. Finally and consequentially, theory and research provide us with only general parameters for interpreting behaviour and determining interventions. These parameters need to be highly individualised (tailored to the child who receives them) and in hands of professionals, not proscribed by research and armchair theorising.

The central argument of this book, therefore, has two main elements: one reactionary, one progressive.

In *reactionary* terms, we are critical of the way in which youth justice policy and practice 'others' children in conflict with the law and the youth justice system and those potentially in conflict with the law and the YJS (for example children considered to be 'at risk' of offending behaviour) and subjects them to (possibly well-meaning) interventions which are ultimately punitive, controlling, stigmatising and harmful. We direct this criticism with particular vigour to the 'new youth justice' policy and practice of the post-Crime and Disorder Act 1998 era (see Goldson 2000), with its emphasis on risk and the demonisation of children – notably through the antisocial behaviour crusade and the criminalisation of the prevention agenda. Our criticism is, however, also a reaction to the welfare and justice philosophies and practices of previous decades – each of which has been shown to have negative consequences for children, such as the indeterminacy of welfarism precipitating interventionism and neglecting children's legal rights to due process and the punitive, stigmatising, marginalising and labelling impacts of justice-based models (see Carrabine 2008; Smith 2006; Daly 2003; Haines and Drakeford 1998; see also Chapter Two for further discussion of justice and welfare models).

In *progressive* terms, we argue that children in conflict with the law and the youth justice system should be treated as children first and foremost. This is both a philosophical, principled position and a policy-practice imperative. We believe that for policies to be clear and to be implemented effectively, they must have a clear overarching objective. The philosophy of treating children in conflict with the law and the youth justice system in a CFOS way is such an objective. If those staff responsible for policy implementation and for working with children are to understand what they do, why they do it, and in the way that they do (and if they are to be able to reflect on and measure the effectiveness of their practice), they need a clear overarching objective for their work (see also Haines and Drakeford 1998). The philosophy of treating children in conflict with the law and the youth justice system as CFOS helps staff to understand why they come into work every day and provides a touchstone against which they can measure their daily practice. In its simplest form, CFOS means de-emphasising the treatment of children in conflict with the law and the youth justice system as offenders or in terms of their offence and emphasising responses to children that recognise their status as children and that are child friendly and child appropriate.

We fully accept that the central elements of our argument are (necessarily) complex and that they contain certain assertions and assumptions that do not, as yet, stand up to scrutiny. There is much to explain and it is to this purpose that the entire book is dedicated. We do not believe that the task of explaining, understanding, demonstrating or evaluating the CFOS approach is necessarily easy – it requires much sustained effort and involves dealing with many complicated, involved issues, arguments and material. Nor do we subscribe to the objective of providing a simple, off-the-shelf prescription for responding to children in conflict with the law and the youth justice system. Those seeking simplistic and easy, ready-made, answers will not find them in this book (or anywhere else for that matter). The way in which society treats its children is complex, dynamic and socially constructed. Locating the treatment of children in conflict with the law and the youth justice system within this broader context is similarly challenging. However, it is a challenge that we feel compelled to address, not least because of the fundamental importance and significance of the answers that we (and others) promote for those children whose lives may be either negatively or positively affected by our actions.

Children First, Offenders Second: a modern and distinctive economic-normative model

We intend to make two interlinked claims for the CFOS approach: that it is a modern philosophy and approach that is fit for our times and that it is distinctive from previous approaches and from other contemporary contenders for a dominating model in youth justice. The basis of our claim that CFOS is modern and distinctive is partly normative and partly consequentialist. Society is ever changing. Different ideas and circumstances emerge and come to dominate our thinking and actions at different times. Fashions come and go in the same way that, at different times, certain actions rather than others become possible or more likely given their fit with broader ideas and beliefs. Broad socio-economic changes thus have consequences for social policy and practice. While some actions and changes become (more) likely or possible, at the same time, some become less likely or less possible. Any discussion of the possible must also take place at the same time as a discussion of the impossible – or less probable.

In advanced Western capitalist countries, in particular, children are a financial burden. Not only are children economically unproductive, they cost money to rear and educate. While a portion of this financial expenditure is met by parents or carers, the state is also called upon and is responsible for paying for services and provision for children. This is not a new phenomenon. Since the invention of the notion of childhood and since the advent of the Industrial Revolution (and its consequences) the payment by the state for services for children has been a defining characteristic of our social history and of our treatment of children (for example Rose 1996; Hendrick 2006). We cannot, therefore, escape some consideration of the economics of childhood and the role of the state. We need not, however, dwell on this matter at length or in any great detail. The argument in this case is quite simple. For at least the last 30 years, successive Western capitalist governments (in the UK, across Europe and more broadly across the globe) have sought to increasingly manage (predominantly a euphemism for cut) state financial expenditure on children.[5] It was possible, therefore, fairly recently in our history to think about and to implement a welfare-based approach to children generally and to children in conflict with the law and the youth justice system specifically – an approach that focused on the needs of children and providing a wide range of services to meet these needs. However, it is no longer possible to even think in these terms, let alone to contemplate providing the finances necessary to create and deliver such holistic, wrap-around services (see Haines 1997; O'Hara 2014). On this central question of economics, childhood and the role of the state, therefore, a consequence of the economic stringencies brought about by governments and globalised capitalism[6] is that notions of welfare and increased spending on children is a non-starter. As we develop our arguments throughout this book, we will demonstrate how CFOS, while not necessarily totally economically neutral (and maybe even economically positive in the sense of cost reducing in the long-term – for example through the reduction of social exclusion and related factors such as youth unemployment and academic underachievement – see Prince's Trust 2007), is distinct from previous youth justice paradigms in that it does not rely on increased government expenditure.[7]

The CFOS model is not only modernist and distinct in its economic outlook, it is also distinct from previous youth justice models in that it is normatively based. Here, we are seeking to place the model in the contemporary social context and within the dominant norms within society – in short, as an idea whose time has come. It is, of course, entirely possible to identify and list a wide range of different ideas and ways of thinking about children and specific sub-groups of children (differentiated

[5] For a more technical and detailed discussion of the issues, see Lash and Urry's (1988) *The End of Organised Capitalism* and their 'hollowing of the state' thesis.

[6] In this respect, the swingeing cuts to services for children wrought by the Conservative-Liberal Democrat coalition government in the UK following the global economic crisis of around 2010, precipitated by unregulated financial markets, are but one (albeit fairly drastic) manifestation of a longer-term trend.

[7] Although the extent of the financial cuts and their associated cuts in services for children wrought by the Conservative-Liberal Democrat coalition government in the name of austerity inhibited the ability of those working at the local level to deliver a range of positive services to children.

by age or behavioural characteristics). It has been argued, for example, that children have been/are viewed as commodities to be exploited (Dottridge 2004), as feral beings in need of taming (Hall 1905), as imbued with risk (Loeber and Farrington 1998) or as immature, helpless, neglected and in need of protection (Gillis 1975; Gelsthorpe and Morris 1994; James and Prout 1997; Hendrick 2003). A whole host of ideas and perspectives, sometimes competing, sometimes contradictory, can be identified as current at any particular time in influencing the way we think and act in respect of children. Without wishing to diminish the significance and impact that these different ideas may have at particular times, however, such ideas are largely transitory and it is important to differentiate between contemporary ideas (which are frequently short lived) and societal norms (which are more enduring). Each generation, it seems, believes that the children of the time grow up faster and earlier. Patently this cannot be true in any absolute sense – or we would witness five-year-olds going to university! But change does happen. Changes in societal norms do occur, they are real and they have real-world consequences for the way, in this case, we think about children and childhood, and the way in which society treats children. These norms also affect the way in which children think about themselves, affect what they expect from society and affect the way in which children act or behave.

Children's rights as a progressive social norm

Just as we have identified economics as the critical (constraining) factor in thinking about and developing services for children, we identify *children's rights* as the dominant norm shaping more progressive thinking about children and in shaping the societal context of what is possible and more likely in terms of the treatment of children, notably (but not exclusively) children in conflict with the law and the youth justice system. To be sure, children's rights are a contested topic internationally and there is far from unanimity of opinion as to whether children have, can have or should have rights (see Scraton and Haydon 2002; Kemshall 2008; Kilkelly 2008). We believe, however, that it is the children's rights agenda that provides the terrain on which major societal debates about children and their treatment is taking place and has done so for 50 years. Moreover, setting aside philosophical questions about whether children can or should have rights, it is the children's rights agenda that is shaping the substance and content of debates (see Towler 2009) about society's treatment of children – more than any other.[8]

Any discussion of children's rights must, of necessity, be placed in the context and significance of the UNCRC. Published in 1958 and ratified by all but two countries around the globe (the US and South Sudan), the UNCRC sets the baseline for all matters concerning children's rights. With 54 articles, the UNCRC is a long and complex document, detailed consideration of which is beyond our scope here (but see Muncie 2009). However, some basic details are necessary. The UNCRC sets out a positive view of children and it seeks to promote and protect the place of children in society and the value and status of children as citizens. While it is invidious to highlight selected provisions of the UNCRC (and the UNCRC is not intended to be used as a buffet) this is both necessary in short compass and justified to the extent that certain provisions are more general in scope and applicability, and have achieved a prominence in debates, as well as in children's rights practices. In addition to its promotion of a positive view of children as citizens, notable among the provisions of the UNCRC are:

- Article 2 (non-discrimination) – sets out the principle of non-discrimination; that children's rights are immutable and applicable to all children, regardless of their age, gender, race, religion, culture, nationality or abilities;

[8] This is not the time or place to fully justify our faith in this statement, but some justification is called for. We suggest that the growth and plethora of research based on the children's rights agenda over the last 50 years is testament to our belief. The recent emergence of state youth strategies, in many countries across the globe, many of which are firmly located in the children's rights agenda, is further testament to the normative importance of children's rights (see Scraton and Haydon 2002; Kilkelly 2008). Other examples can be found in youth justice where rights-based arguments proliferate – particularly in the anti-risk literature (for example Goldson and Muncie 2006; Haines and Case 2011). We return to these discussions in subsequent chapters.

- Article 3 (best interests of the child) – establishes the primacy of the best interests of the child in all decisions affecting them, notably in terms of budgets, policy and law making;
- Article 4 (protection of rights) – asserts that governments should respect, protect and fulfil children's rights;
- Article 12 (respect for the views of the child) – sets out the right of children to express their views and have them taken into account on all matters affecting them, with children's participation appropriate to their level of maturity;
- Article 13 (freedom of expression) – outlines children's right to receive and share information that is not damaging to themselves or others;
- Article 17 (access to information) – establishes that children have the right to information that is important to their health and well-being;
- Article 40 (juvenile justice) – provides that children who are accused of breaking the law have the right to legal help and fair treatment in a justice system that respects their rights.

Not only have the provisions of the UNCRC shaped much of the terrain on which adult debates about the treatment of children have taken place in recent times (Hammarberg 2008; Muncie 2009), but, as we suggested earlier, the norms derived from these provisions have also shaped the way in which children think about themselves, the way they act and the way they expect adults to act in respect of them. For example, in relation to Article 12 of the UNCRC (the right of all children to express their views on issues that affect them), despite persisting blockage impeding children's right to participate in decision making (Kirby and Bryson 2002; Middleton 2006; Kellett 2011), children have exhibited a keen willingness to exercise this right. The literature reflects this willingness and suggests that it is located in a diverse range of areas, including policy development, the evaluation of service provision (Nolas 2011) and decision making generally (Charles 2011). Additionally, due to continuing public exposure, this right in particular has been accepted as a critical policy imperative and has been encapsulated in law and strategy (for example the Rights of Children and Young Persons (Wales) Measure 2011). It is our contention, therefore, that the UNCRC and the children's rights debate more generally, constitutes a dominant social norm and a fundamental social context within which any consideration of the treatment of children and thus equally children in conflict with the law and the youth justice system must be framed. In this regard, we agree with Muncie (2010: 201) when he asserts that: '[C]onsistently restating, promoting and defending these [UNCRC] principles is a vital first step for governments (State Parties) if they are to move towards child-centred and rights-compliant systems of youth and youth justice'.

A cadre of criminologists, policy makers, practitioners and children's rights advocates have been heavily critical of the 'new youth justice' of the Crime and Disorder Act 1998, in particular the risk-based model of youth justice and the manner in which the approach has subsumed and marginalised a focus on children's rights (compare Goldson 2000; Scraton and Haydon 2002; Goldson 2005; Kilkelly 2008; Case and Haines 2009; O'Mahony 2009; Bateman 2011). Critical commentators (compare Goldson and Muncie 2006; Muncie 2008**b**; Creaney and Smith 2014) have highlighted the extent to which the contemporary YJS in England and Wales contravenes a number of articles of the UNCRC and a succession of principles from contemporary youth justice conventions such as the Beijing Rules (1985), Riyadh Guidelines (1990), Havana Rules (1990), Tokyo Rules (1990) and Vienna Guidelines (1997), consolidated more recently by *Access to Justice for Children: Report of the United Nations High Commissioner for Human Rights* (UNHCHR 2013) and the *Ten Point Plan for Fair and Effective Justice for Children* (Penal Reform International and Interagency Panel on Juvenile Justice (PRI and IPJJ) 2012). The essential elements of a principled approach to youth justice that have been neglected by the 'new youth justice' include emphasis on:

- children's rights and well-being (UNCRC; Vienna Guidelines; Beijing Rules; UNHCHR);
- non-discrimination (UNCRC; Beijing Rules);
- proportionality (Beijing Rules);
- increased age of criminal responsibility (PRI and IPJJ);

- child-centred early intervention and multi-agency prevention (Vienna Guidelines, Riyadh Guidelines; PRI and IPJJ);
- diversion (Riyadh Guidelines; Havana Rules; PRI and IPJJ; UNHCHR);
- community-based responses (Tokyo Rules);
- anti-custody (UNCRC;Vienna Guidelines; Beijing Rules);
- children's participation in youth justice processes (UNCRC; Vienna Guidelines; UNHCHR).
- Our view is that the UNCRC and the wider children's rights debate (as illustrated by the different elements of the identified conventions) set parameters to the principles that should inform our approach to youth justice as follows:
- rights belong to all children (committing an offence should not lead to a loss of rights);
- adults, not children, bear the most responsibility for upholding and promoting (through policy and practice) the rights of children;
- certain responses to the behaviour of children are not appropriate simply because they are children (and therefore not fully socially or biologically mature, responsible and legally capable adults);
- certain responses to the behaviour of children are (more) appropriate simply because they are children;
- children are part of the solution, not part of the problem.

As we will go on to explain and illustrate in subsequent chapters, CFOS seeks to give expression to these principles. The answers that we will provide are not definitive – in the sense that we do not believe it is possible, necessary or desirable to set these matters in stone for all children, of all ages, in all circumstances, in all locations, for all time. In our view discretion, flexibility, dynamism, innovation and invention are essential characteristics of all responses to children. Change over time is almost inevitable. We also believe it is practically impossible to leap to a full-blown CFOS approach (as subsequent discussions of our Reflective Friend Research partnership with Swansea YOT will illustrate – see Chapter Four) and that the approach we are advocating here represents an objective, rather than a prescription.

Children First, Offenders Second: a distinctive, positive youth justice paradigm

To foreground the arguments and material to come, and to illustrate our claim that CFOS represents a distinctive approach to youth justice (in addition to a distinct approach to working with children generally), we provide, in Table 1.1, a summary of contrasting models. Certain models have preceded CFOS as dominant animating philosophies for youth justice. Welfare and justice models have articulated youth justice in the UK (and beyond) across the 20th century (for an in-depth review of the welfare–justice debate, see Smith 2005). More recently, risk has dominated youth justice policy and practice (see Table 1.1).

We hope a clear picture is beginning to emerge from Table 1.1 about the particularities and differences in approaches to youth justice and what they might mean for the treatment of children in conflict with the law and the youth justice system, in particular the distinctiveness of CFOS as a modern and progressive model for youth justice. We will expand on our notion of CFOS in the following chapter.

New Labour, 'new youth justice'

On coming to power in 1997, the 'New' Labour government in the UK immediately consolidated their stance as the party of law and order, a government that would be seen to 'do something' about the 'problem' of offending by children. The Crime and Disorder Act 1998 emphasised the need to ground youth justice practice, particularly crime reduction interventions, in a thorough (risk) assessment of the likelihood that children who came to the attention of the YJS would reoffend. The prioritisation of risk (factors) and the sweeping, contested conclusions of risk factor research (see Case and Haines 2009 for a detailed critique) underpinned the application of the risk factor prevention paradigm across youth justice practice (see Chapter Six). As Farrington (2007: 606) asserts: 'The basic idea of risk-focused prevention is very simple: Identify the key risk factors for offending and implement prevention methods designed to counteract them. There is often a related attempt to identify key

Table 1.1: Models of youth justice

	Welfare	Justice	The new orthodoxy	Risk-focused	Children First, Offenders Second
Support	Waterhouse and McGhee 2002; Asquith 1998; Children in Trouble 1968; Children and Young Person's Act 1969	Criminal Justice Act 1991; Morris and Giller (1983); von Hirsch (1976)	Bottoms et al (1990); Tutt and Giller (1987); see also, Haines and Drakeford (1998)	Breaking the Cycle 2010; Youth Justice Board (YJB) (2009); Farrington (2007); Crime and Disorder Act 1998	Haines and Case (2012); Drakeford (2010); WAG and YJB (2004); Haines and Drakeford (1998)
Overall aim	To meet the needs of children	To serve the interests of justice and proportionality	To decriminalise and to divert from the formal YJS	To respond to assessed risk	To promote the interests of the child and to improve outcomes
Process	The needs of children and the causes of their behaviour are investigated and professional expertise and discretion are emphasised	The legal rights of children are safeguarded by the application of the 'due process' of the law	Systems management – targeting decision-making points in the YJS	The nature, frequency and duration of interventions are determined by assessed risk	Promoting the interests of the child and responding to their views
Main concerns	Addressing needs	The law and the determination of guilt	Avoiding the detrimental effects of formal intervention	Risk	The child
Scope	Children in need	Identified offenders	Identified offenders, decision making	Offenders and potential offenders	Comprehensive prevention through to post-custody
Basis of sentencing	The welfare needs of the child and treatment	The offence and proportionality	Diversion and anti-custody	Responding to assessed risk	Normalisation
Type of sentence	Indeterminate	Determinate	Community, intermediate treatment	Offence- and offender-focused	Child-appropriate, child-focused

protective factors against offending and to implement prevention methods designed to enhance them.'

The focus on 'risk' enabled the Labour government to shift the aims of youth justice away from the traditional welfare- or justice-based approaches, which had dominated the youth justice agenda for over a century. Through the prescription of technical, standardised risk assessment processes (Asset, Onset) and risk-focused interventions (dictated by the Scaled Approach assessment and intervention framework), New Labour implemented a managerialist 'new youth justice' agenda (Goldson 2000; see also Chapter Four). The uncritical, routinised and automated completion of the Asset tool (see Pitts 2001; see Baker 2005 for counter-arguments) and an assiduous and uncritical adherence to the Scaled Approach (see Sutherland 2009; Bateman 2011; Haines and Case 2012) has served to individualise and personalise the blame for offending onto individual children. Privileging a risk-based youth justice agenda allowed the government to demonise children in conflict with the law and the youth justice system, using net-widening, punitive, labelling, responsibilising measures, while simultaneously controlling the central–local relationship and the practice of YOTs and their staff via prescriptive and technicised responses to restricted conceptions of offending behaviour by children. The risk-based framework was fit for purpose and fit for its time, offering a managerialist, 'evidence-based' and anti-child form of youth justice to supplant the ostensibly outdated and purportedly ineffective welfare- and justice-based approaches (see Smith 2005).

The deficit-focused negativity and responsibilising nature of the risk paradigm is challenged by the forward-looking, promotional (of prosocial, positive behaviours) and rights-based nature of the CFOS approach.

Children First, Offenders Second: the constraints of complexity

In advocating a CFOS model for youth justice, we are not claiming that this approach is without its problems, tensions and difficulties – all models are redolent with such issues and limitations. Proponents of different approaches, however, rarely recognise these limitations and often seek to proselytise (for example justice – Morris and Giller 1983; welfare – Asquith 1998; risk – Farrington 2000). While this is understandable to a certain extent, it does tend to lead to defensive model building and competition between approaches. Such strategies also tend to produce (sometimes overly) simplified versions of the different approaches, which may be easier to describe, understand and implement, but which are imbued with a lack of reality, absence of sophistication and a failure to learn and make progress over time. Simplified or poorly explicated approaches fail to do justice to the complexity of the problems and issues to be addressed and fail to give policy makers or practitioners sufficient understanding or equipment (theoretical and practical tools) to carry out their roles critically, professionally and effectively. Poorly or inadequately theorised, developed and described approaches also permit the expression of a wide range and variety of practice which, while claiming to give expression to a particular model, may only possess a passing resemblance to the model and which can give rise to poor quality youth justice work (see Haines and Drakeford 1998). This is not a satisfactory situation and these are dangers we must confront. With this caution in mind, it is incumbent upon us to discuss the most obvious and immediate constraints, problems and difficulties associated with CFOS as we see them at this present time. There will undoubtedly be others raised in the future.

Perhaps the biggest difficulty with CFOS is the model's complexity, by which we mean a number of things. CFOS aims to be a comprehensive approach dealing with issues from crime prevention through to how we respond to children convicted of the most serious crimes and made subject to the fullest force of the law. Moreover, it seeks to achieve this by putting our responses to children in conflict with the law and the youth justice system in the wider context of how society responds to children and their place in society. This intention, in turn, necessitates a sensitivity to a whole range of concerns, including: age, relative maturity, personal/social/structural characteristics and circumstances, family issues, the views of children, gender, ethnicity, physical and social geography, the responsibilities of adults, interactions with agencies of formal and informal socialisation (for example school, police, workplace) and the roles of adult stakeholders within these organisations, official representations of children within governmental policies, organisational practices and media outputs at local and national levels – all of which may interact in complex patterns producing a wide range of different outcomes. Accounting for such complexity is necessary for effective practice, but this complexity should not be over-simplified and thus cannot be reduced into simple tablets of stone or off-the-shelf prescriptions.

There is further complexity in the constraints on the approach. Rather than determining or prescribing policy and practice with children in conflict with the law and the youth justice system, CFOS seeks to build parameters within which flexibility, innovation and professionalism must be exercised. These parameters place limits around what is acceptable, limits that give direction and coherence to the approach, but there is much scope and necessity for (professional) discretion. We do not believe 'one size fits all', in all circumstances, in all places – complexity is both necessary and inherent in our understanding of children and childhood, and in our work with children. What is right for some children in some places simply will not work and is not right for others in different places. The social circumstances and localised contexts (historical, political, socio-structural) confronting children living in major cities, for example, are quite different from those faced by children living in rural areas; ethnicity and gender are crucial considerations which may cut across place. It is critical that we locate our understanding of the behaviour of children and our responses to this behaviour in a detailed analysis of these differing personal and social circumstances and localised contexts – for each and every child.

That said, CFOS would not bear critical scrutiny and it would be of very limited use to policy makers and practitioners if it were to be so loose as to offer little more than weak platitudes. The substance and hence value of CFOS is to be found in the strength of the parameters introduced in Table 1.1 and the sense in which the model provides meaning and direction to policy and practice. These matters are further described and discussed in detail in the following chapter. We have also been working in partnership with Swansea YOT and its partner agencies for 20 years to reflectively develop and implement the CFOS approach. There is strength and value to be derived from examples of practice we have utilised (as much as they can be adapted in other areas), the results we have obtained and the outcomes for children achieved; examples and outcomes we go on to detail and evaluate in subsequent chapters.

It will remain evident, however, that CFOS is complex and it defies reduction to simplistic terms. We cannot provide a simple definition or description of CFOS because one does not exist. We will provide details about the principles that inform and shape the CFOS approach, we will set out the parameters of the approach and we will provide examples from practice, but we will not over-simplify. We make no apology for behaving in this way, because we see this stance as inherent to the task. We see it as incumbent upon those who choose to work with children to accept the responsibility that professionalism requires and that children deserve, to make the necessary effort to understand the complexities of the approach, to recognise and respond to critical challenges and knowledge limitations, and to strive in difficult conditions to do their best for children confronted by challenging circumstances.

Central to the CFOS approach is the notion that children are confronted by challenging circumstances and that these circumstances frequently bring children into conflict with the law and the youth justice system. Also fundamental is the principle that practitioners must listen to what children have to say about these circumstances and their impact on their behaviour, and that practitioners must confront these circumstances as priority – over and above (but not to the exclusion of) confronting children with their behaviour and its consequences in child-friendly and child-appropriate ways that are sensitive to age, relative maturity, developmental trajectories and socio-structural circumstances. We argue that the 'othering' and responsibilising of children (and their families) and subjecting them to intrusive, controlling, repressive and punitive offence- and offender-focused interventions is unacceptable (as well as being ineffective in reducing undesirable behaviours or in promoting desirable behaviours). Central to the CFOS approach are the ideas that adults must take responsibility for what happens to children and that any response to children in conflict with the law and the youth justice system must be based on the principle of *normalisation* (see, for example, Pitts 1988). That is to say, we should not respond to children with the imputed status of an offender or in terms of their alleged offence, but we should respond to children in conflict with the law and the youth justice system as children and any interventions should reflect their status as children and promote child-friendly and child-appropriate methods. A central principle[9] of the CFOS approach, therefore, is that the mechanisms and interventions used when children are identified as having committed an offence should be those mechanisms and interventions that exist in society for all children.

The spectre of socio-structural inequalities: normalisation and service provision

In an ideal world, normalisation would be both a sufficient and appropriate principle upon which to base all work with children in conflict with the law and the youth justice system. We do not, however, live in an ideal world. This reality leads us into one of the major potential criticisms and problems of the CFOS approach – the issue of socio-structural inequalities. We live in a rich country that provides a fertile environment and a wealth of positive services and experiences for children, but these resources are very inequitably distributed (Dorling 2014). While some children benefit from what our society provides, other children live in social circumstances of extreme poverty, hardship and deprivation (and, for a minority, even in circumstances which are actively hostile). The socio-structural inequalities in society are vast, very real and more likely to be experienced by those children who come into contact with the YJS (see Goldson and Muncie 2006; Creaney and Smith 2014). Our advocacy, therefore, that interventions in the lives of children in conflict with the law and the youth justice system should be based on the principle of normalisation, may mean that we are normalising children into circumstances of structural disadvantage. This criticism becomes particularly acute in the context that the provisions of the law and the youth justice system are not developed and targeted on children from more

[9] It is important to remember that these are principles not prescriptions. Some children suffer such extreme circumstances that 'normal' provision would be a grossly inadequate response. Some children also exhibit extreme behaviours that call for responses beyond the normal – although even in such circumstances any response should be considerate of their status as children and should be both child friendly and child appropriate (see Chapter Two).

privileged backgrounds or circumstances, but they are developed and targeted on those children who live in some of our most deprived areas and communities.

The existence and the impact on the lives of children of socio-structural inequalities in society pose a serious challenge to the CFOS approach. Children in conflict with the law and the youth justice system tend to come from communities blighted by social and economic disadvantage and are often those who experience the worst that these communities offer. These children are thus multiply and extremely disadvantaged ('the disadvantaged disadvantaged'). The notion of compounded disadvantage reinforces, rather than diminishes, however, the importance of seeing and responding to these children as children, it reinforces the importance of a normalising approach (albeit to higher standards) and it heightens the demand for adults to be children's champions. There is most certainly a strong argument to avoid practices which reinforce the relative deprivation experienced by these children or which effectively blame children for living in poverty – hostile circumstances – when they have no responsibility for this or ability to do anything about it. This is both an ethical/moral position and somewhat pragmatic. While we believe that such pragmatism is often a necessary and, indeed, valuable tool, it will not, however, address the severe problems that socio-structural inequalities cause for children. This is a difficult matter and there are no easy answers, but to the extent that it is real, it is a reality we must confront. In addition to what we have said earlier, therefore, there are a number of implications for a CFOS way of thinking in responding to these issues.

Clearly, social and structural deprivations and inequalities have severe negative consequences and affects children and their families, restricting their life choices and opportunities (see, for example, Pitts 2003; Armstrong 2004; Webster, MacDonald and Simpson 2006; Prince's Trust 2007; O'Mahony 2009; Bateman 2011; Kelly 2012). Socio-structural inequalities, however, also impact upon and impede the actions and abilities of those adults who work in organisations that provide services to children and they constrain the resources available to those organisations (schools, the police, local authorities and voluntary organisations), while also making the problems they face more challenging.

This situation has been compounded over the past 15–20 years by the exponential constriction of funding for mainstream and specialist services focused on children's well-being, coupled with the unsatisfactory plugging of service gaps and funding shortfalls with 'initiatives' (see National Audit Office 2008, 2013), often limited in scope, resource, duration and effectiveness (see Haines 1997).

Responding to socio-structural inequalities first means fully recognising their consequences for all those living and working in deprived communities and circumstances. Consequently, any response to socio-structural inequalities requires joined-up thinking, joined-up working and a whole community strategy.[10] At the very least, this means that all organisations that work with children in conflict with the law and the youth justice system must work together. The creation and maintenance of a safe and positive environment in which children can grow must be the shared responsibility of all relevant agencies. Although each respective agency has its own agenda, this should not mean that they ignore those of others – agencies must work together. The consequences of adults in a range of agencies failing to work together are immediate. For example, the youth service could work constructively at engaging with children within a preventive agenda that promotes positive behaviour, but if police pursue an enforcement approach robustly and indiscriminately, good intentions and positive outcomes will dissolve as children lose trust in adults and responses lose their legitimacy in the eyes of children (see Charles 2011, Hawes 2013).

The broader and more explicit link here is with the prevention agenda (see Youth Justice Board (YJB) 2004; Crime and Disorder Act 1998), which seeks the prevention of negative and deleterious behaviour by children (for example offending, antisocial behaviour, substance use). CFOS addresses this prevention agenda not in an excessively targeted and individualised manner (see

[10] For example, the more holistic approach proposed by the revised Scaled Approach framework, AssetPlus (Youth Justice Board (YJB) 2011 – discussed in detail in Chapter Four) promises a more comprehensive assessment and understanding of the complexities of and interactions between children's personal circumstances, environments and local contexts – a model that fits with the emerging localism agenda (Ministry of Justice 2010), but is not connected or beholden to it.

Kelly 2012), but by refusing to tolerate harmful environments for children or cuts to essential (youth) services or by blaming children for their social circumstances. The prevention agenda requires improvements in the range and quality of services and provision for all children, and ensuring that these improved services/provisions are child friendly, child appropriate and accessible to all children. Unblocking blocked opportunities, ensuring children have access to their entitlements is essential if positive outcomes for all children are to be realised. If this agenda is effectively pursued it provides a context and provision in which responses to children in conflict with the law and the youth justice system can be located. Therefore, socio-structural disadvantage not only means that agencies face bigger problems, but that their resources and those of the community are typically diminished too. Consequently, it is even more difficult in such areas to meet the challenges they face. Responses, therefore, should be joined up rather than fragmented and should prioritise universalism rather than excessive targeting and responsibilisation, in order to enable access to services by disadvantaged groups in under-funded local areas (see United Nations Research Institute for Social Development 2010; Drakeford 2010). Even more importantly, we should refuse to tolerate this situation, which has been perpetuated by a neoliberal responsibilising agenda of localism that exacerbates the cultural and economic disadvantages experienced by the less well off in society (see, for example, Atkinson, Roberts and Savage 2012). Children living in socially deprived areas constitute the 'disadvantaged disadvantaged' in that they are a disenfranchised and vulnerable social group whose problems are compounded by restricted services and provision. Appropriate responses to these children should be socially inclusive, redistributive, transformative and focused on enhancing their strengths and capabilities (see UN Research Institute for Social Development 2010).

Children first prevention

A central principle of the CFOS approach is that 'prevention is better than cure'. However, we are wary of the established prevention agenda, particularly as it has become manifest in

England and Wales following the Crime and Disorder Act 1998 and placed at the forefront of the criminal justice policy proclamations of the new UK coalition government (see Centre for Social Justice 2007, 2011). The Crime and Disorder Act 1998 established that 'it shall be the principal aim of the youth justice system to prevent offending (including re-offending) by children and young people' (section 37). However, the chosen approach served to criminalise the prevention agenda through its emphasis on early intervention and reduction (of reoffending) through neoconservative correctionalism guided by the identification of risk factors for offending – drawing on a restricted body of artefactual risk factor research (Farrington 2000, 2007). Risk assessment instruments have been widely utilised in the YJS to identify children allegedly 'at risk' of negative behaviours and outcomes at some future point and thus in need of targeted intervention. Risk assessment in the youth justice arena has been subjected to intense criticism in recent times for a number of cogent reasons, including its flawed, over-simplistic methodological bases (see Case and Haines 2009), the extent of false negatives and positives produced by such assessment (see Case 2007) and the potential for labelling, stigmatising and further disadvantaging already disadvantaged children (see Bateman 2011) – all of which conspire to undermine the validity and utility of the approach to *prevention*.

Despite our wariness of extant early intervention and reduction masquerading as prevention in the YJS (see Chapter Six), we are equally committed to the prevention of offending by children and assert this approach as a priority over reactive service provision for children once they have been identified as 'at risk' or 'problematic'. Thinking about prevention in a CFOS manner, however, displays some distinctive attributes, notably that offence- and (potential) offender-focused thinking and action should be discontinued in favour of a whole child approach, which focuses on promoting positive behaviour and positive outcomes for all children, including those who come into conflict with the law and the youth justice system (see also WAG and YJB 2004). We therefore reject approaches to the prevention of youth offending that prioritise the targeting of offending behaviour, antisocial behaviour, respect for adults or prioritising victims' rights – in favour of universalised and normalised approaches that work with children to identify the problems they experience in their localities and support them in developing appropriate solutions. This form of 'progressive universalism' underpins the preventive approach adopted within social policy making for children and young people in Wales (Drakeford 2010). Moreover, it is an approach that firmly advocates the principle that 'children are part of the solution, not part of the problem'.

Working with children in conflict with the law and the youth justice system must be set in the context of a strategy for all children. If the negative consequences of normalisation into situations of structural inequality are to be mitigated, this can only be achieved by improving the lives of all children. Children, particularly those who come into conflict with the law and the youth justice system, have been repeatedly demonised in recent years by politicians and the press. Successive governments have not shied away from extremely negative rhetorical posturing about feral youth and the problems posed to society by children. Such political posturing has been accompanied by government policies, laws and changes to the YJS that are extremely prejudicial to children. In some important ways, therefore, the role of those who work in the YJS (that is, all those agencies in the system, including, but not exclusively, YOTs) has become confused. In many ways the system has developed negative norms about children and sees itself as set against them. Practices have developed which focus on managing children and the risk they are supposed to present to society (sometimes as if these children are not part of that society). The interests of children have been set against and seen as a lower priority than the wider interests of society in general, the interests of community organisations and the interests of victims in particular (even corporate victims). This confusion and the plethora of interests to be served by the YJS is, in our view, both unhelpful and wrong. The organisations that make up the YJS and the adults that work in them should very clearly see themselves as working for children (and not against them) and not as representatives of any other interest group or constituency, particularly those who are capable of representing themselves, or who have representatives of their own – not least because this representation is not enjoyed by many children. These points are integral to CFOS thinking and practice – particularly as we make efforts to address the structural inequalities in our society. We do not pretend, however, that the strategy we have described is sufficient to fully mitigate the deprivations of socio-structural inequality, let alone to be an adequate response that seeks to reverse the impact of these deep-rooted, multifaceted and enduring inequalities. Our suggestions, if taken seriously, will reduce (and hopefully put an end to) the extent to which the YJS reinforces structural inequality and disadvantage. We also see the measures discussed as essential steps in a more positive trajectory for practice and for children that, at least, starts the process of beginning to address structural inequality in society 'bottom up'.

There remain, of course, many issues and practical consequences that our suggested approach will not touch and to the (potentially large) extent that this is real, it represents a serious challenge to proponents of a CFOS approach. The impact of structural inequality will continue to disadvantage many children, but much of this lays outwith the purview of youth justice practice and is the responsibility of others. The implication here is that addressing structural inequality necessitates a more holistic, comprehensive, multi-agency and multi-disciplinary approach within which youth justice constitutes a small, yet integral component. As such, CFOS presents a promising way of working with children that encompasses (but is not restricted to) youth justice issues, in conjunction with broader, macro, inter-personal and individual influences in a child's life. CFOS thinking and practice requires a rearticulation in our attitudes and actions towards children generally and towards children in conflict with the law and the youth justice system specifically. Children should be seen as part of the solution, not part of the problem.[11] Indeed, one of the main reasons why prevention and intervention in youth justice policy and practice has not enjoyed much success and has been subjected to such vehement criticism (for example

[11] This approach is exemplified in Wales by 'youth action groups', small teams of 11- to 25-year-olds (typically 3–10 members) in local communities, supported by at least two adults, working on six-month thematic projects related to community safety issues (for example youth crime prevention, antisocial behaviour, substance use, promoting positive images of children, youth inclusion).

Armstrong 2004; Case 2006; O'Mahony 2009; Kelly 2012) is that it has been cast against children and has notably failed to engage them in seeking solutions. As a consequence 'intervention' has become (at least for notable criminologists from Cohen (1985) to Goldson (2005, 2010)) a dirty word. In contrast, in a CFOS approach intervention is not only a good thing, it is essential – but this very much depends upon the nature of the proposed interventions.

Intervention in the youth justice system

Youth justice intervention does not boast a positive history or track record and has been lambasted for (at times) serving to exacerbate the personal and social circumstances that may have influenced offending behaviour in the first place (for example McAra and McVie's (2007) conclusion that contact with the YJS can actually increase the likelihood of future offending by children). We are seeking to make intervention in children's lives respectable again, but only if the nature and delivery of this intervention fits with our agenda for a CFOS model of practice. In all that we have argued, we have sought to place children and their interests in the primacy. We stand by this approach, but there remain certain tensions that require reconciling within the CFOS model – namely the nature of intervention(ism) within the existing system and the necessity for it.

The first of these tensions concerns the fact that society and adults intervene in the lives of children all of the time as part of what we may think of broadly as normal child-rearing practice. The second tension revolves around the fact that, setting aside the power imbalances and socially constructed nature of the law and the youth justice system and the prejudicial manner in which it sometimes goes about its business, some children do commit offences. There is therefore a need for a constant balance between the utility of intervention/non-intervention (with specific individuals, at specific times, in specific contexts) and the need to balance a focus on the child with the offence.

Society, in the guise of state organisations (for example schools) and adults (for example parents and other meaningful adults) intervenes in the lives of children all the time. This tends to be seen as quite normal and acceptable, even desirable. Children are not born as fully functioning adults and so require socialising into becoming responsible adult citizens. The very notions of childhood and the status of being a child are attached to a justification for intervention that is expressly designed to bring about change and for this change to be prosocial – in line with societal norms and expectations. Of course, the intensity and nature of this intervention varies markedly over the course of a child's life depending upon their age (and level of maturity, or ability to respond) and activity or behaviour. For example, responses to 'problematic' behaviours such truancy, antisocial behaviour and offending tend to be more interventionist and punitive than responses to behaviours that do not constitute a breach of societal norms, rules or laws. The intensity and nature of the intervention also depends upon who is intervening and what their objectives are. There are obvious differences (as well as some similarities), for example, in the roles of schools and parents. Just as the state creates schools to educate children and makes participation in education a legal responsibility, it creates other institutions to regulate children and their behaviour. Nowhere is this more clearly illustrated than in the law and the youth justice system, which are designed to respond to the behaviour of children that is either beyond the reach of other socialising processes and institutions or which contravenes social norms to such an extent that some additional intervention is deemed necessary and justified. While any judgement about what behaviour is illegal or undesirable or antisocial remains a socially constructed and potentially contested matter, some children come into conflict with the law and the youth justice system as a result of their behaviour. The existence of the legal norms that children's behaviour can bring them into conflict with is generally taken to justify intervention.

That intervention with children at certain points in their lives is, in principle, both justified and necessary is incontrovertible. The huge question that remains to be answered, however, is: what should be the nature, intensity and timing of this intervention? This is rarely, if ever, an empirical question, but a social and moral matter. As such it is an issue that is unlikely ever to attract a universal answer. The CFOS approach is an attempt to provide one answer. Largely following the social control tradition within critical criminology (see Hirschi 1969; Cohen 1985; Agnew 2005) and in response to the depth and breadth of empirical evidence that shows the propensity for the YJS to do more harm than good (albeit sometimes unintentionally), there are those who argue against the existence of the YJS and the panoply of measures it employs with children (see Goldson 2005; McAra and McVie 2007). There is much merit in these arguments and much that we are entirely happy to agree with. To the extent, however, that these arguments are synonymous with a non-interventionist stance, we depart from them. CFOS is not a non-interventionist philosophy – it is an active interventionist approach.

In this respect CFOS is not intended as a buffet from which to select partially, while other elements can be ignored. The model is intended as a whole child, holistic, coherent approach, wherein every component part must be executed as assiduously and effectively as any other. For example, it is incongruent and counterproductive to attempt diversion via methods that are not seen by children as legitimate, nor can preventive goals be pursued through an offence focus. CFOS is a comprehensive, principled and necessarily complex approach. As such, it eschews intellectual laziness among academics, policy makers and practitioners and demands commitment, professional ethics/principles and rigour to apply effectively. Any response to any child who has been convicted of any offence, for example, must be based on their status as a child – in every sense of what this means, no matter how challenging. Intervention within the CFOS model is built on a series of principled components that will be set out in detail in the following chapter.

Thus far, we have reached a number of firm conclusions about the prevailing youth justice agenda and the potential for a CFOS approach to supplant it. Children are in need of special, nuanced, sensitive treatment by society, including those children in conflict with the law and the youth justice system. This special treatment should not be framed by the punitive, controlling, adulterising and criminalising youth justice agendas of the past (for example welfare or more punitive, justice-based models), but instead should be progressive and principled. CFOS offers a modern and distinctive socio-economic-normative model grounded in the children's rights movement. Through CFOS, we assert that it is crucial to attend to the influence of socio-structural inequalities on children's lives and on the ability of agencies to provide them with effective support services. CFOS is a necessarily complex model, defying reductionist definition or description, which must be delivered holistically and comprehensively, rather than on a piecemeal or ad hoc basis. As such, the approach is not anti-intervention, but neither is it a buffet from which to select interventions. CFOS and the interventions it delivers are child friendly and child appropriate, working to the central tenet that prevention is better than cure and operating from a first principle that children are part of the solution, not part of the problem.

Critical academics are often themselves criticised (notably by politicians and frustrated policy makers) for being solely critical, for pointing out what is wrong with the system, for highlighting its flaws and failings, for being against everything, but for offering nothing by way of an alternative. We believe there is great value in criticism and that it should not be stifled, but encouraged and embraced. We also feel some responsibility to engage proactively in the debate about how we should respond to children in conflict with the law and the youth justice system. Therefore, CFOS is our attempt to structure the answers to the question concerning the nature, intensity and timing of intervention in the lives of children who are, or who may become, in conflict with the law and the youth justice system. We have already begun to set out the terrain and some of the principles that constitute our answer in the preceding discussion and we will go on to further elaborate our approach in the following chapter.

TWO

What is Children First, Offenders Second?

In Chapter One, we introduced Children First, Offenders Second (CFOS), a modern and distinctive model of youth justice that challenges established approaches grounded in welfare, justice, new orthodoxy and risk. CFOS is a principled, progressive and child-friendly model of positive youth justice, underpinned by the special treatment of children, adherence to children's rights and attendance to socio-structural inequalities. CFOS holds the central tenet that prevention (of offending and other problematic behaviours by children) is better than cure and is founded on the belief that children are part of the solution (to preventing problems and achieving positive outcomes), not part of the problem.

In this chapter, we set out the central tenets of a CFOS approach to responding to children in conflict with the law and the youth justice system. As we will show, this approach embraces both children who are identified as offenders and the prevention of offending by children – based broadly on notions of normalisation and inclusion. The central tenets of the CFOS model will be set out and contrasted with the main ideas and practices that have characterised youth justice (see Chapter One, Table 1.1) and which we see as having no place in the youth justice system (YJS) – thus drawing and deepening the distinction between the key tenets of CFOS and those of other approaches. Table 2.1 provides an illustration of the contrasts as we see them, which are explored in subsequent sections. In our view, a CFOS model of positive youth justice is as shown in Table 2.1.

Table 2.1: The central tenets of Children First, Offenders Second

	Children First, Offenders Second	Contrasting approaches
1	Child friendly and child appropriate	Adulterised
2	Diversionary	Punishment/justice- or welfare-based
3	Prevention as inclusionary	Prevention as exclusionary
4	Evidence-based partnership	Programme fetishism
5	Legitimate to children	Labelling and stigmatising
6	Systems management	Unprincipled net widening
7	Partnership with the state	Distrustful of the state
8	Responsibilising adults	Responsibilising children

We build on these contrasting tenets throughout this chapter as a way of outlining and exploring the principles, influences and drivers of CFOS – establishing clearly what the model *is* and what it most definitely *is not*.

Child friendly and child appropriate, not adulterised justice

A CFOS approach to youth justice views offending as 'only one element of a much wider and more complex identity' (Drakeford 2009: 8) for children, which should be addressed by a series of joined-up, inclusive and rights-based social policies. Thus we concur with Drakeford's (2010: 143) assertion that 'a "children first" approach to youth justice must be embedded in a wider and more generic set of policy-making responses to children'.

Children in conflict with the law and the youth justice system should be viewed primarily as children who (sometimes) experience personal and social vulnerabilities and who possess an entitlement to the benefits of living in a rich, advanced, Western society – as befits their growing maturity. This contrasts starkly with traditional ways of treating children primarily in terms of their offence or their offence-related characteristics and through the punitive, repressive, controlling, responsibilising measures that are typically visited upon adults. In other words, CFOS does not seek to treat children who offend as if they are (mini-) adults (that is, in an *adulterised* manner – see Fionda 1998; Fagan and Zimring 2000; Muncie 2008b) as this process ignores children's inherent vulnerability and need for protection and is thus anathema to 'good youth justice' (see Harding and

Becroft 2013). While we fully recognise that notions of justice in the adult criminal justice system are complex and contested (see Sanders, Young and Burton 2010), whatever one's view on the justices or injustices perpetrated by this system, it treats those with whom it deals as adults – as people who are independent, capable and responsible for making their own decisions in life and for bearing the consequences of their decision making.[12]

In direct contrast to the norms of the adult criminal justice system and the adulterising tendencies of the YJS, the CFOS approach disavows the use of the term 'offender' (that is why we have taken care to use the term 'children in conflict with the law and the youth justice system' throughout) because of the narrowing, blaming effect and negative consequences for children that this label entails. A child who commits an offence is not an 'offender'. The status of offender should not become a label or a master status (following Becker 1963) that characterises the whole person just because they have been drawn into conflict with the law and the youth justice system. A child who is on one or more occasions drawn into conflict with the law and youth justice system remains as much someone's child or friend as any other child growing up in a complex (and sometimes challenging) social environment. To respond to a child in conflict with the law and the youth justice system simply as an offender reduces a social being to an object or a thing (a 'dividual' – O'Malley 2010), it acts to responsibilise (Garland 1996; Muncie 2006) the child for their behaviour, it divests the state of its duties towards these citizens and it negates the responsibilities organisations and adults have towards children.

CFOS is a child-friendly and child-appropriate model (see also Goldson and Muncie's 2006 model of 'Principled Youth Justice'[13]) that aims to engage with children in conflict with the law and the youth justice system in 'child sensitive' ways (see UNHCHR

[12] That said, of course, the adult criminal justice system has provisions for mitigating (although not discharging) the degree of responsibility – manifest in differential sentencing. It also has the capacity to discharge this responsibility in cases of mental disorder – although, as research has shown (Peay 2012) it tends to do this quite badly.

[13] Constituted by the six principles of: addressing the socio-economic conditions that lead to poverty and inequality; universality and re-engaging the 'social'; diversion; child-appropriate justice; abolitionism; depoliticisation and tolerance.

2013) on the child's terms and on the basis that they are children (see also Harding and Becroft's 2013 '10 Characteristics of a Good Youth Justice System'[14]). Miniaturising an adult criminal justice system in the form of a YJS is an insufficient and inappropriate approach. Although the establishment of the juvenile court (over 100 years ago) was seen as a progressive, civilising and pro-child development (Behlmer 1998), the juvenile court effectively enshrined a miniaturised criminal justice system in the realm of youth justice. This model of youth justice has proved particularly resistant to (meaningful) change – despite the absence of any evidence that this model works. Children are prosecuted in courts for offences. Although these courts are meant to be less intimidating and, indeed, separate from adult courts (except in the case of those prosecuted in the higher courts), they are still formalised, adult-oriented settings. Children are prosecuted for offences, based on a justice model and there is a prosecutor (who presents formalised evidence against the child) and a defence solicitor. Children are subjected to sentences that resemble (frequently very strongly) the sentences handed down to adults – broadly: fines, community service, community supervision and imprisonment (although usually scaled down in severity). Children are subjected to the same enforcement regimes of sentences as adults.[15] In short, it is hard to make any claim that the current YJS is in any way child friendly – in the sense that the system has been designed for children, in the sense that children are able to understand, appreciate and participate in the system in any meaningful way and in the sense that the

[14] The '10 characteristics' are: (1) limitation upon charging children and young people (and options to discharge young people who perform well in court), (2) minimum and maximum ages for Youth Court jurisdiction, (3) trained specialists working with young people, (4) timely decision making and resolution of charges, (5) delegation of decision making to families, victims and communities, (6) duty to encourage participation, (7) evidence-based therapeutic approaches to offending, (8) ability to refer to care and protection where that is overwhelming need, (9) minimal use of incarceration/custodial sentences, (10) keeping the young person with their family and community. These characteristics and their overlap with CFOS principles are discussed at various points throughout our book.

[15] Which, particularly in the case of community supervision, means being subject to a whole series of 'requirements', failure to comply with which results in a formal 'breach' of the conditions of the order of the court and frequently a return to court.

system works for children. In short, the YJS is in desperate need of radical child-friendly reform.

Diversionary, not punishment-, justice- or welfare-based

CFOS holds a commitment to *diversion* from the formal YJS that goes beyond the recognition and acceptance that the system has iatrogenic properties (compare McAra and McVie 2007) and our adherence to the value of effective systems management (discussed later in this chapter), to the belief that normal child-rearing practices should be prioritised when dealing with the child's behaviour and that the best place to do this is in the context of the family (see also Harding and Becroft 2013). The formal YJS should stay out of the lives of children – right out! This approach is not a clarion call for radical non-intervention, but rather for principled diversionary responses that focus on promoting positive behaviour by and outcomes for children and enabling access to universal entitlements to services, activities, support and information. A progressive and rights-based model of youth justice grounded in diversionary principles runs counter to the interventionist and net-widening tendencies of the formal YJS (following Goldson and Muncie 2006). Therefore, we are not arguing for non-intervention per se, we are arguing for non-*formal* intervention. Diversion from the formal YJS should mean exactly that. Children who demonstrate problems and problematic behaviour (for example low-level offending, antisocial behaviour, substance use) should be *worked with* by practitioners offering supportive services that promote positive behaviour and enhance access to children's rights/entitlements, rather than being *dealt with* by counterproductive, formal youth justice processes that can stigmatise, label and disengage children from positive and nurturing experiences as they grow and develop.

Diversion, not punishment

Through its commitment to diversion from formal youth justice processes, CFOS eschews notions of *punishment*. Although punishment in the criminal justice arena is far from unequivocally defined or understood (see Cavadino and Dignan 2002 for a broader discussion of punishment), for us, punishment has a quintessential retributive quality – rooted in the idea that punishment is justified by some wrongdoing. Retribution can take the form of taking something away from the 'offender' such as money – in the form of fines – or time – in the form of community payback – or restrictions on liberty – in the form of curfews or mandatory attendance/participation in supervision, to the deliberate infliction of pain (for example Muncie, in Goldson 2008a).

Eschewing punishment in favour of diversion is an explicit recognition that youth justice interventions have (more often than not) unintended consequences (see Kelly 2012). What may be done to children with good intentions or with their best interests in mind may be perceived by those children as punitive and/or may exacerbate the problems experienced by children and/or may contribute to further offending rather than lessening it. We also fully recognise that, whether intended or unintended, whether deliberately punitive or not, embroiling children in the formal YJS can, in and of itself, contribute to further offending rather than lessening it (McAra and McVie 2007; Richards 2014). These issues are, however, well established and not the main focus of our concern here.

The focal point of our concern is when the YJS *deliberately* visits punishment on children, when the practices and sentences of the YJS have punishment as their aim.[16] A second, but nonetheless important and related target of our concern is when the practices and sentences of the YJS are perceived by children to be punitive or to have punitive impact – whether or not such motivations were in the mind of those adults responsible for such practices. From our perspective and from that of the children involved, there is no distinction between measures that are deliberately punitive in intent and those that are perceived as being punitive – from the child's point of view they are being punished.

What, then, is so wrong with punishment? Why does the CFOS approach eschew punishment? We have two main

[16] Muncie (in Goldson 2008a: 278) discusses this issue in the Dictionary of Youth Justice under the heading of 'Punitiveness', with which our argument has much in common (see also Muncie 2008b: 308).

responses to these questions: punishment is nasty and punishment is ineffective. Retribution is an inherently vindictive act, not motivated by any attempt to do good. It is simply an act designed to exact revenge for some perceived wrongdoing. Retribution has no aim to make things better in the future (for the young person, the victim or for society), but is simply an attempt to atone for something done in the past. Our main objection to punishment (as nasty retribution) can be expressed quite easily as: what kind of society do we live in where our response to wrongdoing by children is characterised by retribution? Retributive responses, especially when applied to children, are inhumane, antisocial, often knee-jerk/thoughtless and anathema to a principled and rights-facing model of youth justice.

To compound these issues, there is no (compelling) evidence that punishment is an effective mechanism for reducing offending. This situation clearly flies in the face of not only commonsense and human decency, but also concerns for 'evidence-based' and 'effective' practice (see Stephenson, Giller and Brown 2011). In fact, the limited amount of evidence there is on this topic shows that overtly punitive responses to children in conflict with the law and the youth justice system are not just ineffective, they are actively counterproductive. Moreover, the more punitive the response becomes, the more it actually promotes reoffending (see Haines and Drakeford 1998).

Diversion, not justice

As much as CFOS is not *punishment* based, neither is it *justice* based. Justice-based responses to children in conflict with the law and the youth justice system are predicated on one simple principle: that children should receive penalties/punishments that are proportionate to the seriousness of the offence(s) they have been found guilty of.[17] This, in short, is an Offender First,

[17] The justice-based 'just deserts' approach outlined in the Criminal Justice Act 1991 required courts to undertake a balanced consideration of the severity of an offence alongside offender information such as age, attitude, maturity, culpability and reasons for offending, then to select an appropriate sentence from a 'tariff' of sentencing options (see Haines and Drakeford 1998).

Children Second approach and, as such, is in direct contradiction to the approach we set out in this book.

While, over history, traditional responses to children in conflict with the law and the youth justice system have swung between justice-based and welfare-based approaches, there is a strong sense in which justice has been a consequentialist reaction against welfare-based approaches (and their perceived negative consequences, such as indeterminacy, lack of proportionality, excessive practitioner discretion – see Smith 2005). In particular, advocates of justice-based responses to children have seen justice as a way of reducing the severity of the sanctions applied – notably the perceived over-use of custodial sentencing, but also excessively long, excessively interventionist and excessively punitive community-based sanctions. In some ways, therefore, this has enabled advocates of justice-based approaches to argue that they are more child friendly than welfare-based approaches, for example in their adherence to children's *legal* rights through the promotion of due process (see Ignatieff 2000; Daly 2003; Carrabine 2008). This argument, to a certain extent, characterised the 'back to justice' movement in the early 1980s in England and Wales, but was only so to the extent that 'justice' was coupled with systems management (Haines, in Goldson 2008) and other guiding principles (see 'Principles of a children-first youth justice philosophy' – Haines and Drakeford 1998: 91; see also Morris and Giller 1983).

There is, however, nothing inherently child friendly about justice-based approaches and it is troubling that they focus on the link between the adjudged severity of the offence and notions of proportionality. Proportionality is inherently malleable and subject to a wide range of influences: what is considered proportional at one time may be considered lenient (or, indeed, punitive) at others. The venal and retributive excesses of justice-based approaches are no more plainly exhibited than in recent developments in youth justice in the US (see, Winterdyk 2005; Lipsey and Howell 2012), where the focus on the offence (to the exclusion of the child) coupled with a marked political and public opinion set against the offender has resulted in a distinctive and quite nasty punitive turn (see Cavadino and Dignan 2006; Muncie 2008b). This turn has been accompanied by the excessive use of imprisonment and other retributive and punitive measures for children, such as the absence of a clear minimum age of criminal responsibility in certain states (King and Szymanski 2006), increased accountability for children who offend (Hazel 2008), adulterised sentencing practices (Cavadino and Dignan 2006) and repressive crime control initiatives (Jepsen 2006). The consequentialist and relativist properties of justice-based approaches are further (beyond their prioritisation of the offence over the child) reasons to question their validity and applicability to youth justice.

Diversion, not restorative justice

Even more specifically, CFOS is not an approach that integrates, supports or resonates with *restorative* justice – probably the fastest and biggest growing area in criminal and youth justice since it exploded internationally with John Braithwaite's publication of *Crime, Shame and Reintegration* in 1989.[18] In terms of youth justice, restorative justice has risen to occupy a very high profile in official policy (Crawford and Newburn 2003) and it has proliferated in practice – where, in both policy and practice spheres, it is regarded in a highly positive manner (compare Ministry of Justice 2010; Independent Commission on Youth Crime and Antisocial Behaviour 2011; see also Robinson 2014). Similarly, in academic terms, books and journal articles extolling the virtues of restorative justice now abound (and run into the hundreds).[19] Policy makers, practitioners and (most) academics seem to be of one mind; restorative justice is a good thing and

---

[18] Interestingly, *Crime, Shame and Reintegration* was not a manifesto for restorative justice, but Braithwaite's analysis of why some countries/cultures have lower crime rates than others. It nevertheless spawned one of the biggest international revolutions in criminal justice.

[19] In a subsequent section in this chapter ('Partnership with the state'), we discuss how criminology is frequently characterised by critical analysis and an associated criticism of state policy and youth justice practice. In the field of restorative justice, however, an unusual harmony exists between criminology, the state and practice – in the UK and internationally. Published criticisms of restorative justice are relatively rare (although see Haines 1996; Delgrado 2000; Gelsthorpe and Morris 2002; Johnstone 2002; Haines and O'Mahony 2006).

it should be used, as much as possible, at all points of the YJS from diversion to custody.

However, there are two major long-standing problems with restorative justice that, in our view, mark it out for special criticism and distinguish it from CFOS. First, no one knows what restorative justice is and, secondly, restorative justice is rooted in the victims' movement. The first problem raises the issue of exactly who is being restored by restorative justice. The second problem actually answers this question ('the victim'). Either way, however, the child is not at the heart of the process and does not appear to benefit from it – counter to the CFOS approach.

After many years of quite fervent debate (Braithwaite 2002) and notwithstanding the schisms within the restorative justice movement (for example relational justice – see Casanovas 2008), the academic community reached a consensus on the definition of restorative justice – that put forward by Tony Marshall (1996: 37): 'Restorative justice is a process whereby all the parties with a stake in a particular offence come together to resolve collectively how to deal with the aftermath of the offence and its implications for the future.'

Thus, restorative justice seeks to restore and repair the harm caused by the conduct of an 'offender' (Marshall 1996), but beyond this notion much remains uncertain. Perhaps reflecting the distance between restorative justice protagonists, or perhaps reflecting the elusive quality of restorative justice itself, this agreed definition hardly qualifies as a definition at all because of its imprecision and the room it leaves for interpretation (and, indeed, misinterpretation). What precisely does 'repairing the harm done by the crime' mean? Is it the harm to an individual victim? The victim's family? The neighbourhood? A corporate victim? Society generally? The 'offender' or their family? Or is it 'all of the above'? In both policy and practice, the answer has been 'all of these, at different times, in different places'. Moreover, who is responsible for 'repairing the harm'? Is it society, the state (in whatever guise), criminal justice agencies? The answer (so far) is that it is variously 'some or all of these, at different times, in different places'. Most frequently, however, the answer to this question is that it is the 'offender' who is responsible for repairing the harm. Probing more deeply, what precisely is the 'harm' to be repaired? Is this harm material, financial or emotional? Is symbolic reparation sufficient? If so, for whom? Yet still more difficult questions arise, such as 'who decides all of this'? Despite the proliferation of restorative justice in the work of proselytising academics, policy and practice, there are no satisfactory answers to these questions. This absence of agreement on all these critical questions, rather than causing the exercise of caution and restraint, have provided the scope for diversity in academic, policy and practice spheres to flourish – all in the name of restorative justice, but without any clear definition as to what it is, what it is trying to do and any idea as to how you would recognise it if you saw it.

Whatever the answers to the questions just posed (answers that vary considerably within academic, policy and practice discourses and that are seldom satisfactory in any way) and whatever the rhetoric about restorative justice being a constructive and positive response to crime, there is one consistent theme – the 'best interests of the victim'. No one doubts that the experience of being a victim of crime runs from inconvenience to devastating. No one would (dare) argue that victims of crime do not suffer and that they do not deserve better treatment. It is quite a different position, however, to argue that justice (in whatever guise) should serve the best interests of the victim. It is this quality that marks restorative justice out as a victim's movement.[20] While in the adult sphere one might be able to justify such a position (at least in part), it is wholly unjustified when applied to children. Seen from this perspective restorative justice is a *Victim First, Child Second* approach and this brings it into direct conflict with CFOS. This conflict is readily evident at the level of principle, but it exists too at the level of policy and practice. A host of policy and practice documents advocate restorative justice as a means of meeting the needs of victims (for example Domestic Violence, Crime and Victims Act 2004; *Developing Restorative Justice: An Action Plan* guidance document –YJB 2008b). This focus is consolidated by law and policy that

[20] Perhaps paradoxically, the contribution of John Braithwaite to this debate marks him out from the vast majority (see Braithwaite 2002; Braithwaite and Mugford 1994).

places the victim at, or near, the centre of restorative justice processes (for example Referral Order Panels, Youth Restorative Disposals – see Chapter Five). Research continues to place the victim's concerns at the centre of evaluations of restorative justice practices/projects (Sherman and Strang 2007; Zernova 2007), as do actual restorative justice projects, where the needs/interests of the victim are given primacy over the needs/interests of children (Wilcox 2004; Department of Justice Northern Ireland 2011).[21]

For all these reasons, restorative justice is not CFOS.

Diversion, not welfare

CFOS is not a welfare-based approach that advocates delivering interventions that address the underlying social welfare needs of children and their families. The welfare model privileges needs over deeds, care over control and deprivation over depravation – seeking either to 'correct' individual deficiencies through treatment (Harris and Webb 1987) or to ameliorate the consequences of social deprivation (Goldson 2000). Setting aside the unintended consequences of welfare-based youth justice as it has been practised (for example indeterminism producing interventionism and net widening, lack of demonstrable effectiveness) (see, for example, Haines and Drakeford 1998) and the political/economic arguments (set out in the previous chapter) as to why welfare is no longer feasible, a welfare-based approach to youth justice is predicated on responding to the (adult-defined) needs of the child in the manner of providing a safety net below which no child must be allowed to fall (Hill, Lockyer and Stone 2007). While the offence is very much a secondary consideration in welfare-based approaches and, at face value, therefore, may appear coincident with CFOS – it is not. The welfarist emphasis on identifying and responding (for example through treatment) to children's needs promotes an adult-centric service delivery model that can neglect working with children as agentic, active constructors of their own positive

[21] Arguably, the Swansea Bureau diversionary programme (see Chapter Five) is the only example of restorative justice-like processes that place the child at the centre (see Hoffman and MacDonald 2011; Nacro 2011; Centre for Social Justice 2012).

futures, in favour of adult interpretations of the needs and requirements of children. Consideration of children's rights and entitlements is relatively overlooked, as is the responsibilisation of adults to facilitate children's access to these rights and entitlements and their access to child-friendly, child-appropriate services and support. Welfare-based approaches are rooted in pseudo-psychosocial notions of problematic childhoods, in adult-centric assessments and in adult-determined interventions. This is anathema to CFOS, which is rooted in notions of children as part of the solution, not part of the problem, of effective engagement with children and a focus on enhancing positive outcomes.

The main difference between welfare-based approaches and CFOS, however, is to be found in the underlying motivations of these different approaches and of the adults that populate them. Welfare is wedded to notions of treatment and of providing a safety net. It is an approach, therefore, which is, at best, retrospective and, at worst, backward looking. In contrast, CFOS is an approach which is not so concerned with the past, but is much more proactive, forward looking and ambitious. The CFOS approach is, among other things, focused on the future, on working with children to achieve positive outcomes.

Prevention as inclusionary, not prevention as exclusionary

Following the Crime and Disorder Act 1998, 'prevention' (or, rather, 'prevention, prevention, prevention' – see Garland 2002) became the overarching goal of the YJS. Prevention has, however, been somewhat disappointingly implemented by Youth Offending Teams (YOTs) and their partners over the last decade or so. This has been the fault of three main actors: government, the Youth Justice Board (YJB) and critical academics.

Despite the punitive shift in youth justice policy ushered in by the Labour government following its election in 1997, New Labour never really was 'tough on the causes of crime' as it promised, nor was it truly 'tough on crime' (Labour Party 1997), but it most certainly was tough on children.[22] For all its

[22] Indeed, Muncie (1999) described the Crime and Disorder Act 1998 as 'institutionally intolerant' of children.

rhetoric about the harm caused by social exclusion and the need to promote inclusion (Lister 1998; Social Exclusion Unit 2000), New Labour set about what was arguably a deliberate strategy of demonising children in conflict with the law and the youth justice system (Pitts 2003). The whole ASBO (Antisocial Behaviour Order) crusade (for that is what it became, see Squires and Stephen 2005; Burney 2009), for example, did much damage to the position of youth in society. New Labour's political strategy, therefore, made a 'tough on children' approach more politically and publicly acceptable than any attempts at dealing constructively with the problems faced by children. Furthermore, the linking of 'intervention, intervention, intervention' with 'prevention, prevention, prevention' effectively served to draw more and more children into the formal YJS, subjecting them to offence and offender-oriented interventions – largely in response to the social distress experienced by many such children. The much lauded *Every Child Matters: Change for Children* policy framework (Department for Education and Skills (DfES) 2004), which committed to build services around children that would 'maximise opportunities and minimize risk' (DfES 2004: 2), deliberately excluded children in conflict with the law and the youth justice system, as those children who offended or behaved antisocially were to have their opportunities forcibly removed (Haines 2009b; see also Kemshall 2008; Robinson 2014). This standpoint was exemplified by then Prime Minister Tony Blair's statement in 2004 that those 'who play by the rules are not going to see their opportunities blighted by those who don't' and his proclamation that children should have 'no rights without responsibilities' (Blair, speech to the Labour Party Conference, 2004). New Labour, therefore, did much to ramp up the role of the formal YJS in a context where the responsibility for offending by children and its consequences were firmly fixed on the individual children involved. All of this made it very difficult for Youth Offending Teams (YOTs) to engage positively in the prevention agenda – they were much too preoccupied with individual identified offenders. New Labour failed children politically, in policy terms and in practice.

For much of its lifetime, the YJB has been preoccupied with regulating the work of YOTs in the processing of individual children, ably assisted by the Probation Inspectorate whose narrow-minded focus on process – to the exclusion of almost everything else – has done serious damage the work of YOTs and the relationship between YOT staff and children. In the context of increasing workloads (with more and more children being brought into the remit of the formal YJS[23]), YOTs have struggled to meet the managerialist requirements for processing children imposed by the YJB. Consequently, they have taken their eyes off the prevention agenda. This state of affairs has been compounded by a confusion (or a lack of clarity) over whether the main purpose of the YJS is the prevention of offending or the reduction of *re*-offending – two very different objectives. While both aims have been promoted (see Case and Haines 2009), the emphasis of the YJB and Probation Inspectorate has been on managing the processing of identified offenders[24] alongside the identification and management (through risk-based early intervention) of children 'at risk' of offending in the future[25] (coupled with the absence of focus in any key performance indicators on the prevention of offending) at least partly explains why YOTs, generally, have paid scant attention to the primary prevention of offending.

The voices of critical youth justice academics have been quite influential in drawing attention to the negative (even if unintended) consequences of prevention work (see Kelly 2012), but largely to the exclusion of putting forward a positive prevention agenda based on constructive intervention (although

[23] Although we should note that this trend has recently been reversed, at least partly, by the introduction of a key performance indicator for YOTs to reduce the number of 'First Time Entrants' (FTEs) into the YJS (see, Haines and Case 2012). Notably, however, the widespread reductions in FTEs has not been achieved by a burgeoning of preventative work on the part of YOTs, but must be explained by other causes (for example better systems management coupled with a renewed emphasis on diversion).

[24] In reality, the focus has been on *reconviction* rather than reoffending, as the latter category can include (unmeasured, unrecorded) offending behaviour that has not come to the attention of the formal YJS and agencies within it.

[25] To reiterate – we do not intend to over-simplify, caricature or homogenise youth justice practice; nor are we suggesting that all YOTs behave in this way. We remain attendant to local variations in the mediation of policy and the delivery of practice (compare Smith 2014).

see Case and Haines, 2015a). The broad argument of many critical youth justice academics (from Cohen 1985 onwards) has been that *any* involvement of those who work in the formal YJS with children (and especially that which aims to do good – such as involvement of a preventive nature) is actually and actively harmful to those children (see, for example, Pitts 2003; Goldson and Muncie 2006; McAra and McVie 2007; Bateman 2012). To be sure, from the critiques of the justice-based model (see previous section) and critiques of welfare-based approaches to youth justice (see, for example, Cohen 1985; Smith 2005), the evidence tends to be on their side. But this evidence also tends to miss one important point: that the majority of prevention work that the critics are so critical of tends only to take place with identified offenders (or those deemed to be antisocial) – thereby reflecting the confusion over the prevention of offending or prevention of reoffending issue – and tends only to happen by drawing those children, in some way, into the formal YJS.[26] Following this logic, the opportunities for genuine prevention of offending work are missed.

Conversely, CFOS takes the prevention of offending seriously. We believe that the prevention of offending is a proper, even the primary, goal of the YJS and will even go so far as to extend this belief into an argument for intervention that utilises children's inclusion, participation and engagement to prioritise the *promotion* of positive behaviours and outcomes (see Chapter Six). We believe YOTs must be centrally involved in delivering these prevention services, not just because prevention is inherently better than cure, not just because the formal YJS has so many iatrogenic properties that children are best kept out of it, but because (when you place children at the heart of the system) it is the right thing to do and because YOT staff possess the requisite knowledge and skills to take forward a strategic youth

[26] Or by prejudicing the position of children engaged in preventative work in the face of future formal engagement with the system – as happened, for example, in the case of Intermediate Treatment in the 1970s and 1980s when voluntary engagement in Intermediate Treatment programmes was seen, on a subsequent court appearance, as having been tried and failed, resulting in the up-tariffing of children (see, Haines and Drakeford 1998).

crime prevention agenda. Such an agenda can only effectively be progressed, however, in adherence to CFOS principles:

- adopting a whole child, child-friendly perspective;
- *diversionary intervention* conducted outside the formal YJS;
- legitimate to children;
- systems management and a partnership approach as vital;
- recognising the *responsibilities of adults* towards children;
- taking a *long-term* perspective.

It is essential that the CFOS approach to youth justice is not taken as a buffet-style menu where one is free to choose the tasty morsels, leaving some dishes untouched. CFOS is a comprehensive approach in which the various elements are interdependent and mutually reinforcing. Taking crime prevention seriously is an essential and critical part of the CFOS approach, but its realisation is dependent upon all other aspects of the approach being developed and implemented simultaneously. Accordingly, the prevention of offending by children is an objective best achieved through the provision of universal services within and outwith the YJS (whole child) that safeguard children (child friendly), that enable children to avoid the deleterious impact of formal system contact (diversionary), and that are normalising, decriminalising, meaningful and considered moral and fair by children (child appropriate and legitimate). Services and interventions should be underpinned by considered decision making at key stages of the youth justice process (systems management) that holds the child's best interests as paramount (child friendly) and are developed, implemented and evaluated in partnership though the participation and engagement of children (child-friendly and child-appropriate approach to evidence-based partnership) and researchers (Reflective Friend Research – see Chapter Four). Access to these supportive and promotional services and interventions must be facilitated by responsibilised adults, not responsibilised children. Many of these services will already exist[27] – albeit from which too many children are excluded – but some new services may need to be developed.[28]

It is essential that the development and implementation of a prevention of offending strategy takes a long-term perspective. Prevention of offending strategies will be doomed to fail from the outset if a quick fix is the expected outcome. It takes time (sometimes a long time) to identify and engage with all relevant local stakeholders. It takes time (sometimes a long time) to find sufficient common ground between all the relevant stakeholders to begin developing a joint strategy. It also takes time (sometimes a long time) to re-articulate existing service provision, to change organisational behaviour or to develop services that are designed, at least in part, to prevent offending. Once these *organisational* matters are attended to (as far as is possible and it is important to see these as aspects of service delivery that require ongoing attention), it also takes time (sometimes a long time) to realise the objectives of a CFOS strategy in terms of outcomes for children. Therefore, CFOS is not a superficial quick fix, but is intended as a long-term, sustainable approach to delivering social justice.

Evidence-based partnership, not programme fetishism

For responses to children in conflict with the law and the youth justice system to be properly inclusionary and legitimate (see next section), as necessitated by CFOS, they should be underpinned by genuine *partnership* working that is *evidence based* (compare the 'good youth justice' of Harding and Becroft 2013). Notwithstanding what we have said earlier about the centrality of YOTs in local prevention of offending strategies, it is absolutely clear that YOTs cannot effectively carry out this work alone. Partnership is critical to the success of prevention of offending and this partnership needs to be evident at the strategic

[27] Although many services for children have been cut as a result of the austerity measures imposed by the Conservative/Liberal Democrat Coalition Government from 2010 onwards (Robinson 2014).

[28] In every local area, there are a number of children who experience levels of personal distress and social hardship that cannot be effectively addressed by universal services and, for these children, additional targeted services are necessary to prevent further suffering.

level and in practice and delivery. The reflective development, implementation and evaluation of child-friendly, meaningful and legitimate services and interventions should be guided by evidence-based partnership between children (and their families), youth justice practitioners, policy makers and researchers. The policy maker–practitioner–child/family relationship has been conceived of by some as a 'trialogue' (see Williamson 2011) – a three-way dialogue – but such a focus on dialogue/discussion downplays the child's potential to contribute to the services they receive through meaningful participation and engagement. It also neglects the potential for academic researchers to engage with key stakeholders (children, families, practitioners, policy makers) in reflective research partnerships that facilitate children's engagement and offer critical friendship to youth justice staff when reflecting on their practice and provision.

It was Leon Britton (writing as Home Secretary) who first expressed the view that it was legitimate (indeed essential) for government to have a coherent criminal justice policy and to expect that the various agencies that make up the criminal justice system should work together to achieve that (common) goal (Britton 1984). Since that time, inter-agency working and notions of partnership have become central features of government criminal/youth justice policy and critical academic discourse (Bailey and Williams 2000; Burnett and Appleton 2004; Kelly 2012; Robinson 2014). While we fully recognise the politics of this issue and do not deny the difficulties involved in developing successful partnerships, we fully believe that it is only through a partnership approach (one involving children) that children can be best served by a prevention strategy linked to the promotion of positive behaviours and outcomes for children (see Chapter Six).

The Crime and Disorder Act 1998 made it a legal requirement for local authorities to establish a strategic approach to youth crime. Through the Act, multi-agency Community Safety Partnerships (known as Crime and Disorder Reduction Partnerships in England) were created in every local authority area in England and Wales (see Burnett and Appleton 2004).[29] In practice, however, these partnerships have been somewhat lacklustre and disappointing (Hughes 2004, 2007; Loveday 2006; Edwards and Hughes 2009; Houghton 2011). For example, some partnerships have experienced longstanding difficulties in engaging certain statutory partner agencies (for example health) in crime prevention and reduction activities (National Audit Office 2008) and certain partners (for example health again) have struggled to identify and understand their role in these multi-agency partnerships (see Nacro 2001; Case 2004). The development of effective partnership working has been hampered, in some areas, by a lack of willingness on the part of some agencies to engage in partnership-based approaches and by the reinforcement of intra-agency perspectives and priorities (Hughes et al 2009). Clarity of structure and sustainable resourcing have been long-term problematic issues for many partnerships (see Nacro 2001; Morgan 2009). There has been an over-riding tendency for partnerships to prioritise the *reduction* of risk factors and reoffending over preventive work and a tendency for local partnerships to 'consult' with local communities rather than directly involving them in key decision-making processes (Edwards and Hughes 2009).

Additionally, anathema to the central principles of CFOS, has been the lack of involvement, participation and engagement (and possible active exclusion) of children from partnership approaches. We believe that effective prevention of (re-)offending strategies and practices need to be developed in partnership with children, the very group that they are aimed at and structured for. All too often children are seen as a problem to be fixed by local partnerships. Conversely, CFOS does not see children as part of the problem, but, as we have said, as part of the solution.

Notwithstanding the difficulties and deficiencies in partnership working, identified above, partnership approaches and partnership working are central to a CFOS model. The negative

[29] These provisions were included in the Crime and Disorder Act 1998 largely as a reaction to the *Misspent Youth* report (Audit Commission 1996) and its castigation of the YJS for being inefficient, ineffective and uneconomical – typified by youth justice agencies working poorly together (or not working together at all).

consequences of a failure to generate and implement effective partnerships are manifest, for example poorly executed, poorly evidenced and inconclusive community crime prevention (see Newburn and Souhami 2005) and the politically motivated and subjective risk judgements characterising the *Communities that Care* programme in England (see France and Crow 2005). These negative consequences are most keenly felt by those children who are (and who continue to be) let down by those agencies whose purpose is to serve children. The positive outcomes to be achieved by effective partnerships are equally manifest and are well documented in those localities where effective partnerships have been forged, for example reductions in first-time entrants into the YJS (FTEs) and reoffending rates through the Bureau project (see Haines, Case, Charles and Davies 2013; see also Chapter Five) and increased engagement and problem-solving ability in children evidenced by both the Flintshire Community Reparation Project and the Rhonnda Cynon Taf Safety Zone Project (see Hughes et al 2009).

A crucial but important benefit of a partnership approach is the extent to which it guards against the tendency of individual agencies, acting alone, to become excessively introspective and the associated tendency for such agencies to pursue simplistic, often off-the-shelf, approaches to working with children. Thus, the evidential and reflective partnership bases of CFOS mean that the model avers *programme fetishism*. The term was introduced by Rod Morgan (2002: 8) in his annual report as Chief Inspector of Probation as a critical comment on the manner in which probation services had responded to the effective practice agenda. Any discussion of programme fetishism hinges on the definition or understanding of the term 'programme'. For many academics, the term 'programme' means a planned sequence of learning opportunities (McGuire 2001). Thus, according to Durnescu, 'a programme is an organized and systematic intervention directed towards specific objectives' (Durnescu 2012: 194). However, following the critical intent of Morgan, in practice, programme fetishism has embodied a more narrowing and specific definition and set of consequences: 'The 1990s saw a "programme fetishism" reflected in a preoccupation with identifying the activities that had most impact on offending – as if the training of offenders in anger management, for example, or in literacy skills or in relapse prevention, was the critical feature of successful practice.' The programme fetishism, of which Morgan was so critical, has a number of distinctive features, tending to privilege programmes which:

- emphasise the *integrity* of programme delivery;
- are defined primarily in *pseudo-psychological* terms;
- come '*off the shelf*' in accredited packages;
- are strictly offender and/or offence focused;
- *de-humanise* and *de-socialise* those subjected to them.

It is our contention that although the debate discussed earlier has focused on adult criminal justice, programme fetishism has come to dominate and characterise youth justice practice. The edifice of youth justice that has been built up under the stewardship of the YJB has managed programme fetishism into the centre of youth justice assessment and practice. The evidence for this is to be found in the structure and outcome of Asset-based risk assessments in the YJS (as it currently exists[30] – see Chapter Four) and the type of interventions privileged. The Scaled Approach to assessment and intervention in the YJS has been underpinned by the Asset risk assessment tool – a tool which is designed (by intent or by default) to deliver programme fetishism. Asset measures (practitioner perceptions of) a child's exposure to risk factors in 'psychosocial' (psychological and

[30] The YJB has recognised and responded to this criticism by rejecting the current version of Asset and the Scaled Approach (and its over-reliance on risk assessment, offence and offender focus, and preoccupation with narrowly defined risk and related programme delivery), to be replaced by a revised Scaled Approach, to be known as AssetPlus (YJB 2011; 2013). This revised approach will focus on: enhancing children's *strengths* rather than prioritising risks/deficits; addressing *needs* alongside risks, promoting *desistance* from offending, accessing *children's voices* rather than privileging adult prescriptions and understandings of 'risk' and children's lives, enabling more *practitioner discretion* in assessment and intervention planning and in focusing on achieving positive outcomes for children.

immediate social) risk domains[31] and pursues an *integrity* of (risk-based) programme delivery that is frequently lacking in a robust evidence base or detailed, long-term evaluation outcomes (see Case and Haines 2009). This inevitably produces definitions and explanations of youth offending couched in reductionist, *pseudo-psychological* and risk-focused terms[32] (see Chapter Four for further discussion of this reductionism). These assessments shape subsequent interventions, which are taken from an off-the-shelf menu of (largely pseudo-psychological) accredited 'what works' programmes (for example cognitive-behavioural, anger management, victim empathy, moral reasoning, social skills – Wikström and Treiber 2008), in line with the YJB's *Key Elements of Effective Practice* (KEEPs). Asset and the structure placed around it by the YJB, therefore, represents programme fetishism in practice.

There are a number of problems with this programme-fetishised response. The psychosocial risks measured by Asset and the psychosocial programmes that inevitably result from this assessment serve to *individualise* the causes, responsibility and blame for offending onto the child, rather than looking to broader, meso- and macro-level explanations and responses in socio-economic, socio-structural, political and demographic domains (Pitts 2003; Case 2007; France and Homel 2007; Muncie 2008b; O'Mahony 2009; Smith 2011). Programmes 'favoured' by Asset and the YJB's accompanying KEEPs are typically offender and offence focused – reflecting both the political demonisation of youth and the inherently individualising responses of a psychosocially dominated paradigm. The consequence is a potentially deleterious focus on offending that can serve to *dehumanise* and *desocialise* children by subjecting them to abstract assessment and interventions that neglect the realities of their

[31] Family and personal relationships, education, training and employment, neighbourhood, lifestyle, substance use, physical health, emotional and mental health, perception of self and others, thinking and behaviour, attitudes to offending, motivation to change, indicators of serious harm to others.

[32] This is, in fact, hardly surprising given the theoretical foundations of assessment and intervention in Asset are based on risk factor research, which is dominated by a developmental psycho-social paradigm (see Case and Haines 2009).

lives and lived experiences rather than promoting their active and willing participation and engagement in socially meaningful and age-appropriate, non-stigmatising processes (see also Goldson and Muncie 2006). Furthermore, the evidence for the effectiveness of offence- and offender-focused programmes in reducing offending is partial and, at best, quite poor.

Programme fetishism aims to achieve a quick fix. Its basic rationale is to try to identify (often in an overly simplistic, unitary, manner) the root cause of offending behaviour by children and to implement an accredited programme designed to correct the deficiency in the individual – in the belief that changing this root cause will prevent further offending. Setting aside questions as to whether offending behaviour (and particularly reoffending behaviour) can ever be understood in terms of a single cause and the imputed link between cause and effect, it is important to ask: What evidence is there that these programmes actually work in reducing offending? What evidence is there that these programmes are more effective than other forms of intervention? These are, in fact, very difficult (and contentious) questions; our answer to which is, as things currently stand, that there are problems (often of a methodological nature) with much existing research (for example, see Sherman and Strang 2004) and too little research of a broad enough compass to answer these questions adequately, let alone definitively.

Therefore, our objections to programme fetishism are rooted in its *Offender First, Children Second* focus, the manner in which it responds to children in terms of their offending behaviour (and not as whole children, with complex lives), its frequent reliance on narrowly conceptualised (and individualised) notions of risk and its use of offence- and offender-focused interventions that are founded on partial research and scant evidence of their effectiveness. On balance, we do not believe that there is convincing evidence of the effectiveness of 'programmes' in reducing offending – comprehensive evidence that would allow for a definitive answer to questions concerning the effectiveness of interventions is simply not available. An answer to this ongoing dilemma is to move away from the misguided reliance on the partial (psychosocial) and ostensibly 'evidence-based' programmes that are, in reality, seldom reinforced by a comprehensive, reliable and robust range and depth of actual evidence. Programmes and interventions recommended by the CFOS model are 'evidence based' in the sense that they are grounded in research and evaluation conducted in reflective partnerships of key stakeholders – practitioners, policy makers, children, families and researchers. Such interventions would not discount psychosocial influences on offending behaviour, but would promote whole-child and child-appropriate responses founded on an holistic assessment of the personal, social and structural circumstances and histories of children and their families. Thus, subsequent intervention would not fetishise risk and the prevention of negative behaviours/outcomes, but would prioritise promoting positive behaviours/outcomes, enabling access to universal rights/entitlements and working in partnership with children to reflect on and enhance programmes. The collection and utilisation of *evidence* is crucial to this agenda. However, the nature of this evidence would be open minded, reflexive and bottom up, rather than restricted, prescriptive and top down, developed in locally sensitive partnership with children and other key stakeholders.

Legitimate to children, not labelling and stigmatising

Central to the CFOS approach and crucial to any effective YJS is the principle that systemic responses to children must be seen as *legitimate* in the eyes of children. The concept of legitimacy has gained considerable ground in criminology in recent times, due, in large part, to the work of Tom Tyler (see Tyler 2004, 2006, 2007; see also Weber 1978; Quinney 1980; Cole 1999; Bobo and Thompson 2006; Tankebe 2008; Hawes 2013). Legitimacy has been employed to explore general questions of social order and to more explicitly understand the role legitimacy plays in explaining 'why people obey the Law' (Tyler 2006). The general thrust of the legitimacy argument is that the maintenance of social order is the main preoccupation of rulers. Social order can be maintained (broadly) through the use of rewards or coercion (by buying the consent of the people), or it can be maintained through suppression and punishment – both the threat of and the administration of (frequently very severe) punishments, or it can result from particularly charismatic leadership. Alternatively, social order can be achieved and maintained by the consent of the people and this is most likely to be manifest when the people see the authority and the discharge of authority by leaders or rulers (or their agents) as *legitimate*.

For Tyler, in this context, legitimacy is rooted in the internal beliefs of the people and what they consider to be moral, right or just (Tyler and Huo 2002). In short, if people consider the law to be moral, right or just (and fair) they are more likely to live their lives within the confines of the law and social order will be promoted. This symbolic quality of the law is important, but so too is the administration of the law by the agencies of the state. Thus if, in their interactions with the agencies and agents of law and order, the people perceive the behaviour and actions of, for example police officers, courts and youth justice staff, as moral, right, just and fair, they are more likely: (1) to perceive their treatment as moral, right, just and fair (even if this involves censure or punishment) and (2) to obey the law in the future. Conversely, if the people perceive the law as illegitimate (immoral, unjust and unfair) a deficit in legitimacy accrues and social order is likely to break down. This may manifest itself in general social disorder (public disturbances or riots) or in acts of individual resentment (crime). Similarly, if people perceive the behaviour and actions of the agents of law and order (in their individual interactions) as illegitimate – immoral, unjust or unfair, they are likely to resent their treatment and this has a deviance amplificatory effect.

The legitimacy of state authority and of the rule of law, therefore, is to be found in the complex interplay between the extent to which the public perceive state authority to be moral, right, just and fair *sui generis*, and the extent to which the public perceives their individual treatment by the agents of law and order as moral, right, just and fair de facto. Moreover, the greater the extent to which state authority and the rule of law is perceived by the public as legitimate, *sui generis* and de facto, the lower will be the amount of general social disorder and individual crime in society.

For us, legitimacy plays a central role in the promotion of a CFOS approach. This means, broadly, at least two things: that children must perceive the *authority* of the state to be legitimate and that children must perceive their *treatment* by agents of the state as legitimate. However, all too often in contemporary society, children do not view their treatment by the state and its agents of social control (for example police officers, teachers, YOT staff) as legitimate. This view is reflected in recent developments such as the backlash of UK riots in 2012 and in the scrapping of the Educational Maintenance Allowance in England in 2012 (alongside a raft of ongoing so-called austerity measures), which gave a clear message to children that they are a low priority (to the point of not mattering) to the current UK government. Furthermore, children often view their treatment by state agents as 'illegitimate' in the sense of punitive, coercive, controlling and disproportionate (see, for example, Jamieson 2005; Phoenix 2009; Case, Charles and Haines 2012; Hawes 2013). Conversely, participatory research (see Hawes 2013) has shown that when state agents act in a manner that promotes their legitimacy in the eyes of children, social order is promoted.

CFOS explicitly embraces legitimacy through its foci – reflexive partnerships between children, families, practitioners, policy makers and researchers, wherein the child's voice is paramount as the provider of evidence to inform and drive the provision of services for and with children. We discuss this issue further in Chapter Four (children in the YJS), Chapter Five (diversion) and Chapter Six (prevention).

Systems management, not unprincipled net widening

> Systems management is a strategic approach based on the belief that outcomes for individual children and the way in which the Youth Justice System as a whole works can be changed by managing processes and targeting specific decision-making points within the system itself. (Haines, in Goldson 2008: 349)

CFOS is facilitated and enabled by a *systems management* approach (after Tutt and Giller 1987, see also Haines and Drakeford 1998), which views the YJS as an interconnected, mutually reinforcing series of decision-making points (for example decisions to arrest, bail, remand, sentence, divert, imprison, punish) that can be targeted to meet specific goals. Seen through a systems management lens, the YJS is a huge machine that is out of control and has been traditionally constituted by 'disparate bodies of professionals [who have] made the wrong decisions about the wrong children at the wrong time' (Thorpe et al 1980: 3). The goal of systems management is to bring that machine back under control. The processing of children by the YJS and the outcomes they are subjected to are the product of long sequences of individual decision making. Taken together, all the decisions made about all individual children constitute the behaviour of the (youth justice) system (the diversion 'rate', the custody 'rate', the reconviction 'rate'). Someone, usually a single person working in one of the many agencies that comprise the YJS, must decide whether a young person is diverted from the YJS or prosecuted. If the decision is to 'divert', the child enters a 'diversion system' in which a series of subsequent decisions about the treatment of the young person ensues. If the decision is to 'prosecute', the young person enters the formal YJS, which triggers a sequence of subsequent decisions. Every decision made in respect of an individual child has consequences for subsequent decision making and for the individual child concerned. The number of decisions required to determine a final outcome for each individual young person can run into the hundreds. Systems management thinking teaches us to see the ultimate outcomes for individual children as the product of this series of decisions. It teaches us that each of these decisions is not immutable, in other words, that it is possible to influence or change every decision that is made about how the YJS treats individual children. It teaches us that by targeting these decisions, we can change them to alter the treatment of individual children by the YJS and thus the behaviour of the system as a whole.

There is nothing inherent within systems management thinking or practice, however, that dictates particular decisions or outcomes as right or wrong (see Bell and Haines 1991; Haines and Drakeford 1998). Systems management thinking is simply a way of conceptualising how the YJS operates and of understanding how the outcomes for individual children are arrived at, and it provides a methodology for interventions that are designed to change the decisions made in respect of individual children. Systems management could bring the youth justice machine under control or it can facilitate the opposite. Goldson (2010), for example, portrays the YJS as a 'bulimic' system, widening its net and gorging on expanding numbers of children prior to regurgitating them in damaged form at a later stage. CFOS, however, enables a systems management approach with a coherent philosophy (children first), an explicit sense of purpose (prevention is better than cure, children as part of the solution not part of the problem), clear goals (responsibilising adults, evidence-based partnership working) and clearly articulated, desirable outcomes for children (promoting positive behaviours and outcomes, enabling access to rights/entitlements) – giving direction to (the changes in) decision making.

Systems management thinking is a powerful tool for understanding the way in which the YJS operates and how it produces different outcomes (some good, some bad) for children. It is essential to utilise systems management practice in the service of CFOS – as a tool to animate the objectives and principles of a CFOS approach.

Partnership with the state, not distrustful of the state

Criminology is a discipline with a long, distinguished and proud track record of critical research. Rigorous and methodologically robust criticism is, in some ways, the hallmark of academic criminology – yet what distinguishes criminology has not always served the discipline well. Because criminal justice is largely a state-run activity, the work of criminologists often brings them into conflict with the state (see Hope and Walters 2008). Some academics distrust the legitimacy, credibility and transparency of the state in its dealings with researchers, research processes and research findings (see Hope 2005; Hope and Walters 2008), reflected in Pitts's depiction of a state run by deaf idiots (Pitts, in Haines and Drakeford 1998). Similarly, some state representatives (particularly politicians and state officials) believe that criminology is anti-state and inherently negative, always showing what is wrong, or what does not work in terms of criminal justice policy and practice, and incapable of offering positive alternatives, reflected in the ongoing debate regarding 'public criminologies' and the need to balance a policy- and practice-relevant criminology with one that maintains academic rigour and critical reflexivity (Carrabine 2008; Loader and Sparks 2010; Uggen and Inderbitzen 2010). There are, indeed, huge frustrations on both sides.[33]

The negativity of criminology is overstated, as is the negativity of the state (although the state is and has been responsible for some fairly atavistic criminal and youth justice policies and practices!). It is important, however, to bring a fresh perspective to this situation. There is a very proper place for criticality within criminology. Methodologically robust criminological research[34] will provide insights into the nature, causes, effects and treatment of crime. Some of these insights will be positive and constructive, while others will be critical and negative. Where the critical and negative brings criminology, in some way, into conflict with the state (as the provider of criminal justice) this is right and proper. Where the relationship between criminology and the state breaks down, however, occurs when criminology evinces an inherent distrust of the state.

This distrust of the state, however, is not a criminological problem or phenomenon (it is just vividly exposed by criminology because the focus of our work is on state activity). The distrust of the state is a social phenomenon (see Beck 1992; Marková and Gillespie 2007), of sociological significance and it affects criminologists as it affects others within society. The contention here, therefore, is that the anti-state or distrust of the state phenomenon is a distinctively (albeit not exclusively)

[33] The debates surrounding the respective negativity of criminology and the state are amply illustrated by the emergence of the so-called administrative criminology in the 1980s (see Young 1999; Hudson 2003; Scraton, in Goldson 2008).

[34] We must recognise, of course, that within the discipline of criminology what constitutes methodologically robust research is often a contested matter (see Case and Haines 2014a). There is a proper place within criminology for these debates (as there is in other disciplines).

English state of mind that is deeply rooted in English history[35] (Giddens 1990). When criminologists evince an inherent distrust of the state, therefore, they are not doing so as criminologists, but as members of English society.

This distrust of the state, however, is not ubiquitous, nor is it inevitable. These arguments are reflected in the work of a Welsh criminologist, Mark Drakeford, who has written at length about political developments in Wales in the post-devolution era (for example Drakeford 2009, 2010), notably how Welsh social policy for children and children has adopted a rights focus and how youth justice in Wales is becoming distinctive or 'dragonised' (see Edwards and Hughes 2009; see also Haines 2009b). To date, a CFOS approach to youth justice has found its fullest expression in relation to the emerging principles of Welsh social policy for children since the process of devolution began in 1999. Although the work in Swansea we report on this book began in the mid-1990s and pre-dates devolution, Welsh policy for children and Welsh youth justice strategy has developed symbiotically with the CFOS approach and, as such, makes for an interesting case study. Consequently, we turn our attention to exploring the policy differences and divergences between Wales and England in the next chapter. In short, an institutionalised lack of trust between researchers and the state is an unhelpful impasse that both sides need to work to overcome. The state, at both central and indeed local levels, is a critical partner in developing effective youth justice policy, strategy and practice, and while many problems remain in the relationship between researchers and the state, it should be clearly articulated as a matter to be addressed.

[35] This was illustrated at an international symposium of juvenile criminologists focused on the 'dialectical relationship between research, policy and practice'. Presentations on this topic were made by criminologists from Belgium, Wales, Germany, Ireland, the Netherlands, Finland and England. Following some debate, the quizzical expression on the face of one of the German representatives turned into a smile and she said, "I finally get it, you guys," pointing towards the English representatives "are anti-state. I've always wondered why the English always seem to be so critical and angry, when the majority of us take a more positive view of youth justice research and the role of the state, and now I finally understand. You guys are anti-state."

Responsibilising adults, not responsibilising children

Children are, by dint of their age, not fully afforded or accorded the status of independent adulthood. Children cannot (fully) make their own independent decisions about their behaviour or lead their own independent lives (Koocher and Keith-Spiegel 1990; Such and Walker 2004; Freeman 2007). There is much about a child's life that is decided by adults. There is much about the lives of children that is the responsibility of adults. Children are not given the full social responsibilities of adulthood; it is wrong to invoke this responsibility when and if they come into conflict with the law and the youth justice system. Adults, on the other hand, must (fully) accept their responsibilities towards children.

Children cannot decide the fiscal priorities of government or the services government chooses (or not) to provide and at what level of quality, they cannot decide whether to attend school (or often which school they must attend), they cannot decide on the quality of their education, they cannot decide on the provision, quality and availability of cultural, sporting or leisure-time activities in their community or neighbourhood, they cannot decide in which neighbourhood they live, they cannot decide on local policing priorities or practices, they cannot decide how adults behave – yet children bear the consequences of all these (and more) decisions made by adults. The special place of children in society must, therefore, be recognised and acted upon.

The United Nations Convention on the Rights of the Child (UNCRC) provides an important context for a discussion of CFOS principles – particularly the emphasis on children's entitlements and rights. The UNCRC is a convention of (near) universally agreed,[36] non-negotiable, interdependent minimum standards for children's rights (civil, cultural, economic, political and social), formalised across 54 articles that adhere to four core principles: (1) non-discrimination, (2) devotion to the best

[36] The UNCRC was ratified in the UK in 1991 and has now been incorporated into Welsh legislation through the Rights of Children and Young Persons (Wales) Measure 2011, which places a duty on Welsh government ministers to have due regard to the UNCRC and to be responsible for making sure that it is complied with.

interests of the child, (3) promoting survival and development (for example rights to food, shelter, formal education, leisure and recreation, cultural activities, protection from abuse and exploitation – including within the criminal justice system) and (4) respect for the views of children (participation rights – freedom to express opinions on matters affecting children's social, economic, religious, cultural and political life, rights to information). According to Whyte (2009: 226), the significance of the UNCRC is clear: 'the near universal ratification of the UNCRC has placed importance on providing "a level playing-field" of values and principles for all children through universal prevention and early social intervention measures'.

There is, however, an important point of departure in CFOS from the UNCRC. In its ambition to provide 'a level playing field' for all children the UNCRC is inherently restricting its ambition to guaranteeing universal *minimum* standards for the treatment of children (Drakeford 2010; Case and Haines 2014b; Case and Haines 2015b). In contrast, CFOS is not interested in minimum standards. CFOS has as its central ambition the promotion of *maximum outcomes* for all children. As such, CFOS is derived from the children's rights movement, but not beholden to it.

On an individual level, for every child, there are a host of adults who make decisions that affect their lives every single day. Setting aside macro social policy making and focusing on micro everyday decision making, parents, community members, shopkeepers, teachers, youth workers, police officers, social workers, YOT staff and many other adults, make hundreds of decisions for and in respect of every child. The outcomes of these decisions and their consequences have very significant implications for children and their behaviour. Adults have choices, where children do not. Adults are responsible for decisions, where children are not. Adults can choose to discipline children, or reward positive behaviour. Adults can choose to create opportunities for children and facilitate their access to these opportunities, or they can decide to exclude children.[37] Recognition of the responsibilities of adults for decision making in respect of children and the outcomes for these children is a central feature of Extending Entitlement (see Chapter Three) and it is fully endorsed within a CFOS approach.

A unique element of the Welsh Extending Entitlement strategy is the manner in which it responsibilises adults (for example service providers, policy makers) to ensure that children have full and unobstructed access to the support, services and information that can enable them to access their universal entitlements (see Chapter Three). The English approach to social policy for children, articulated in *Every Child Matters: Change for Children* (Department for Education and Skills (DfES) 2004) and *Youth Matters* (Department for Education and Skills (DfES) 2005) sets out 'a series of global objectives for children's well-being in positive terms' (Smith 2011: 173) to be pursued through universal services. However, critics have argued that the policy is more focused on reducing risk and responsibilising children to take advantage of the opportunities offered to them or, indeed, of having these opportunities removed as a result of offending (Hoyle 2008; Case and Haines 2011). This responsibilising approach has been consolidated in practice by the management of antisocial behaviour (for example the use of Acceptable Behaviour Contracts and ASBOs). Therefore, while in England *opportunities* for children are conditional upon their behaviour,[38] in Wales adults are responsible for ensuring that children achieve, to the maximum possible, specific *outcomes*. Many of the children targeted by social and youth justice policies are likely to be already disadvantaged, socially deprived, thus less able to access support and services and less likely to be in a position to

[37] In stating this, we do not intend to paint a picture of children as the passive recipients of adult decision making, nor do we seek to present children as the helpless victims of their circumstances, devoid of personal agency. This would run counter to our previous arguments and to other research evidence (for example *The Teeside Studies* – Webster, Simpson, MacDonald, Abbas, Cieslik, Shildrick and Simpson 2004; MacDonald and Marsh 2005; see also Charles 2011). However, we do seek full recognition of the responsibilities of adults for their decision making in respect of children and we seek to make adults responsible for the consequences of these decisions.

[38] It is also very important to recognise that for far too many children (particularly those who do not live in wealthy families) these opportunities are hollow.

comply or engage with this support. Ironically, they could then be penalised and criminalised as a result of non-compliance (for example breaching an ASBO is a criminal offence), an example of 'repressive welfarism' (Phoenix 2009; see also 'no rights without responsibilities' – Giddens 1998: 65). There is no excuse for making children responsible for the consequences of adult decision making, whether this be at the level of government, or at the local level or in terms of individual decisions made in respect of individual children. A central feature of the CFOS approach is the extent to which it makes adults responsible for the outcomes that children achieve.

Conclusion: Children First, Offenders Second?

So what does a CFOS approach to youth justice look like? As we said in the previous chapter, there is no simple or single answer to this question. In the chapters that follow, we will describe how we have sought, through a long-term partnership with Swansea YOT, to implement a CFOS approach (however imperfectly) as *an* example, but not a prescription, for practice. The notion of a CFOS youth justice was originally set out in Haines and Drakeford (1998, mostly in Chapter 3, see also Drakeford 2010) and our aim, throughout this book, has been to elaborate on this concept.

The CFOS approach does not seek to dictate to policy makers or to tell practitioners *what* to do when engaging children in conflict with the law and the youth justice system. At its core, the CFOS approach seeks to establish key principles for youth justice policy and practice that establish a consistency to *how* children are engaged by the system. CFOS puts the child at the heart of the system and makes service delivery and the achievement of specific outcomes primarily the responsibility of the adults involved. In order to achieve this, we believe that practitioners must understand why they come into work every day, what it is that they are employed to do, to have singularity of purpose – but an essential element of freedom in selecting what methods they employ in achieving this purpose. In saying this, we do not mean that practitioners are free to choose any method (as the first part of this chapter makes clear). Youth justice practice, particularly a *positive* youth justice, must be consistent with the guiding principles of CFOS.

A CFOS positive youth justice is *child-friendly and child-appropriate*, maintaining sensitivity to the status of 'child', children's universal entitlements and the inherent responsibilities of adults in all dealings with children. The objective of 'special treatment' of children is pursued through the *normalisation* of everyday childhood behaviour and the normalisation of the treatment that children receive following demonstration of need, deprivation or problems. Accordingly, children should be diverted from the potential iatrogenic consequences of the system contact they receive in response to their behaviours and circumstances, as opposed to the state and adults seeking to inflict retributive punishment, administer punitive justice or impose adult-centric, needs-led welfare to admonish or cure the child. The CFOS model emphasises *diversion and minimum necessary level of intervention* with children, eschewing the interventionist and net-widening excesses of punishment, justice and welfare models. Positive youth justice prioritises *inclusionary prevention* through the *legitimate participation and engagement* of children and their families in evidence-based partnership with practitioners, rather than subjecting children to disengaging and inequitable treatment that could result in social exclusion, stigmatisation, marginalisation and further offending. CFOS centralises the responsibilities and *responsibilisation of adults* (practitioners, policy makers, politicians, parents, researchers) to ensure positive youth justice through *child-focused decision making* across the YJS and beyond (systems management), *evidence-based partnership* with children, families, other practitioners, researchers, agencies and the state and the *promotion* of children's universal entitlements, universal rights and capacities to realise positive behaviours and outcomes.

THREE

The context of Children First, Offenders Second positive youth justice: evolution through devolution

The opening chapters have established a pressing need for an alternative, positive model of youth justice to counter the *offender first* excesses of traditional approaches to working with children in conflict with the law and the youth justice system. The modern context of youth justice is one rife with paradox in its negative views of children as: responsible for their (offending) behaviour, yet not responsible or capable to change their behaviour and circumstances without formal intervention from adults; in need of protection from harm and risk, yet posing harm and risk to a society which must be protected from them; and active beneficiaries of universal, unconditional rights, yet rights that can be withdrawn once the child enters the formal youth justice system (YJS). We have outlined how the 'new youth justice' of the Crime and Disorder Act 1998 has portrayed offending by children as the deterministic result of exposure to psychosocial risk factors and has individualised the blame for this exposure and subsequent offending, responsibilising children and their families to resist risk factors and to desist from offending by engaging and complying with enforced, adult-led, offence- and offender-focused interventions.

In Chapter One, we made a case for a positive model of youth justice, Children First, Offenders Second (CFOS), which subverts the current dominant, deterministic view of children who offend and likewise the appropriate ways of responding to these children, their behaviour and their lives. CFOS provides a modern paradigm that views children as active constructors of their experiences, circumstances, context and behaviours, but often with their ability to influence outcomes being restricted by entrenched socio-structural inequalities and adult-centric decision making guided by managerialist processes and negative, offender-first perspectives of the child. The model is underpinned by the notion of children's rights as a progressive social norm, extending this principle beyond the need for adults to provide children with minimum standards of service to meet their rights (in line with the United Nations Convention on the Rights of the Child 1989 (UNCRC)) and into an *entitlements*-focused pursuit of maximum outcomes for children through child-friendly and child-appropriate service provision and intervention guided by a view of offending as a normalised childhood behaviour.

The second chapter expanded upon the central principles of the CFOS model of positive justice and how these contrast starkly with the negative and deleterious features of punishment- and justice-based models of youth justice. We set out the parameters of CFOS as a child-friendly and child-appropriate approach to understanding, assessing and responding to children in conflict with the law and the youth justice system, as opposed to an adult-centric model that 'does to' children by treating them as mini-adults within a miniaturised and adulterised YJS. Central to these child-friendly principles is the prioritisation of diversion from the damaging effects of formal contact with the YJS, whether this be welfare or justice based, and the pursuit of an inclusionary prevention agenda that promotes positive behaviour through evidence-based partnership with children (contrary to programme fetishism) to identify their needs, problems, influences on their behaviour and how best to address these. Diversion and positive, inclusionary prevention facilitate an emphasis on legitimate treatment (not labelling and stigmatisation) that children view as fair, just and moral and are therefore more likely to comply, participate and engage with in constructive ways. At the broader systemic level, CFOS is driven by a targeted systems management approach (to counteract indiscriminate net widening) with a coherent philosophy of CFOS, 'prevention is better than cure' and 'children are part of the solution, not part of the problem' and a clear goal to responsibilise adults to ensure children's access to their entitlements. The central features of the CFOS model have evolved through and are supported by an overarching partnership with the state (for example as espoused by the Welsh government), rather than a distrust of the state and its managerialist and harmful prescriptions for youth justice policies and practices (as largely pertains in England).

This chapter is about *policy*, more specifically the policy divergences between England and Wales in relation to children and the geopolitical conditions under which CFOS has emerged at national (policy) and local (practice) levels. We begin by analysing the manner in which youth justice policy in England and Wales developed into a 'new youth justice' (Goldson 2000) of risk-focused (neoconservative correctionalist) individualisation and (neoliberal) responsibilisation under the Labour government that took office in 1997 and how successive pieces of legislation consolidated this approach. We continue by exploring the influence of partial devolution of Wales in 1999 on the development of a distinct (from England) national identity in terms of social policy making for children and young people and how this has, in turn, influenced an emerging Welsh youth justice identity at the policy level. We acknowledge the tension inherent in presenting these broad national divergences as we see them, while at the same time recognising the realities of unevenness of policy within and between localities in each country, emerging from local mediation and inconsistent implementation of policy (rhetoric) in practice. That said, the distinct nature of social policy making for children and young people in Wales and the extent to which it has been inhibited by centralised (English) directives remains central to the CFOS arguments in this book.

The evolution-devolution of youth justice in England and Wales

The hegemonic direction and ethos of youth justice in England and Wales has changed irrevocably since the *Misspent Youth* report by the Audit Commission, an organisation charged, among other things, with auditing the 'economy, efficiency and effectiveness' of the agencies that constituted the YJS (Audit

Commission 1996: 3). The resultant recommendations for reorganising and refocusing the YJS proved highly influential, coming as they did in the year prior to a change of government in the UK. The Audit Commission concluded that the YJS, as it was constituted and operated in the early 1990s, was *ineffective* in preventing and reducing offending, *inefficient* at administering justice and enabling agencies to work together and *uneconomical* in its methods, largely due to prioritising of expensive and ineffective sentencing approaches such as custody. The report's recommendations were largely technical and systemic in nature, focusing on helping the YJS to more effectively and efficiently *manage* the operation of its constituent agencies and the children they worked with. Alongside suggesting increased levels of multi-agency partnership working (following the Morgan Report 1991), *Misspent Youth* recommended a greater emphasis on prevention through early intervention in the lives of children experiencing problems and identified as 'at risk' of entering the YJS or experiencing social exclusion, a recommendation underpinned by the growing hegemonic body of risk factor research that informed understandings of offending by children (for example Graham and Bowling 1995; Catalano and Hawkins 1996; Farrington 1996; Utting 1999; see Case and Haines 2009 for a detailed critique of this movement). Practice, it suggested, should be 'evidence-based', informed by technical risk assessment and risk-appropriate intervention identified through robust evaluation as 'effective' and 'what works' (typically in terms of reducing reoffending by identified offenders). Consequently, *Misspent Youth* articulated a move away from traditional welfare- and justice-based models of youth justice, towards more technical *system first* and individualised *offender first* conceptions of how to understand and respond to offending behaviour by children in a neoconservative correctionalist manner as the product of individual deficit (exposure to risk factors that predict and lead to offending) that demands adult-led management through intervention informed by risk assessment. The culture shift towards a technical, 'administrative' form of youth justice focused, therefore, on risk-based reduction (as prevention) that individualised the 'causes' of offending and thus individualised responsibility for this behaviour (that is, blamed children for not resisting the influence of risk factors).

The neo-correctionalist individualising and neoliberal responsibilising tone of *Misspent Youth* was consolidated by the 1997 White Paper *No More Excuses: A New Approach to Tackling Youth Crime* from the incoming Labour government (Home Office 1997). Written in Labour's first year of office, the *No More Excuses* White Paper (Home Office 1997: Preface by the Home Secretary) sets out the new government's stance on offending by children:

> An excuse culture has developed within the youth justice system. It excuses itself for its inefficiency, and too often excuses the young offenders before it, implying that they cannot help their behaviour because of their social circumstances. Rarely are they confronted with their behaviour and helped to take more personal responsibility for their actions ... This White Paper seeks to draw a line under the past and sets out a new approach to tackling youth crime.

As its name suggests, the *No More Excuses* White Paper established the Labour government's responsibilising approach to preventing and responding to offending by children (see also Bessant, Hill and Watts 2003) by representing offending behaviour as the product of individual deficit (exposure to and failure to resist risk factors), rather than by addressing the needs of children or their (all too often deleterious) socio-structural circumstances. The thoroughgoing risk focus of *No More Excuses* was employed to justify recommendations for pre-emptive early intervention to prevent 'at risk' children from becoming offenders (disregarding the attendant potential of this approach to label, stigmatise and criminalise – see McAra and McVie 2005; Hine 2006) – precipitating the (in)famous political (evidence-free) sound bite (Home Office 1997: 3, emphasis added): 'There will be a new focus on *nipping crime in the bud* – stopping children at risk from getting involved in crime and preventing early criminal behaviour from escalating into persistent serious offending.'

The recommendations of *Misspent Youth* and *No More Excuses* underpinned the central piece of legislation during the Labour government's tenure (1997–2010), the Crime and Disorder Act 1998. The Act reoriented and reformed the YJS to the point that it was virtually unrecognisable from the welfare-, justice- and new orthodoxy-informed systems of the past (see Chapter Two). The Crime and Disorder Act 1998 established that:

> It shall be the principal aim of the youth justice system to prevent offending but children and young persons. (section 37(1))

Under the Crime and Disorder Act 1998, all local authority areas had a statutory obligation to audit levels of local crime and disorder and to produce a Crime and Disorder Reduction Strategy to address these issues. Reduction strategies were formulated and monitored by Crime and Disorder Reduction Partnerships in each local authority area (called Community Safety Partnerships in Wales). The 'prevention' of offending (see Chapter Six for a fuller discussion) was to be addressed along a continuum from targeted (pre-offending) early intervention with children identified as 'at risk' of entering the YJS (for example by demonstrating the new social construction of 'antisocial behaviour') to targeted (pre-conviction) diversionary activity with children through two newly created pre-court orders: Reprimands and Final Warnings (replacing the previous cautioning system), to targeted (pre-reoffending) reduction activity with children convicted of an offence and given one of an increased range of statutory courts orders. At all points along this prevention continuum, children were to be subjected to structured risk assessment in order to measure their exposure to risk factors and to target (purportedly) appropriate evidence-based, effective (risk-focused) interventions as a response.

The emphasis of the Crime and Disorder Act 1998 on risk-focused assessment and intervention formally introduced into youth justice policy and practice an overriding individualised, *offender first* understanding of offending by children, wherein, according to Turnbull and Spence (2011: 954): 'Larger social concerns such as disadvantage, poverty and racial inequality are also individualised in a similar way, with young people subject to interventions designed to shape their responses to these structural forces, irrespective of the limited agency of young people in such circumstances.'

Children entering the YJS were to be assessed on the basis of their exposure to a series of risk factors in their personal lives (psychological, emotional) and immediate social lives (family, education, neighbourhood, peer group) and 'treated' by way of risk-focused early intervention across the system. Individualising the causes of, and blame for, offending behaviour was used as the basis for pressing a responsiblisation agenda that held children and their families (rather than the government itself) fully responsible for their social circumstances (compare Rose 1996; Kemshall 2008) and which was used to justify increased intervention (*interventionism* – Goldson 2000). Children and families were responsibilised for preventing future offending in a variety of punitive and controlling ways: through surveillance into their lives (Smith 2006), even in the absence of demonstrable problems or negative behaviours (see McAra and McVie 2005), through conditions attached to court-ordered interventions, through the introduction of restorative justice approaches and through certain punitive measures such as Parenting Orders. Government legislation represented and understood children as possessing a degree of agency (constituted by, among other things, responsibility and self-control) that allowed them to resist and negotiate risk, or 'choose' to accept its negative influences (see Kemshall 2008). Therefore, responsibilisation and agency were seen as a consequence of, and solution to, structural inequality (see also Turnbull and Spence 2011).

The reoriented *offender first* and *offence first* prevention focus of the 'new youth justice'[39] (Goldson 2000) emanating from the Crime and Disorder Act 1998 were to be monitored and

[39] The 'new youth justice' was 'new' in that it superseded the traditional concerns with meeting children's welfare needs and/or delivering justice through the YJS with modernising, managerialist, preventative, risk-focused and interventionist approaches to dealing with children. In other words, the 'new youth justice' was a largely technical approach to render the YJS more effective, efficient and economical (compare Audit Commission 1996) rather than underpinning practice with a guiding philosophy.

managed (from April 2000) by two bespoke new structures: a Youth Justice Board for England and Wales (YJB), a non-departmental public body (or 'quango' – quasi-autonomous non-governmental organisation), created to oversee the functioning of the YJS, and multi-agency youth offending teams (YOTs), created to implement the youth justice-related requirements of the Crime and Disorder Act in every local authority area in England and Wales. The dual role of the YJB was conceived in terms of providing 'independent' expert guidance and advice to the UK government on the operation of the YJS (see Pitts 2001; Souhami 2011), while being charged with developing consistent standards and a coherent approach to youth justice. This the role of the YJB encompasses:

- monitoring the operation of the YJS;
- advising the Secretary of State on the operation of the YJS, National Standards, and on how the aim of preventing offending by children and young people can most effectively be pursued;
- identifying and disseminating effective practice across youth justice services;
- making grants to YOTs and other organisations to support development and delivery of effective practice;
- commissioning a distinct secure estate for young people;
- placing young people in custody. (YJB 2012: 4)

Following the Crime and Disorder Act 1998, the YJB was tasked to coordinate, monitor, inform (for example by recommending 'effective' and 'evidence-based' practice) and fund the practice of multi-agency YOTs.[40] YOTs were formalised in April 2000 in every local authority area in England and Wales as the means of delivering youth justice services and meeting the statutory requirements of the Crime and Disorder Act. Each YOT was required to co-opt representatives from the four statutory agencies: police, local authority (predominantly social

[40] Formerly known as Youth Justice Teams. In some areas of England and Wales, Youth Offending Teams have become known as Youth Offending Services (YOSs).

services), probation and health (predominantly mental health) and to include the voluntary and charitable services where partners considered this to be appropriate. Under the Crime and Disorder Act, YOTs were charged with reducing and preventing youth crime, tackling locally specific criminogenic influences identified in local crime and disorder reduction strategies (based on local crime and disorder reduction audits), and delivering youth justice assessment, supervision and interventions to local children. A central driver of the YJB's approach to its statutory responsibility to *monitor* the performance of the YJS has been the collection of *statistical data* on YOT workload and attainment of key performance indicators (measuring first-time entrants (FTEs) into the YJS, reoffending rates and custody rates[41]) and the provision of detailed practice guidance relating to National Standards, case management and evidence-based *Key Elements of Effective Practice* (YJB 2008a; see Chapter Four for a more detailed discussion).

The evolution of a 'new youth justice' (Goldson 2000) approach based on managerialism and technical, risk-focused assessment and intervention (in contrast to a welfare or justice focus), was legislated into existence by the Crime and Disorder Act 1998. It animated the deleterious features of youth justice policy and practice (see Chapter Two), hence our characterisation of these developments as representing a 'devolution' (in the sense of a negative regression) of youth justice. Pursuing an evidence-based, effective practice agenda that privileged risk-focused youth justice (albeit arguably in the spirit of supportive early intervention), the Act responsibilised children for their offending behaviour and adulterised understandings of offending. Consequent (preventive) responses and interventions have been typically adult-centric, widening the net of influence cast by the YJS, yet simultaneously excluding children from contributing to decision-making processes that affect them (see Phoenix and Kelly 2013; see also Chapter Four). The managerialist and prescriptive overtones of the Act, centred on effective, efficient, economical and evidence-based practice, served to: fuel

[41] For YOTs in Wales, key performance indicator data is also collected relating to education, training and employment, substance use and accommodation.

programme fetishism (for example standardised, psychologised responses to 'at risk' populations, rather than interventions sensitive to the individual), deprofessionalise practitioners away from exercising discretion and expertise (see Pitts 2001) and extinguish the potential contribution and influence of critical and dissenting academics.

The *offender first* features of the 'new youth justice' created under the Labour government 'evolved' unabated following the Crime and Disorder Act 1998, consolidated and exacerbated by subsequent legislation:

- **Youth Justice and Criminal Evidence Act 1999** – introduced a new Referral Order sentence for all children pleading guilty and convicted for the first time in court. Following sentencing, referral is then made to a Youth Offender Panel (also known as a Referral Order Panel) of laypeople led by a YOT practitioner, who then target the prevention of reoffending through planning restorative justice-based intervention (see Haines and O'Mahony 2006). The potentially full, unmitigated responsibilising impact of the Referral Order (due to its overriding restorative emphasis on children accepting responsibility for their behaviour) is mediated somewhat by the consultative and inclusive nature of the assessment and decision-making processes of the Youth Offender Panel, which offers tentative indications of a child-friendly and child-appropriate method of implementing youth justice through partnership with children and enabling their participation and engagement in decision-making processes.
- **Antisocial Behaviour Act 2003** – built on a government White Paper entitled *Respect and Responsibility: Taking a Stand Against Antisocial Behaviour* (HM Government 2003), which made recommendations to allow the government to provide local authorities and the police with wider and more flexible powers to address nuisance crime and low-level incivility. The Act widened the use of Antisocial Behaviour Orders (ASBOs) to allow local authorities, registered social landlords and the British Transport Police to apply for them. In addition, police and community support officers were empowered to issue Dispersal Orders to any group of two or more people, within

a designated area, whose behaviour they believed likely to cause harassment, alarm or distress to members of the public. The Act also broadened the availability of Parenting Orders to parents of children who had truanted or been excluded from school (rather than restricted to parents of children who had offended) and created a statutory basis for Parenting Contracts, wherein parents had to agree to comply with the requirements of the order (HM Government 2003). The broadening of antisocial behaviour powers expanded the net-widening and interventionist influence of the YJS by drawing in children who had not offended and subjecting them to formal intervention (for example ASBOs, notices to disperse, Parenting Orders) which, if breached, constituted a criminal offence – archetypal criminalisation of childhood behaviour in preference to the normalisation of offending behaviour.

- **Youth Crime Action Plan 2008** – outlined a 'triple track' approach to youth justice policy and practice, consisting of: 'Tough enforcement to tackle problems, non negotiable support to tackle the causes of problems and early intervention and prevention to nip problems in the bud' (HM Government 2008: 30). The tripartite approach prioritised risk-focused early intervention and 'positive and engaging' intervention to meet the aims of preventing (first-time) offending, reducing reoffending, increasing public confidence, supporting victims and ensuring that children who offend are able to achieve the five outcomes set out under *Every Child Matters: Change for Children*[42] (see later in this chapter). The *Youth Crime Action Plan* (YCAP) risk focus consolidated the government's ongoing punitive project of responsibilising and stigmatising children and their parents/families. The *enforcement* emphasis progressed this punitive project still further, with the

[42] A set of reforms to promote the well-being, success and inclusion of children and young people in England (Department for Education 2004) through a focus on: being healthy (for example physically, emotionally, mentally, sexually), staying safe (for example from bullying, crime and antisocial behaviour, discrimination), enjoying and achieving (for example education, personally, socially, recreationally), making a positive contribution (for example to community, decision making, positive relationships, self-confidence) and achieving economic well-being.

government pledging to 'set clear boundaries of acceptable behaviour' (HM Government 2008: 1). Crucially, it was viewed as the responsibility of the child and their family to accept and engage successfully with these interventions or else they would face punitive sanctions (HM Government 2008: 5): 'For those who are struggling we will offer more support; and those who do not take their responsibilities seriously we will challenge them to do so.' Thus, the YCAP tempered its ostensibly supportive and preventive tone with a focus on *non-negotiable* support, challenge and enforcement – an emerging (responsibilising) feature of the government's ostensibly supportive early intervention agenda (Blyth and Solomon 2009). It was proposed that children and their parents who did not accept or engage with the support offered to them would have punitive enforcement action taken against them and sanctions levied (for example the increased use of Parenting Orders and ASBOs).

Coalition risk-based youth justice: revolution or evolution?

Since the general election in May 2010, the incumbent Conservative-Liberal Democrat coalition government in the UK has been relatively silent and largely static on youth justice issues. Reflective of and attendant to the context of widespread socio-political insecurity and anxiety due to a globalised economic crisis in which the coalition came to power, early policy 'developments' were tentative and piecemeal, typically rehearsing the new youth justice of the outgoing government. A series of policy statements (governmental position pieces, consultations and acts) and independent reviews have outlined the coalition's proposals for the future shape and nature of youth justice in England and Wales, notably:

- ***Breaking the Cycle: Effective Punishment, Rehabilitation and Sentencing of Offenders 2010*** – the *Breaking the Cycle* Green Paper (Ministry of Justice (MoJ) 2010) reinforced much Labour policy direction, outlining the coalition's proposals to improve the YJS by preventing offending and reoffending by children through a set of key objectives:

more emphasis on prevention and diversion from the YJS; an enhanced focus on public protection and reparation to victims and communities; more effective use of sentencing and incentivising local agencies to prevent offending through a payment-by-results model. *Breaking the Cycle* articulated the government's continued commitment to risk-based preventive early intervention as 'our best chance to break the cycle of crime' (MoJ 2010: 68). The report also consolidated the YCAP recommendation that parents be made to take greater responsibility for crime prevention, for example by increasing support for the development of parenting skills and by enforcing more Parenting Orders where 'parents refuse to face up to their responsibilities' (MoJ 2010: 68). Restorative justice was expounded as an 'informal intervention' to enable children to 'face up to the consequence of their crime, provide reparation and prevent further offending' (MoJ 2010: 68). *Breaking the Cycle* consolidated much of what came before in terms of, among other things, the managerialist control and responsibilisation of children, parents, local authorities and multi-agency partnerships, despite the government framing their proposals as a movement towards developing more effective local governance and flexibility in delivering youth justice. The proposals were grounded in the (risk-based) individualisation of offending behaviour and the consequent responsibilisation of children (via continued risk assessment and restorative justice measures) and their parents to address the causes of offending and to engage with (risk-focused) supportive early interventions. Notwithstanding this seeming consolidation of much previous policy and practice direction, there were some encouraging signs of a progressive move towards increased levels of practitioner discretion and localism, couched as 'radical and decentralizing ... to give providers the freedom to innovate, increase their discretion to get the job done, and open up the market to new providers from the private, voluntary and community sectors' (MoJ 2010: 37). However, the subsequent official response to the Green Paper, *Breaking the Cycle: Government Response* (MoJ 2011) appeared to temper much of this ambition, excluding the term 'discretion' entirely and introducing a new element of centralisation to its decentralising claims (see Drake, Fergusson and Briggs 2014). The response document qualified the government's commitment to 'end the current high level of central performance monitoring … based on the principles that youth justice services will be locally determined and driven' with the centralising caveat that these local services must 'maximize value for money, be publicly accountable … We want to target those Youth Offending Teams that are underperforming' (MoJ 2011: 33–5). Of most concern in the Green Paper is the proposal to introduce an austerity-based (centralised) *payment by results* model regarding the reduction of reoffending which, when considered in the context of increased localism and practitioner discretion, raises the spectre of YOT practice being manipulated under pressure and prescription to meet system-first performance targets (systemic outputs rather than outcomes for children – see Puffett 2012; Briggs 2013; Drake et al 2014).

- **The Independent Commission on Youth Crime and Antisocial Behaviour: Time for a Fresh Start 2011** – the Police Foundation established the Independent Commission on Youth Crime and Antisocial Behaviour (ICYCAB 2011) through funding provided by the Nuffield Foundation to provide 'a blueprint for reform' of the YJS based on the assertion that 'we need a fresh start in responding to youth crime because of intractable and deep-rooted problems that current systems can't reform' (D.J. Smith 2010: 1). The reform objectives were to identify a set of principles for responding fairly, effectively, proportionately and humanely to offending behaviour by children through sustainable and evidence-based services (ICYCAB 2010). The Independent Commission's report *Time for a Fresh Start* castigated the YJS in England and Wales for the 'questionable nature' of its guiding youth justice policy and its 'unimpressive [record of] deep rooted failings' (ICYCAB 2010: 17). Furthermore, contemporary youth justice responses were lambasted for a 'lack of coherence', 'adultifying' tendencies (treating children as adults), the discriminatory targeting and criminalising of 'young people from deprived backgrounds', 'inflated use of penal custody' and wasting money on 'expensive and ineffective and probably harmful' youth justice responses (ICYCAB 2010: 23). The report concluded with a series of recommended reform principles for the YJS: an increased emphasis on *prevention, early intervention*, use of *restorative justice* measures and the *integration* of children who have offended into mainstream society (for example through limiting the use of ASBOs and custodial sentences).

The report reflected a significant and growing body of critical literature from academics, non-government organisations, progressive practitioners and children's rights organisations, much of which had been neglected by politicians, policy makers and (ironically) by several of the authors cited within the report itself (Goldson 2011; see also Case 2011). However, the 'fresh start' recommendations for reform retained faith in much 'conventional youth justice apparatus' (Goldson 2011: 7) – notably risk-based early intervention – stating confidently that 'an understanding of "risk" and "protective" (or "promotive") factors provides a valuable basis for planning and implementing prevention strategies' (ICYCAB 2010: 39).

The promotion of risk-based early intervention, alongside an enhanced role for restorative justice, illustrates a thoroughgoing responsibilising tendency within the Independent Commission report. Children in conflict with the law and the youth justice system are encouraged to 'face up to the consequences of their actions and accept responsibility for them' (Salz in ICYCAB 2010: 5), thus reflecting an overriding responsibilisation and adulterisation in the representation of children in the YJS. The Independent Commission produced a confused and disparate set of well-rehearsed criticisms and recommendations, ultimately settling on a slightly modified version of the YJS that remains wedded to risk, targeted early intervention and responsibilisation over broader considerations of the universal prevention and children's rights agendas, both of which are held to be key features of the emerging Welsh youth justice context that is overlooked by the Independent Commission (Case 2011;

see also later in this chapter). Early intervention programmes have been demonstrated in reports (for example National Audit Office 2013) as largely ineffective, failing to achieve the results required. Reports do not say why this may be the case (beyond targeting issues), but we suggest that excessively targeted and insufficiently universal methodologies rooted in the notion of 'trouble' neglect to focus on achieving positive outcomes for children and are thus lacking in effectiveness.

- **Legal Aid and Sentencing and Punishment of Offenders Act 2012 (LASPO)** – the LASPO Act 2012 offered the first indications of coalition intent to evolve youth justice policy and practice through its explicit attack on the formulaic and inflexible approach of the Crime and Disorder Act 1998. A series of new out-of-court disposals were created to replace Reprimands and Final Warnings and to re-emphasise the utility of diversion from the formal YJS. Crucially, since their inception in April 2013, each diversionary disposal can be administered to the same child on multiple occasions (including those with a prior conviction), removing the previous inflexible escalatory progression system from pre-court to court sentence.[43] The new pre-court disposals are:

  - Community Resolution – a police-administered first-stage disposal requiring children's agreement to participate and taking victims' perspectives into account;
  - Youth Caution – a second-stage disposal, typically determined in partnership between the police and the YOT locally, requiring assessment and intervention by the YOT;
  - Youth Conditional Caution – a third-stage, pre-court disposal with proportionate rehabilitative, punitive and reparative conditions, seen as an alternative to prosecution. YOTs are charged with monitoring compliance and non-compliance can result in prosecution for the original offence.

[43] The LASPO Act 2012 makes provision for an equivalent flexibility to be applied to the court-based Referral Order.

The LASPO Act 2012 prioritised an out-of-court, diversionary approach that attempts to progress youth justice beyond punitive and inflexible systemic responses and into non-criminalising, systems management-led responses. As such, the Act raises issues for the local authority areas and YOTs charged with implementing these new approaches in terms of decision-making processes regarding what structures and processes should be put in place locally to facilitate decision making and how children can be provided with appropriate early support mechanisms and services in the absence of formalised interventions (Hart 2012). These questions implicate the local mediation of centralised policy: an issue that is pivotal to the examples of the CFOS model of positive youth justice provided throughout this book. Notably, we will explore the diversionary Bureau model in the context of the new out-of-court processes that have emerged from the LASPO Act 2012 (see Chapter Five).

The early positioning of the coalition government regarding youth justice represented very much more of the same (new youth justice) approach of individualisation and responsibilisation through *system first, offender first* and *offence first* models of risk-focused early intervention(ism) and the managerialist control and prescription of practice. Like its predecessor, the government was producing youth justice policy that threatened net widening and labelling through identifying 'at risk' and 'high risk' children in need of adult intervention, in direct opposition to the diversionary, anti-punishment, minimum necessary intervention and best interests principles of contemporary children's rights contraventions (see Chapter One). Proposals for increased practitioner discretion within a decentralised, localised agenda for shaping and delivering youth justice have been driven by deficit reduction goals (in this case, economic deficit rather than perceived deficits in the child) in a period of economic austerity, evidenced by proposals for payment-by-results financial models for practice (Puffett 2012). Economically driven policy and practice, however, actually run the risk of reducing practitioner discretion by pressurising staff into meeting tightly prescribed performance targets and by generating what Drake et al (2014: 26) conceive as:

> [S]mall-scale centralism, whereby newly empowered local managers replace the paraphernalia of centralist controls with their own closely monitored strictures over the discretions of front-line staff, in pursuit of easy-to-show targets that measure outputs not outcomes. Austerity budgets could exacerbate these tendencies amongst ever-more accountable YOT managers labouring under the gaze of an ever-more-watchful YJB and Ministry of Justice.

Consequently, there is the paradoxical potential for centralisation at the *national* level to be expanded through the decentralised localism and practitioner discretion agendas, particularly where economic concerns take precedence over the principled treatment of children. It is already clear that austerity measures have resulted in severe cuts to youth justice services in England and Wales, notably regarding prevention (see Creaney and Smith 2014). These cuts introduce a further centralisation-decentralisation potentiality at the *local* level. Faced with drastic and unavoidable cost cutting, it is possible that multi-agency partnerships (for example YOTs, Crime and Disorder Reduction/Community Safety Partnerships) will opt for a retrenchment of their services, taking them in house. Conversely, multi-agency partnerships may seek to utilise their limited funding in more innovative, outward-looking ways, incorporating more external (non-youth justice) agencies and services into their partnerships and pursuing more universal provision (for example social enterprise, careers/work experience companies) as a means of delivering child-friendly youth justice. Economic austerity is a dangerous development in the context of a youth justice policy and practice that already prioritises neoliberalist, managerialist and financial (cost-effectiveness) objectives through the targeting of children by short-term projects and interventions such as Sure Start and YOT interventions attached to court-ordered disposals (privileged in English social policy) over a more principled, child-friendly agenda of long-term, universal and mainstreamed provision (promoted by Welsh social policy – see later). Taken together, neoliberalist targeting and the diminution of social provision tend to disproportionately and adversely affect the children of the 'not rich', such that austerity creeps up the social class ladder (National Audit Office (NAO) 2013; Yates 2012), exacerbating existing social inequalities and encouraging organisations working with children to withdraw into *offender first* mentalities. There are encouraging signs within the LASPO Act 2012, for example, of the emergence of a more flexible, diversionary, child-focused approach to pre-court processes (see Chapter Five), consolidated in the formal YJS by the introduction of a more holistic, child-friendly assessment and intervention framework (AssetPlus – see Chapter Four). However, it remains to be seen how these nascent and proposed enhancements will be realised and mediated in practice locally and to what extent the government asserts a centralised, performance management approach to their monitoring and evaluation. It also remains moot as to the extent to which these progressive developments will shape the YJS, rather than functioning as peripheral elements of an otherwise punitive, negative-facing and *offender first* system.

The geo-political context of Children First, Offenders Second

It is important to stress that the socio- and geopolitical contexts of England and Wales differ markedly. Indeed, England has a different social context and class system to other Celtic countries. Since the Magna Carta, 'Englishness' has been associated with freedoms (read 'opportunity'), whereas Wales and the other Celtic countries (in common with a broader European norm) have more in common with the tradition of the Napoleonic code and its associated notion of 'rights'. Freedoms and rights represent very different ways of thinking and acting. The CFOS approach to youth justice has been foregrounded at the national policy level by social policy developments in Wales since (partial) devolution in 1999 and facilitated at local practice level by local government reorganisation in 1996. Both contexts have provided important geopolitical conditions within which CFOS could emerge and evolve. It is essential to explore in order to evaluate CFOS in both policy and practice terms.

National devolution: the birth of a partially devolved Wales

The UK is 'a complex legislative and constitutional entity' (Haines 2009: 231), essentially one country consisting of one large country (England) and three smaller countries (Wales, Scotland and Northern Ireland) and governed from Westminster, London (England). According to 2010 mid-year estimates (Office for National Statistics [ONS] 2011), the UK population is just over 62 million (62,261,967), with 89% of the population based in England (52,240,475), 8% in Scotland (5,222,100), 5% in Wales (3,006,430) and 3% in Northern Ireland (1,799,392). In relation to the legislative bases of the individual countries within the UK, Northern Ireland ceded from direct English rule in 1998 following the ratification of the Good Friday Agreement and the establishment of the Northern Ireland Assembly. Scotland partially devolved from English rule in 1999 following the Scotland Act 1998 and the formation of the Scottish Parliament in the nation's capital, Edinburgh. Scotland has independent control over a number of policy areas, including criminal justice, policing and the courts, education, health and housing, but other areas remain under Westminster rule (for example local government, trade and industry, social security, defence). Similar to Scotland, Wales achieved partial devolution in 1999 following the Government of Wales Act 1998, which established the National Assembly for Wales in Cardiff. The subsequent Government of Wales Act 2006 catalysed a range of primary law-making powers and created an executive body, the Welsh Assembly government (known as the Welsh government since 2011), separate from the National Assembly legislature (see Haines 2009b). The Welsh government holds devolved responsibility for certain policy issues (for example education, health, housing, local government), but other areas are non-devolved, notably criminal justice, youth justice and policing. Consequently, Wales shares a YJS with England.

Post-devolution social policy for children and young people

Social policy for children and young people in England, immediately following the devolution of Wales, has prioritised the negative behaviours and outcomes targeted within youth justice policy, namely offending, substance use and antisocial behaviour, alongside broader (non-offending) problems such as social exclusion, academic underachievement and unemployment. In March 2000, the month prior to the official inception of the YJB and YOTs in England and Wales, the UK government's Social Exclusion Unit published their *Report of Policy Action Team 12: Young People* (SEU 2000). The report characterised children and young people as potentially 'at risk' of exposure to risk factors and consequent negative behaviours, reflective of the Crime and Disorder Act 1998 focus on risk reduction and (ostensibly) the prevention of offending (but, see Chapter Six), but expanding these foci beyond the youth justice arena and into the broader lives of children. The UK government Department for Education and Skills (DfES) followed up this report with their *Every Child Matters: Change for Children* policy framework for children in England (DfES 2004). Despite its grounding in the Children Act 2004 (an amendment to the Children Act 1989), which stated that the welfare of the child be paramount in all legal proceedings, *Every Child Matters* introduced a greater emphasis on the prevention of negative behaviours and outcomes (educational failure, antisocial behaviour, substance use, offending, ill-health, teenage pregnancy) through risk-focused early intervention. To this end, the policy promised more coordinated, multi-agency and responsive services for children and their parents that would 'maximise opportunities and minimize risk' (DfES 2004: 2). Therefore, not only did *Every Child Matters* retain a distinct risk and negative behaviour focus that privileged individualised, deterministic explanations for personal and social problems experienced by children, but it also responsibilised children and their parents to take advantage of the 'opportunities' given to them and to adhere to social norms and rules (for example do not offend or behave antisocially) or have these opportunities forcibly removed (Goldson 2003).

Furthermore, the responsibilisation of children and their parents has been inextricably bound together with children's rights discourses in England, not least through Blair's proclamation that children should have 'no rights without responsibilities', rendering children's rights 'conditional' on acceptable behaviour (see Kemshall 2008). The Labour government followed up *Every Child Matters* with *Youth Matters* (DfES 2005), a strategy aimed at meeting needs, improving services, increasing opportunities and enhancing support for 13- to 19-year-olds in England, while also committed to 'challenging' children to 'appreciate and respect the opportunities available to them' in order to strike the 'right balance between rights and responsibilities' (DfES 2005: 4). *Youth Matters* outlined a twin-track approach committed to 'engag[ing] more young people in positive activities and to empower[ing] them [while providing] ... personalised intensive support' for young people with serious problems and/or those in trouble with the law (DfES 2005: 5). The *Youth Matters* policy framework extended the multi-agency and responsive service provision ethos of *Every Child Matters*, but similarly retained a focus on risk-focused targeted early intervention to address negative behaviours and outcomes (adding educational exclusion, unemployment and victimisation to the list of negative behaviours and outcomes targeted within *Every Child Matters*) and responsibilising rhetoric couched in the language of meeting needs. Subsequent social policies for children and young people, such as the *Children's Plan* (DfES 2007) and the *Youth Task Force Action Plan: Give Respect, Get Respect – Youth Matters* (Department for Children, Schools and Families 2008), further pursued the foci of risk reduction and preventing negative behaviours and outcomes, expanding the latter to incorporate underachievement and disaffection (see Turnbull and Spence 2011). However, social policy making for children and young people in England specifically has continued to prioritise the prevention of offending by 'at risk' children (see Department for Children, Schools and Families 2008) and has thus reflected the risk-laden negativity of the views of children perpetuated by youth justice policy since the Crime and Disorder Act 1998.

Social policy for children in Wales: children's rights and entitlements

Following (partial) devolution, the Welsh government sought to create and develop its own distinctive social and legislative identity. The founding principles of the devolved National Assembly for Wales were social justice, diversity, community regeneration, social inclusion, equality of access and the Welsh language (Drakeford 2009). Accordingly, social policy making in respect of children in Wales has been underpinned by a set of fundamental collectivist and rights-based principles since devolution,[44] which include commitments to:

- The advantages of *universal services* – rather than narrowly targeted means-tested services;
- *Equality of outcome*, not simply equality of opportunities;
- For children, in particular, processes of *engagement and participation*. (Drakeford 2010: 142, emphasis added)

The social policy-making principles for children in Wales have been animated by the children and youth inclusion strategy Extending Entitlement (National Assembly Policy Unit 2000, 2002), which established a set of 10 universal entitlements 'which are, as far as possible: free at point of use; universal and unconditional' (Morgan 2002). Under the Extending Entitlement strategy, every young person in Wales (with 'young person' defined as anyone aged between 11 and 25 years old) has a basic entitlement to:

- Education, training and work experience – tailored to their needs;
- Basic skills which open doors to a full life and promote social inclusion;
- A wide and varied range of opportunities to participate in volunteering and active citizenship;
- High-quality, responsive, and accessible services and facilities;
- Independent, specialist careers advice and guidance and student support and counselling services;
- Personal support and advice where and when needed and in appropriate formats – with clear ground rules on confidentiality;

[44] These principles are explicated and elaborated within the document *One Wales: A progressive agenda for the government of Wales* (Welsh Assembly Government (WAG) 2007).

- Advice on health, housing benefit and other issues provided in an accessible and welcoming settings;
- Recreational and social opportunities in a safe and accessible environment;
- Sporting, artistic, musical and outdoor experiences to develop talent, broaden horizons and promote rounded perspective including both national and international contexts;
- The right to be consulted, to participate in decision-making and to be heard, on all matters which concern them or have an impact on their lives. (National Assembly Policy Unit 2002: 10; see also Haines, Case and Portwood 2004)

Although the 10 entitlements within Extending Entitlement were not explicitly linked to the UNCRC, they were clearly informed by it to the extent that they adopt a language of entitlement that marks 'a shift in the conceptual basis towards a rights based approach' (Save the Children 2007: 4). The Welsh government has directly addressed the requirements of the UNCRC explicitly through its *Seven Core Aims* of policy-making for children, set out within their *Children and Young People: Rights to Action* document (WAG 2004) – policy prescriptions that apply to *all* children, including those in conflict with the law and the youth justice system. These core aims state that all children in Wales:

1. have a flying start in life and the best possible basis for their future growth and development;
2. have access to a comprehensive range of education, training and learning opportunities, including acquisition of essential personal and social skills;
3. enjoy the best possible physical and mental, social and emotional health, including freedom from abuse, victimization and exploitation;
4. have access to play, leisure, sporting and cultural activities;
5. [are] listened to, treated with respect and have their race and cultural identity recognized;

6. have a safe home and the community which supports physical and emotional well-being; and
7. [are] not disadvantaged by child poverty. (WAG 2004: 1)

The *Seven Core Aims* have been championed by Keith Towler, the current Children's Commissioner for Wales,[45] as demonstrating progress in realising children's rights across Wales (Towler 2009). The Commissioner has been supportive of what he perceived as the preventive, needs-led and rights-based structures and governance in Wales, highlighting in particular a distinct approach to youth justice in Wales, which is 'tied directly to the UNCRC' and which contrasts with the non-compliant English system, which is 'dominated by a punitive approach' (Towler 2009: 42).

National progress towards meeting the requirements of the UNCRC is formally monitored by the multi-agency Wales UNCRC Monitoring Group, a partnership of academics from Welsh universities, representatives from children's organisations (for example Funky Dragon,[46] NSPCC, Barnardos, Save the Children) and observers from the Welsh government, Welsh Local Government Association, the Equalities and Human Rights Commission and the Children and Young Peoples Partnership Support Unit. The Monitoring Group, which is chaired by the Children's Commissioner for Wales, has an official duty to report back to the United Nations (UN) on Wales's progress

---

[45] An independent, non-government advocate who meets regularly with children (aged 0–18 years old), key stakeholder adults and child-focused organisations in Wales to discuss, monitor, advise, advocate and publish on children's rights issues and child-focused policies and practices. For example, the Office of the Welsh Children's Commissioner monitors national compliance with the UNCRC and the concluding recommendations of the UN Committee on the Rights of the Child.

[46] Funky Dragon, also known as the Children and Young People's Assembly for Wales, is a peer-led organisation that represents children and enables them to have their voices heard on issues that affect them. Funky Dragon consists of a Management Committee (four adult representatives, four young people aged over 18, four children aged below 18) and a Grand Council of 100 children and young people from across Wales (including from local authority areas, schools councils, voluntary services and equality organisations), which feeds into local children and youth forums.

towards addressing the 'Concluding Observations' within the UN Committee's periodic reports. The post-devolution progress made in Wales towards realising children's rights has been detailed in a series of reports:

- *Rights in Action: Children and Young People's Rights in Wales* – the *Rights in Action* report (WAG 2007) promotes the 'distinctive strategy' pursued in Wales (since 2002) in implementing a children's rights agenda, detailing the extent to which each of the *Seven Core Aims* and the entitlements within Extending Entitlement have been grounded in the UNCRC. The Children's Commissioner role was heralded as providing independent advocacy for children's rights and welfare needs, alongside providing representations, recommendations and guidance to the Welsh government and key stakeholders working with children and young people in Wales. The report stated that a set of national outcome measures for children's rights were under construction and would contribute to the development of Children and Young People's Plans in each local authority area, a statutory requirement of Children and Young People's Partnerships under the Children Act 2004.
- *Stop, Look, Listen: The Road to Realising Children's Rights in Wales* – the *Stop, Look, Listen* report (Save the Children 2007) was the Wales UNCRC Monitoring Group's NGO alternative report to the WAG's *Rights in Action* response to the UN Committee. The report highlights the Welsh government's clear commitment 'to establish systems and structures based on children's rights. … the establishment of the first children's commissioner in the UK, the establishment of Funky Dragon (the children and young people's assembly for Wales) and the development of national policy that is explicitly underpinned by the UNCRC' (Save the Children 2007: iv). However, this enthusiasm was tempered by a recognition of the need to raise awareness of children's rights in Wales, to enhance service delivery to levels that more effectively address children's rights, to produce a Welsh implementation plan for children's rights and to encourage the UK government to work more closely with the Welsh government towards solutions more appropriate to the Welsh policy context (Save the Children 2007). Funky Dragon's *Our Rights Our Story*

– the *Our Rights Our Story* (OROS) study (Funky Dragon 2007; see also Penman 2010) accessed the views of 12,205 children (with 94% aged between 11 and 15 years old) from across Wales, consulting on their perceived ability to access their rights under the UNCRC. The consultative research took the form of a national questionnaire survey (10,035 children), interviews with children (37 in total) from special interest groups (for example children in the YJS, disabled children, black and minority ethnic children) and a series of 40 workshops. Children were asked for their views about living in Wales, education, health, information and participation. The issues identified for special attention (for example service improvement, interventions, information provision, policy change) in order to improve access to rights were: education (for example bullying, personal and social education, teaching methods, careers advice, school discipline); health (active participation in service planning, access to health care and professionals, healthy lifestyles); information (for example GCSE choices, Welsh language, health, different cultures); and participation (for example in consultations, in school councils, children as active citizens). Children's responses therefore formed the basis of a series of recommendations made by Funky Dragon for improving young people's access to their rights/entitlements and thus for improving Welsh government compliance with the UNCRC.

- *Getting it Right 2009* – this Welsh government report (Welsh Assembly Government (WAG) 2009) outlined a five-year rolling plan for implementing the government's key priorities in response to the *Concluding Observations of the UN Committee on the Rights of the Child 2008* (UN Committee on the Rights of the Child 2008). The report noted Welsh progress in responding to the previous 2002 UN Committee's observations and made explicit reference to the *Rights in Action, Stop, Look, Listen* and *Our Rights Our Story* documents, along with the evidence given to the UN Committee in Geneva by Funky Dragon representatives in 2007. *Getting it Right* identified 16 priorities for Wales, agreed through collaboration between the Welsh government and the NGO Monitoring Group. Priority 16 was 'working to ensure that

> children and young people from Wales in the YJS can claim their UNCRC and human rights' (WAG 2009: 5).

It is evident that social policy making for children in Wales following devolution has been grounded in a serious commitment to children's rights, articulated in a series of policy/strategy documents and reports. This children's rights focus has culminated in the ratification of the Rights of Children and Young Persons (Wales) Measure 2011, which requires all Welsh government ministers to have due regard to the rights and obligations in the UNCRC when making strategic decisions regarding practice with children. According to Rhodri Morgan, the former First Minister of the Welsh government (in a speech to Texas universities, June 2014):

> What is the key to the UNCRC law is that it takes child protection and welfare one step further. Traditionally, children are seen in law as having interests but not rights. They were objects of protection not holders of rights .... Now Wales has pioneered the move to a rights-based approach – fit for the twenty-first century.

However, the promotion of the *entitlements* concept within Extending Entitlement introduces a potential for confusion with the notion of children's 'rights' (in line with the UNCRC) that guides the documents outlined earlier. The concepts of entitlements and rights are not synonymous. While we support rights-facing approaches to working with children to enable them to receive the *minimum standards* of protection, participation and promotion that they should expect under the UNCRC, this approach does not go far enough for CFOS. We prioritise the principles of an entitlements-led agenda – to embed prospective and proactive ways of working wherein adults facilitate the *maximum outcomes* that children should expect from support, services and interventions. Both entitlements- and rights-led models require consultation and engagement with children in the development and implementation of services, but the concepts are philosophically and practically distinct, notably because the pursuit of children's entitlements responsibilises adults for children's access to and engagement with systemic responses. For these reasons, a CFOS model of positive youth justice privileges entitlements.

Developing Children First, Offenders Second positive youth justice policy in Wales

Despite its distinct social policy-making identity, the Welsh government possesses no formal legal or policy-making powers in respect of youth justice, which remains a non-devolved area subject to the law, policy and practice prescriptions from the UK government based in Westminster. The YJS encompasses England and Wales, thus requiring that children in conflict with the law and the youth justice system in Wales are dealt with under the auspices of the Crime and Disorder Act 1998, via multi-agency YOTs that are governed and (part) funded by the YJB (which itself is governed by the Ministry of Justice[47] based in England). The non-devolved nature of youth justice in Wales, however, highlights an area of significant constitutional complexity (see, Haines 2009b), as most associated issues and organisational arrangements in Wales are devolved, including education, social services, housing, health and probation – all of which sit within the statutory agencies that contribute to the formation and funding of YOTs. Therefore, it is practically and financially impossible for (non-devolved) youth justice to function in Wales without the cooperation of devolved stakeholders and 'anything that the YJB hopes to achieve in Wales can only be obtained with the assistance and agreement of the devolved administration' (Drakeford 2010: 140).

This complexity has been heightened by the apparent divergence in policy orientation between the YJB in England and the Welsh government. Both organisations subscribe to a youth crime *prevention* agenda (the principal aim of the YJS under

[47] A government department with responsibility for monitoring the criminal justice system, the judiciary, courts, probation service and the YJS, with the key objectives to reduce reoffending, protect the public, facilitate access to justice, increase public confidence in the criminal justice system and uphold civil liberties.

the Crime and Disorder Act 1998), but they each pursue this agenda in diverse ways. The YJB has committed to a risk- and deficit-reduction agenda (although an imminent move away from this has been proposed via the AssetPlus assessment and intervention framework – see Chapter Four), while the Welsh government has pursued a more entitlements- and rights-based agenda wherein the principles of Extending Entitlement and the *Seven Core Aims* apply equally to children in conflict with the law and the youth justice system. Social policy divergences between England and Wales and their implications for the development of youth justice policy in Wales, have been managed and reconciled since devolution by the Youth Justice Committee for Wales (now known as the Wales Youth Justice Advisory Panel – see later in this chapter).

In Focus • All Wales Youth Offending Strategy

In 2004, the All Wales Youth Offending Strategy (AWYOS) was published as a partnership document by the Welsh Assembly government (led by the Social Services Minister, Edwina Hart) and the YJB for England and Wales (led by the Chair, Professor Rod Morgan). The AWYOS was intended to provide a 'national framework for preventing offending and reoffending among children and young people in Wales' (WAG and YJB 2004: 1), working from the principle that 'whenever we can prevent offending there is benefit for us all ... the best way to stop offending is to prevent it from happening in the first place' (WAG and YJB 2004: Edwina Hart's foreword). The AWYOS is most notable for initiating unique, Welsh-focused youth justice context whereby 'young people should be treated as children first and offenders second' (WAG and YJB 2004: 3), which directly challenges the risk-focused, responsibilising, adulterised and adult-centric youth justice policy (and social policy) emerging from England.

The AWYOS reflected the divergences and tensions between UK/English government youth justice policy and Welsh government social policy for children in its simultaneous support for the English social policy/youth justice principles of prevention through 'early intervention, restorative justice measures, appropriate punishment and supported rehabilitation', and the more 'children first' Welsh principles of prevention through 'promoting the welfare of children and children' (WAG and YJB 2004: 3).

The AWYOS coalesces with the Extending Entitlement children youth inclusion strategy, which places responsibility on adult gatekeepers (for example YOT staff, teachers, social workers, health workers) to enable children to access their universal entitlements and to participate in the services offered to them. The AWYOS, therefore, officially marks a point of divergence from the English approach to youth justice in terms of:

- **Principles** – the 'children first and offenders second', rights-based and promotional (of positive behaviour) orientation of youth justice policy in Wales contrasts with the more punitive, repressive, responsibilising and risk-based pursuit of youth justice objectives in England (see Muncie 2008b; Goldson 2003). By viewing children and young people as 'children first', the WAG has created a conceptual space for a broad range of policy and services to respond holistically and in a joined-up manner to the rights, strengths and needs of children and young people, rather than artificially restricting the responses of key stakeholders to the reduction of risk
- **Policy and strategy** – the AWYOS pursues prevention, rehabilitation, restorative justice and appropriate punishment via a principled 'children first offenders second' approach that promotes positive behaviour and equality of access to universal services, in contrast to the responsibilising and risk-based rhetoric of *Every Child Matters* in England and the Youth Crime Action Plan 2008, which also emphasises prevention, but through more punitive and repressive measures such as enforcement, risk-based and targeted early intervention and non-negotiable support.

The development and implementation of the AWYOS is monitored and guided by the Wales Youth Justice Advisory Panel (see later in this chapter). In April 2009 the Welsh government and YJB published the *All Wales Youth Offending Strategy: Delivery Plan 2009–11* (WAG and YJB 2009), which committed to working with the Welsh Children's Commissioner to enable 'mainstream and embedded consultation with, and the participation of, children and young people in the youth justice system' (WAG and YJB 2009: 10). The AWYOS Delivery Plan asserted that children and young people's entitlements to express their views should be reflected and implemented at every stage of the criminal justice process (see also Nacro Cymru 2009[48]), outlining the priority themes to be addressed and the actions to be taken in order to deliver the AWYOS. Six priority areas were identified, which mapped into the Welsh Youth Justice Indicator Set (WYJIS) – the key performance indicators against which Welsh YOTs are measured by the YJB (see Chapter Four): reducing FTEs into the YJS, reducing reoffending, reducing custody rates, increasing engagement with education, training and employment, increasing access to suitable accommodation and increasing access to appropriate substance use assessment and treatment (WAG and YJB 2009). The AWYOS Delivery Plan commits to pursuing these objectives through continued *funding, monitoring and support* (for example for targeted prevention programmes, for the Safer Communities Fund, mental health provision, Children and Young People's Partnerships, Nacro Cymru, family and in-school support programmes, restorative justice), an emphasis on *multi-agency partnership working* (for example incorporating police, health boards, substance misuse agencies, careers companies, social services), the increasing *professionalisation* of the youth justice workforce through training, accreditation and qualifications frameworks, and dedicated *evidence gathering*, evaluation and reflection on best practice within strategic guidance (WAG and YJB 2009; see also Chapter Seven, which reviews the updated AWYOS).

Devolving a Children First, Offenders Second positive youth justice in Wales

> The political and organisational context in Wales, with partial devolution of relevant issues ... and a distinctive policy orientation for young people (rights- and entitlements-focused), provides conceptual and practical space for progressive youth justice. (Case and Haines 2012: 40)

[48] The 2009 Nacro report *Youth Justice and Participation in Wales* was intended to assist YOTs in meeting Article 12 of the UNCRC and participation requirements in their work. The report identified the main benefits of children's participation as better understanding of criminal justice processes/procedures, contributing to effective planning of preventive and reductive interventions, promoting engagement and compliance, and enhancing children's potential and confidence (Nacro Cymru 2009).

> When things go wrong in the lives of children and young people, the Welsh focus has been on trying to put right flaws in the systems on which they depend, rather than on focusing on the 'deficits' in young people themselves. (Drakeford 2010: 141)

According to Drakeford (2010: 141; see also Haines and Drakeford 1998), 'the term "children first" in a Welsh youth justice context is used to denote an attitude of mind, in which offending is understood as only one element in a much wider and more complex identity'. Consequently, offending by children should be addressed by a series of joined-up, inclusive and rights-based social policies within which children in conflict with the law and the youth justice system are viewed primarily as children who (sometimes) experience personal and social vulnerabilities and who possess entitlements to the benefits of a rich, advanced Western society – as befits a growing maturity.[49] There is a strong case to be made for the delivery of youth justice in Wales to receive special consideration on the basis of its (partial) devolution settlement and its social policy foci regarding children and young people. While youth justice remains non-devolved, many of those who work in YJS in Wales are employed by organisations providing services under devolved authority. The tensions here readily become clear. The context of partial devolution has complicated the delivery of youth justice *services* in Wales due to the multi-agency composition of YOTs and the non-devolved status of youth justice. The practice of Welsh YOTs is monitored and influenced from the centre (YJB in London) in certain respects (for example requirements to provide data returns, adherence to prescribed National Standards for practice, statutory obligations to prioritise the prevention

[49] This contrasts starkly with policy recommendations for responding to children who offend in England in terms of their offence and their adulterised offence-related characteristics, evidenced in practice by punitive, repressive, controlling and responsibilising measures, according to the *UK Children's Commissioners' Report*, which stated that 'there is a very punitive approach to misbehaviour by children and … the criminal justice system is used too readily' (UK Children's Commissioners 2008: 5).

of offending[50]), yet they employ staff from devolved agencies (for example social services, education, substance use) working alongside staff from non-devolved agencies (for example police, probation) who may be working to different 'national' agendas and organisational priorities (for example enforcement vs. entitlements).

This structural tension has been further complicated by the *principles* of social policy making for children and young people in Wales, which are distinct from those in England. As stated, the Welsh government has forged its distinctive social and legislative identity in relation to working with children and young people, underpinned by collectivist and rights-based principles, promoting universal services over the more narrowly targeted (for example offender-first and risk-based) and responsibilising provision typifying the 'English' approach (a similar 'devolution and difference' distinction between rights and responsibilisation has been made in relation to 'Sex and Relationships Education' – see Oerton and Pilgrim 2013). Welsh social policy for children and young people emphasises equality of *outcome* over the English focus on equality of opportunity (see Haines and Case 2011) and prioritises the engagement and participation of Welsh children in decisions and services that affect them (Drakeford 2010; see also Haines 2009b). However, it is important to stress the nascent and rhetorical bases of the broad policy distinctions we are drawing between youth justice in England (as risk focused) and Wales (as rights focused). Beyond notable local examples, there is a paucity of rigorous empirical evidence to support conclusions that such distinctions have transferred into *practice* at the national and local levels; or that there is anything other than an unevenness of practice across localities (in Wales and England) based on the local mediation of national policy. What we are seeking to argue here is that *policy* documents and NGO reports in Wales provide cogent evidence of an emerging, distinctive and principled Welsh

[50] The prevention agenda, paradoxically, is poorly serviced by YOTs in England. Although it is emphasised in Wales by the Welsh government through the AWYOS (WAG and YJB 2004) and *Youth Crime Prevention in Wales: Strategic Guidance* (WAG and YJB 2008), it is also moot as to the extent this agenda represents primary and universal prevention as opposed to targeted, early intervention and reduction priorities (see Chapter Six).

youth justice *policy* identity, particularly regarding children's rights and entitlements, universalism and advocating children's participation and engagement (see Drakeford 2010; Haines and Case 2012; Case 2014). Much still remains to be done to see these principles brought into practice.

Devolving a Children First, Offenders Second positive youth justice in Wales: political reviews

The Welsh government has been officially debating the devolution of youth justice to Wales since the 2007 publication of *One Wales: A Progressive Agenda for the Government of Wales* (WAG 2007), which committed to 'ensuring an effective youth and criminal justice system [by exploring] the potential for devolution of *some* ... of the criminal justice system' (WAG 2007: 29). *One Wales* prioritised the devolution of funding and delivery mechanisms in youth justice, the continued emphasis on preventive intervention, diversion from custody and effective non-custodial sentences for children and the promotion of cross-cutting practice between the YJS and (already devolved) areas closely related to youth justice, such as education, housing and mental health services (WAG 2007). The emerging political, structural and operational emphases on a distinct Welsh or 'dragonised' youth justice (Haines 2009b) has gained significant momentum in the past five years, in policy terms, though not necessarily in *practice* across Wales. Two simultaneous political agendas have progressed these emphases: the UK coalition government's incremental critical reviews of the YJB in England and Wales and the Welsh government report on devolving youth justice.

UK government reviews have indicated that the role of the YJB in England and Wales should incrementally diminish through: recommendations in the *Breaking the Cycle* Green Paper (MOJ 2010) for its abolition as a cost-cutting measure in the age of austerity, a suggestion that was downsized by subsequent decisions for the maintenance of current functions (albeit in a reduced capacity) in the UK Public Bodies Act 2011 and most recently the reduction of YJB independence to make it more accountable to ministers, expressed in the triennial *Functions Review* (Ministry of Justice (MOJ) 2012). It could be argued, however, that any reductions in the YJB's role have been more in perception than reality – with the reviews making recommendations for changes to functions that are actually already in place (so not changes or reductions in any substantive sense), but inconsistently applied in practice (for example Ministry of Justice representation at YJB meetings, more interface between the YJB and government ministers). Similarly, none of the functions of YJB Cymru (the YJB organisation/division for Wales – see later in this chapter) have been reduced and two in particular have been strengthened: the power to give grants to YOTs (due to being enabled to hold YOTs to account for performance through an escalation process) and the ability to request ministerial intervention in poorly performing YOT areas (Case 2014). Furthermore, the coalition government's 'localism' agenda has enabled YJB Cymru (within its existing legal powers and functions) to more fully realise its effective practice dissemination function by promoting practice more sensitive to the Welsh policy agenda through its Practice Development Panel and the use of the Correctional Program Assessment Inventory (a tool to evaluate criminal justice programme integrity).

In Wales, the Welsh government commissioned a report from Professor Rod Morgan (the former chair of the YJB) on the 'benefits and risks involved in devolving youth justice' (Morgan 2009: 2) and endorsed the recommendations of this report in a Cabinet briefing paper entitled *Devolution of Youth Justice* (Welsh Government 2011). The *Report to the Welsh Assembly Government on the Question of Devolution of Youth Justice Responsibilities* (Morgan 2009) was informed by a broad consultation exercise with key stakeholders in the arenas of policy making (for example government ministers, the YJB, the Welsh Children's Commissioner's office), management (for example police, courts, YOTs), custodial institutions, academia and children in custody, complemented by documentary analysis and analyses of baseline youth justice data. Morgan (2009: 2) conducted a detailed assessment of:

- the current interface between devolved and non-devolved functions as they relate to youth justice and youth crime prevention, with particular focus on the key risk factors that are associated with offending and antisocial behaviour by children and young people;
- the likely benefits and risks to delivery of plans and strategies for tackling youth offending;
- the likely financial implications;
- the benefits to Welsh children and young people that would accrue if the system was devolved.

The report emphasised that the Welsh government was already responsible for the *delivery* of a range of youth justice services (for example community sentences) and youth justice-related children's services in Wales in areas both mainstreamed and devolved (for example education, social services, health), but that it retained limited control over the *demand* for services in the (non-devolved) youth justice domain. However, Morgan concluded that a distinctive Welsh YJS is emerging and that 'the youth justice service is already the most devolved part of the criminal justice system' (Morgan 2009: 7). The report asserted that the devolution of youth justice to Wales constitutes something of a 'red herring' inasmuch as there is a great deal of scope for improvement to the system from within the current constitutional arrangements, in particular, recommending:

> - working with the four police forces in Wales … to reduce the criminalisation of children and young people and bolster alternative early preventive and informal control measures;
> - closer working between the YOTs and the local authority Children and Young People's Partnerships;[51]

[51] Multi-agency framework partnerships established in every local authority area in England and Wales, with a statutory obligation under the Children Act 2004 to produce a Children and Young People's Framework Partnership Plan establishing a local vision for the planning, prioritisation and delivery of support and services to children and young people and for enhancing their participation in decision-making processes locally.

- fostering good practice networks between youth court sentencers and YOT managers in Wales;
- building portfolios of positive activity and opportunity in every YOT area. (Morgan 2009: 11)

Of particular importance to this book is Morgan's (2009: 8) conclusion, following his extensive consultation, that: 'Almost everyone favours the rights-based doctrine of *Extending Entitlement*, with children being treated in a more welfare-oriented manner as children first and offenders second. The visionaries see devolution offering more opportunity to pursue a rights and welfare approach to children in trouble more consistently.' However, at the practical level, the report mirrored the findings of a recent YOT inspection report, *Joint Inspection Findings of Youth Offending Teams in Wales 2003–2008*, which identified 'wide variation in the way in which YOTs have been constituted, funded and managed' (HMI Probation 2009: 47) and concluded that fragmentation and disparities across Wales were not necessarily the responsibility of individual YOTs, but were at least equally attributable to divergences in local government performance and in the delivery of child-related services in local authority areas (HMI Probation 2009). Morgan's report echoed the inspection conclusions that certain Welsh YOTs were operating as distinct and relatively invisible entities within their local authority areas; thus detaching youth justice from child-related services in structural and cultural terms. Nevertheless, the report highlighted that some YOT managers traded on this lack of engagement and consequent autonomy, utilising their relatively invisible status locally and the complex legislative arrangements nationally as a 'policy shield' that enabled them to resist and embrace the YJB/English *managerialist* approach and the Welsh government's 'children first and offenders second' ethos when it suited. The perception that some YOT managers were 'playing both sides' was reflected in the YOT Managers Cymru organisation (the committee of all YOT managers in Wales), which was viewed as operationally stronger as a corporate body than its English counterpart, the Association of YOT Managers. YOT Managers Cymru was seen to maintain a more 'combative' relationship with YJB Cymru than did the

Association of YOT Managers with its respective regional offices. According to Morgan (2009: 33) 'Welsh YOT managers are to some extent able to resist both sides on the grounds that they must do the bidding of the other'. Morgan (2009) identified that despite widespread support for the 'children first' ethos of the AWYOS, there remained a reticence among some YOT managers to support the devolution of youth justice to Wales as this could draw them more closely into partnerships providing services to children, thus threatening their relative autonomy locally and exerting greater pressure to realise the rhetoric of the AWYOS and Extending Entitlement. In other words, Morgan concluded that despite rhetorical support for CFOS, elements of this approach had yet to make their way consistently into embedded, explicit practice within and between YOTs in Wales and that despite national distinctions in policy formation, there were no discernible differences in youth justice practice or outcomes for children between England and Wales.

A subsequent *Devolution of Youth Justice* Cabinet briefing report outlined 'a vision for increasing Welsh government influence over the delivery of services to children and young people who are offending or at risk of offending' (Welsh Government 2011: 1), requiring Cabinet to examine the implications of the full devolution of youth justice, using the *One Wales* policy document and Professor Morgan's devolution review as touchstones. The briefing reiterated Morgan's acknowledgement that the Welsh government already retains strategic and policy-making powers in several areas that influence youth offending and youth justice (for example substance misuse, poor parenting, education, employment and training, mental health issues, housing) such that 'it is not necessary to secure the further devolution of powers to intervene decisively in areas' (Welsh Government 2011: 2). The briefing report recommends ways to 'strengthen the position of children and young people made vulnerable through offending' (Welsh Government 2011: 4), namely (and somewhat paradoxically, by) increasing risk-based early intervention, restorative justice measures as alternatives to formal charging (led by the police) and the more effective management of community sentences, all of which accord with the recommendations of the English-based *Breaking the Cycle* Green Paper and the *Independent*

Commission on Youth Crime and Antisocial Behaviour: Time for a Fresh Start report. The *Devolution of Youth Justice* Cabinet briefing was particularly concerned to enhance the profile and role of YOTs in Wales; identifying and emphasising the piecemeal manner in which YOTs have been integrated within local partnerships and local governance arrangements across the country. For example, it is highlighted that YOT management boards are not statutory and that there has been a persistent separation between children and family services and youth justice services (leading to the neglect of the broader social needs of children in the YJS), precipitating the conclusion that 'too often, youth offending services are marginalised under current arrangements' (Welsh Government 2011: 3).

Overall, the key difference between the English publications (*Breaking the Cycle*, *Independent Commission on Youth Crime and Antisocial Behaviour*) and the Welsh devolution documents (with the partial exception of the Cabinet briefing) is philosophical; namely the Welsh recommendation that youth justice objectives be pursued using an entitlements- and rights-based approach to supporting children, grounded in the UNCRC (Welsh Government 2011: 4): 'The principle is a focus on the needs of the children and young people, rather than on their offending behaviour. The vision is for a rights-based approach: where children or young people are not enjoying their rights, this can contribute to offending behaviour.'

A recent Welsh government Green Paper, *Proposals to improve services in Wales to better meet the needs of children and young people who are at risk of entering, or are already in, the Youth Justice System* (Welsh Government 2012) has moved discussion forward regarding how the Welsh government can most effectively utilise its existing powers to progress a rights-focused youth justice context in Wales that benefits children in the YJS. Most recently, the Welsh government has been tentatively exploring the potential for a devolved youth justice settlement based on the recommendations of the Silk Commission on Devolution in Wales (recommendations not supported with detailed discussion, evidence or justification), notably the second report which advocated that key stakeholders in youth justice in Wales (for example YJB Cymru) should have more responsibility and influence and that youth justice powers should be devolved through a new Government of Wales Act by 2017 (Commission on Devolution in Wales 2014).[52]

Risk has become arguably peripheral to overarching outcomes-led and rights-focused principles within Welsh youth justice and these foci coalesce with wider national policies concerning children in Wales (see Chapter Two), particularly the desire to increase children's access to their universal entitlements and to treat children who offend as 'children first'. The political context of devolving youth justice responsibilities to the Welsh government is pivotal to the agenda of this book – although successive UK governmental (and associated) publications continue to champion risk-led youth justice approaches, this orientation is disavowed in Wales and it is difficult to see how Wales can fully break free from English-led and dominated policy as long as youth justice remains a non-devolved matter.

Devolving a Children First, Offenders Second positive youth justice in Wales: structures and processes

A series of bespoke structures have been created to develop the youth justice agenda in Wales in accordance with the distinct Welsh social policy identity. A significant move towards addressing the policy and practice tensions in the context of an emerging 'distinct' Welsh youth justice was the creation of the YJB Cymru (Wales) division, which sits alongside the Corporate Services, Effective Practice, Community and Secure Estate divisions on the YJB for England and Wales Executive Management Group. YJB Cymru has the responsibility for both implementing and mediating YJB policy in the Welsh context – advising its parent body on Welsh matters and monitoring, supporting and advising YOTs in Wales (YJB Cymru 2012). YJB Cymru is sub-divided into three branches: Policy and Planning, Oversight and Support, and Effective Practice and Innovation. In its *Blueprint for Promoting Effective Practice and Improving Youth*

[52] http://wales.gov.uk/consultations/people-and-communities/improving-services-for-young-people-in-youth-justice-system/?lang=en.

Justice Performance in Wales, YJB Cymru (2012: 5–6) outlines its official role as:

> Working with UK Government
>
> - providing advice to ministers and working with officials in the Ministry of Justice to help them to take account of the potential impact of devolution when developing policy and legislation;
>
> Working with Welsh Government
>
> - developing a joint youth justice strategy and delivery plan for Wales [the AWYOS];
> - collaborative monitoring of youth justice outcome information;
> - joint government oversight of youth justice delivery;
> - exchange of relevant information;
> - collaboration in pursuit of effective and innovative practice;
> - reciprocal advice on the interface between devolved and non-devolved policy;
> - jointly convening the Wales Youth Justice Advisory Panel;
> - accessing the voice of the young person – to ensure that the views and experiences of young people are taken into account.

At the structural level, the Head of YJB Cymru sits as an equal partner on the YJB's Executive Management Group (EMG). A key part of this role for YJB Cymru representatives is to provide expert advice to the EMG and its 'Informational Decision Papers', each of which contains a standing 'Issues for Wales' section.

The Wales Youth Justice Advisory Panel (WYJAP) is a quarterly meeting between the Welsh government and YJB Cymru, which also includes representatives from the YJB for England and Wales, Welsh YOTs, the Secure Estate, Courts, Probation,

Police, academics from the Welsh Centre for Crime and Social Justice and the voluntary sector. The meeting is co-chaired by the Welsh representative on the YJB and the Deputy Director of the Welsh Government Community Safety Division. The WYJAP provides expertise, challenge and scrutiny on the range of strategic, policy, practice and research issues relevant to youth justice in Wales and has the 'primary purpose to assist the Welsh Government and the YJB to implement policy that prevents offending and reoffending by children and young people in Wales' (Welsh Government and Youth Justice Board 2014: 1). The Head of YJB Cymru is a member of the WYJAP and YJB Cymru reports to each WYJAP meeting on the standing item of 'Wales youth justice performance'.

Within the Welsh government, youth justice now sits as part of the Crime and Justice Team within the Community Safety Division. The Crime and Justice Team has responsibility for the interface between Welsh government and criminal justice-related policy from the Home Office and Ministry of Justice, including youth justice. The Crime and Justice Team's role is to liaise externally with YJB Cymru and internally with government colleagues in child-focus departments (for example mental health, education, social services, housing, substance use) in order to shape and influence policy development. There is also the YOT Managers Cymru, a committee of all YOT managers in Wales (represented on the WYJAP), which meets to consider the implications of legislation, government guidelines and policy on youth offending in Wales and to determine effective responses (YOT Managers Cymru 2013). The monitoring and delivery of youth justice, sensitive and appropriate to the Welsh context, is further supported by a single Welsh representative on the YJB (one of the 12 individual board members), who also jointly chairs the WYJAP. The Welsh representative[53] works closely with YJB Cymru in a critical and developmental capacity because

[53] The post of YJB member representing Wales evolved from recognition (for example by the Chair of the YJB) that Westminster-based UK government and the (partially) devolved Welsh government needed to cooperate through a balanced approach that provided the YJB with insight into issues that may require adjustment (to the Welsh context) prior to discussion. In this respect, the Welsh representative and YJB Cymru have a similar remit.

of their remit in working through sensitive political and policy issues. Welsh interests and the devolved youth justice services relationship in Wales are acknowledged and addressed by the YJB through the work undertaken by the Welsh representative on the YJB and YJB Cymru. Liaison between these two is essential and plays a significant role in their approach to gaining recognition and integration with new approaches that require implementation in Wales.

Children First, Offenders Second positive youth justice in Wales?

This chapter has set out the broad divergences in social and youth justice *policy* making for children between England (targeted, risk-based, focused on freedoms, opportunities and responsibilities) and Wales (universal, rights- and entitlements-based, focused on maximising positive outcomes) and the implications of these conflicting policy identities in creating distinct geopolitical contexts for, and national approaches to, youth justice. The geopolitical conditions of Welsh devolution in the non-devolved context of youth justice have simultaneously promoted and inhibited the potential for a CFOS model of youth justice in Wales. The Welsh social policy principles of universalism, entitlements, engagement and participation, reflected in strategic position statements and guidance, encourage YOT practitioners in Wales to pursue CFOS-informed elements of youth justice practice in partnership with the state (for example Welsh government, WYJAP). However, in reality, such practice has been variable (as it has in England), inhibited and distorted by local mediation of the policy and practice prescriptions of the YJB in England and the absence of an overarching, guiding philosophy of practice. Consequently, the implementation of devolved, distinct social *policy* principles in Wales has yet to be evidenced consistently or uniformly in youth justice *practice* at the local and national levels. The forthcoming chapters draw upon local evidence-based examples in order to discuss what forms a CFOS approach could take in practice.

FOUR

Putting children first in the youth justice system

The previous chapter focused on *policy*, the divergences between England and Wales in terms of social and youth justice policy for children and the implications and potentialities for a distinct Welsh youth justice. We set out the evolution of a negative, restricted, managerialist approach to youth justice in England and Wales since the Crime and Disorder Act 1998 that was grounded in a 'new youth justice' of neoconservative correctionalism/individualisation that was animated by risk assessment and risk-focused intervention and the neoliberal responsibilisation of children and families via coerced engagement with non-negotiable 'support' mechanisms. This managerialist 'third way' for youth justice was contrasted with the distinctive, children's rights-focused youth justice policy that has emerged in Wales since its partial devolution in 1999. The intended contrast was grounded in policy divergences – an English form of youth justice driven by risk-focused and responsibilising social policies for children compared to the potential for a distinct, progressive and principled form of Welsh youth justice putting children first. However, conclusions regarding national divergences remain at the policy level and local unevenness and variations in implementation at the practice level persist.

In this chapter, we explore the potential for a Children First, Offenders Second (CFOS) model of positive youth justice with children who have entered the formal youth justice system (YJS) and are subject to statutory court-ordered disposals: Referral Orders, Youth Rehabilitation Orders and Detention and Training Orders (Chapter Five explores the use of pre-court disposals). Embedding a CFOS model with children in conflict with the law and the youth justice system requires the adoption of a *systems management* approach (see Tutt and Giller 1987; see also Haines and Drakeford 1998) to negotiating the stages and processes of decision making regarding children across the youth justice system YJS. We advocate that systems management be facilitated by *evidence-based partnership* between children (and their families), youth justice practitioners, policy makers and researchers, which prioritises the *relational* aspects of practice, notably the participation and engagement of all parties (especially children) in the development of youth justice practice. CFOS practice in the YJS is presented, therefore, as an antidote to the *system first managerialism* of the new youth justice, wherein the technical, administrative management of children's behaviour and the work of Youth Offending Team (YOT) practitioners is prioritised over principled, ethical, humanising and engaging responses that empower children and that embrace practitioner expertise and discretion.

In order to translate policy successfully into practice, a CFOS approach must elicit the expert contributions of the two most important and neglected (front-line) stakeholders in the youth justice process: children and practitioners, while engaging with policy makers and adding the valuable contribution of a fourth (often neglected) stakeholder – researchers. We will analyse the deleterious features of managerialist youth justice, paying particular attention to the risk-based assessment and intervention that begets offender-first practice, which in turn precipitates (systemic) interventionism, net widening and programme fetishism, (organisational) practitioner deprofessionalisation and the (individualised) responsibilisation, stigmatisation and disengagement of children in conflict with the law and the youth justice system.

There follows a critical discussion of the proposed partial evolution of youth justice away from a reductionist, *offender-first* approach and towards a 'whole child' assessment and intervention framework that offers children more voice and practitioners more discretion in youth justice practices. The chapter concludes with a detailed evaluation of the nature and identity of a CFOS practice model for the YJS based on an evidence-based partnership between children, practitioners, policy makers and researchers, drawing upon applied practice examples and empirical research linked to the work of a local YOT in Wales.

Enter system-first managerialism

The radical reforms to the YJS contained within the Crime and Disorder Act 1998 were explicitly *managerialist*, intended to address concerns over the excessive discretionary and indeterminate nature of much welfare-based practice and the perceived lack of success of justice-based approaches, while simultaneously rendering the system more effective, efficient and economical – in direct response to the central criticisms of the *Misspent Youth* report (Audit Commission 1996; see also Chapter Three). The Crime and Disorder Act 1998 moved forward this managerialist agenda through the modernisation of the YJS – introducing centralised control processes and more prescriptive, technical working practices founded in the management of performance generally and risk specifically. A government quango, the Youth Justice Board for England and Wales, was created to advance the central aim of the YJS to prevent offending (more accurately conceived of as the reduction of reoffending – see Chapter Six) by coordinating, monitoring, informing and funding the practice of multi-agency YOTs and their practitioners. Consequently, the prevention agenda was pursued centrally through the simultaneous *management of practice* via performance monitoring measures and the *management of risk* through assessment, supervision and (risk-focused) interventions with children in receipt of a raft of new pre-court and court orders. Souhami (2007: 25) encapsulates this climate of cultural change as: '[a] marked departure from the accustomed ethos of youth justice work ... The formation of YOTs demanded the development of new, multi-agency practice, new routines and ways of working.'

The managerialist turn in youth justice policy and practice that followed the Crime and Disorder Act 1998 was exemplified by the introduction of a series of centrally prescribed organisational and individualised performance guidelines, targets and management measures for YOTs and practitioners, in order to standardise practice and to increase organisational and practitioner accountability, transparency and demonstrable 'effectiveness'. At the systemic and organisational levels, these performance-related measures were animated as key performance indicators (KPIs) – standardised performance statistics gathered from YOTs on a quarterly and annual basis by the Youth Justice Board (YJB), taken from the Police National Computer (PNC) and the Youth Justice Management Information System (YJMIS). KPIs related to:

- **first-time entrants into the YJS** – the number of children receiving a pre-court disposal or (court-based) conviction for the first time, according to the PNC, based on the proportion of first-time entrants (FTEs) per 100,000 children in each local authority area;
- **reoffending rates** – the frequency of reoffending (measured as a somewhat simplistic binary yes/no) among a rolling cohort of children within each YOT area who have received an outcome (pre-court or court disposal) according to the PNC;
- **custodial sentences** – the number of custodial sentences per 1,000 of the general population of 10- to 17-year-olds, according to YJMIS.

In addition to the three main KPIs for England and Wales, there were four Wales-specific KPIs[54] known as Youth Justice Indicators:

- **education, training and employment** – the number of hours of education, training and employment (ETE) offered and hours attended by children (aged under 16 years) subject to a disposal and percentage change in hours between the start and end of this disposal – with the provision of adequate levels of ETE considered to be protective against reoffending;
- **accommodation** – the number of children (aged 10–15 and 16–17 years) on a pre-court or court order who are in suitable accommodation before and after their disposal;

[54] Developed by YJB Cymru in co-operation with YOT Managers Cymru and signed off by the Wales Youth Justice Advisory Panel.

and the percentage change between these two figures – with satisfactory/suitable accommodation considered to be protective against reoffending;
- **substance use** – the number of children identified as requiring substance use assessment who receive this within five and 10 working days – with timely substance use treatment considered to be protective against reoffending.
- **mental health, emotional health and well-being** – the number of children identified as requiring mental health assessment who commence this within 10 working days of the screening date.

The raft of performance measures were complemented at the organisational level by the creation and implementation of the following:

- **Case Management Guidance** – a document to assist and support case managers and operational managers in YOTs to work through the key stages of a child's case, from arrest to court to planning and managing post-sentence interventions (YJB 2009). Produced as part of the introduction of the Scaled Approach (see later in this chapter), Case Management Guidance constitutes a 'how to' guide for practitioners, covering a variety of practice areas such as out-of-court disposals, court work, bail and remand management, assessment, writing reports for court and Youth Offender Panel, planning and delivering interventions (in the community and custody), resettlement into the community and transfer to secure hospital.
- **YOT Core Case inspections** – Her Majesty's Inspectorate of Probation (HMI Probation) conducts Core Case Inspections of all YOTs within a rolling three-year programme that began in April 2009. YOT practice is assessed through YOT case studies (at least 38 YOTs in each inspection administration) and interviews with staff, children and victims. The inspection criteria are: assessment (risk of harm to others, likelihood of reoffending, safeguarding); intervention (protecting the public, reducing the likelihood of reoffending, safeguarding); and outcomes (achieving outcomes, sustaining outcomes).

At the individual practitioner level, bespoke practice performance measures and guidelines were introduced relating to the following:

- **National Standards** – a framework of National Standards for youth justice services was identified to establish 'the minimum expectations of staff and managers in the youth justice system' (YJB 2004: 19), to be used in conjunction with the Case Management Guidance and Key Elements of Effective Practice (see later). Standards relating to governance, planning, service delivery (for example assessment) and performance management are set by the Secretary of State for Justice and the Secretary of State for Children, Schools and Families following advice from the YJB. National Standards for youth justice services currently address: preventing offending, out-of-court disposals, bail and remand management, assessment for interventions and reports, court report, work in courts, work with victims, planning and delivering interventions (in the community and custody) and custodial work.
- **Key Elements of Effective Practice** – identified as the 'essential elements of practice with all children at all stages of the YJS' (YJB 2003: 6), the YJB has proscribed a series of Key Elements of Effective Practice (KEEPs): ETE, mental health, substance use, young people who sexually abuse, offending behaviour programmes, parenting, restorative justice, mentoring, targeted neighbourhood prevention, final warning interventions, swift administration of justice, (now subsumed within/attached to Youth Rehabilitation Orders) supervision and surveillance programmes, custody and resettlement, and assessment, planning interventions and supervision. KEEPs are accompanied by bespoke guidance manuals written by the YJB and drawing heavily on evidence of 'what works' interventions in youth justice (see following section).

The raft of performance management measures that standardise, guide and shape youth justice practice with children have been exponentially managerialist in nature since the Labour government legislated its 'new youth justice' into existence following the Crime and Disorder Act 1998. The organisational practice of YOTs and the individual practice of YOT staff has been subject to ever closer scrutiny, monitoring and control from the centralised YJB. This YJB monitoring has been framed and intended as supportive and constructive guidance from an expert organisation independent from government. However, it has arguably depersonalised and deprofessionalised practice by under-emphasising the relationships between and the potential contributions of two main stakeholders in the youth justice process – children and practitioners, not to mention overlooking other salient stakeholders such as parents and researchers – as well as drawing on a rather restricted evidence base. According to Goldson and Hughes (2010), the simultaneous policy and practice centralisation (monitoring and prescription by the YJB) and decentralisation (the creation of local multi-agency crime and disorder reduction audit/strategies and YOTs – see Chapter Three) was indicative not of confusion, but of a growing *responsibilisation* of children, families, local authority areas and communities by central government (see Bandalli 2000; Kemshall 2002; Muncie 2006) for the reduction of youth offending at the local level (that is, illustrating the central control–local responsibility dichotomy). The Crime and Disorder Act 1998 reoriented youth justice to 'empower' local authority areas and make them more responsible for the measurement, reduction and prevention of locally specific issues related to offending by children. The responsibilisation of children to address their own offending behaviour and its consequences ran throughout the reforms, which focused on marginalising the responsibilities of others for creating and exacerbating the individual and social conditions influencing crime and pushing responsibilisation down the age range and into less and less 'serious' behaviours.

As we go on to discuss in the second half of this chapter, the post-New Labour UK coalition government has begun a steady process of decentralising and localising youth justice, re-empowering local practitioners to utilise their expertise and experience in a more child-friendly way. However, proposed enhancements to existing youth justice practice have much work to do if they are to reverse the unintended consequences on children and practitioners of the managerialist aspects of the new youth justice. The CFOS model offers just such an approach – at once child friendly, promotional, positive and anti-managerialist.

Managing practice and managing risk: anathema to Children First, Offenders Second principles?

> Management systems prioritise the construction of regulatory systems and routines intended to standardise practice and thereby limit, or even eliminate, variations in practice. (Turnbull and Spence 2011: 942)

Youth justice performance measures were established to promote the managerialist aim of standardised, 'evidence-based' and 'effective' practice across YOTs and to deliberately circumvent the threat of the excessive discretion and indeterminacy allegedly demonstrated by foregoing welfare-based approaches and to address the purported ineffectiveness and inefficiency of justice-based approaches. For example the National Standards and KEEPs are intended to enable staff and their organisations to better structure, focus and manage their work. However, as with the organisational performance measures, the National Standards embody technical and administrative objectives that are bereft of principles or a philosophy of practice to guide practitioners' work with children (for example focusing on enhancing the beneficial relational aspects of practice), while lacking the flexibility to enable practitioners to exercise meaningful discretion or local mediation of policy. This runs the risk of producing somewhat automated, unreflective responses to a set of guidelines that could be viewed as prescriptive and that depersonalise practice into adult-centric instruction done to and received by the child, rather than child-friendly, meaningful work developed in partnership between practitioners and children. The evidence base of so-called 'effective practice' that underpins the KEEPs is similarly partial (in the sense of biased and limited) – constituted by a highly restricted, pseudo-psychological, offender-first collection of empirical studies wedded to the identification, measurement and targeting of risk factors. For example the central KEEP, Assessment, Planning Interventions and Supervision (APIS), which serves as the foundation for all other KEEPs, outlines the 'foundation activities which guide and shape all work with young people who offend' (YJB 2003: 6), yet the YJB prescribes that these 'foundation activities' must be based on 'dependable methods for analysing the risks that young people will continue to commit crime, and for recognising the criminogenic needs [risk factors] that interventions should address' (YJB 2003: 5). In other words, the YJB advocates a risk-management approach to youth justice. The 'dependable methods' prescribed by APIS are deliberately restricted to the Asset structured risk-assessment instrument and risk-focused interventions that have been evaluated as 'what works' (see later in this chapter), leaving little room for practitioner discretion and expertise in how best to generate the evidence (for example through partnership) with which to access and understand the lives of children.

Our argument does run into a potential problem here, at least ostensibly, in that FTEs and the numbers of children sentenced to custody have been declining rapidly in recent years. These recent declines, however, have followed previous expansions in both FTEs and custody rates, while the rates of reoffending (of children brought into the system) remain high. We see the latter as the product of a flawed understanding of children's behaviour and an inappropriate model of intervention, and the former (reductions in FTEs and custody) as primarily the product of (albeit implicit) systems management thinking applied to the processing of children (see, for example Chapter Five).

Managing risk: reductionism and de-individualisation

The governmental predilection for *risk management* (see Case and Haines, in Goldson and Muncie 2015) is animated by Asset (YJB 2000), which is employed to 'identify the risk factors associated with offending behaviour and to inform effective intervention programmes' (YJB 2004: 27). Asset is essentially a risk factor questionnaire completed by a YOT practitioner during and following interview with a child who has been referred to the YOT due to coming into contact with the YJS following arrest.[55] Asset contains a series of statements based on 'dynamic' (that is, purportedly malleable) risk factors categorised within 12 risk domains: living arrangements, family and personal relationships, education/training/employment, neighbourhood, lifestyle, substance use, physical health, emotional/mental health, perception of self and others, thinking and behaviour, attitudes to offending, motivation to change. Each domain is given a risk rating (0–4) by a YOT practitioner relating to the perceived likelihood of the child reoffending on the basis of their experience of risk factors in that domain (giving a potential total Asset risk score of 48). Asset contains four further sections focused on: 'positive factors' (more akin to protective factors mediating risk, such as coping strategies and family support), indicators of vulnerability, indicators of (risk of causing) serious harm to others and a 'what do you think?' self-assessment section asking the child for their views on the risk factors they experience.

The 'rigorous evidence-based assessment' (YJB 2003: 20) afforded by Asset has been championed as a (managerialist) way of structuring, informing and complementing practitioner decision making, intervention planning and resource allocation in a manner (allegedly) not possible using traditional clinical and discretionary modes of practice (Baker 2005). The Asset risk assessment tool heralded a new era of actuarialism and structured decision making in the YJS, but it can be heavily criticised for constructing individualised and offender-first explanations of offending behaviour and for fostering technical, 'routinised' and 'deprofessionalised' practice (Pitts 2001; see also Case 2006, 2009; Case and Hester 2010; Paylor 2010; Bateman 2011; Haines and Case 2012; Phoenix and Kelly 2013). Asset prescribes, produces and promotes simplistic, offender-first developmental understandings of children's offending behaviours as the (irresistible) product of exposure to risk factors at early stages in their lives (see Case and Haines 2009 for a fuller description and

[55] An equivalent risk assessment instrument known as Onset is completed by YOT practitioners with children who have not officially offended but who are considered to be 'at risk' of offending following their referral to a Youth Inclusion Programme or a Youth Inclusion and Support Panel (discussed in more detail in Chapter Six).

analysis). Childhood exposure to risk factors, it is supposed, leads to/predicts adolescent offending, adolescent exposure to risk factors, leads to/predicts offending in early adulthood and so on. Consequently, these purportedly 'predictive' risk factors should be identified by practitioners through assessment and targeted through intervention – classic, common-sense prevention.

A major weakness with this approach to working with children lies, however, in its excessive *reductionism* – reducing, restricting and oversimplifying potential understandings of children's lives to an uncritical pursuit of risk. The very act of oversimplifying potentially complex and dynamic aspects of children's lives, experiences, perceptions and thoughts into readily quantifiable and targetable risk 'factors' does not nor can it ever hope to represent the lived realities of children (France 2008). Understandings children's lives as restricted bundles of risks is reductionist in its own right, but these understandings are even further reduced by focusing only on risks in *psychosocial* (psychological and immediate social, such as family and education) domains of children's lives rather than examining socio-structural influences related to, among other things, social class, gender, poverty, unemployment, social deprivation, neighbourhood disorganisation and ethnicity. Understandings of risks in each dynamic psychosocial domain are yet further reduced by requiring practitioners to simplistically identify whether they are present (yes/no) and provide a summative aggregated rating for each domain of 'the extent to which the child's lifestyle is associated with the likelihood of further offending (0 = not associated, 4 = very strongly associated)' (Youth Justice Board (YJB) 2000). The most alarming aspect of this ostensibly common-sense approach to assessment and intervention is, therefore, its reliance on a staged process of reductionist quantification that renders risk a static 'artefact' or factor that harms passive and helpless children, thus incrementally moving understandings of children's lives away from any grounding in the dynamic complexities and nuances of reality, experience, agency and social construction (Webster, MacDonald and Simpson 2006; France and Homel 2007; Case and Haines 2009).

Managing intervention: fast-tracking programme fetishism

The reductionist and prescriptive nature of youth justice assessment processes has been complemented by an equivalent bias in the nature of the interventions privileged and standardised by KEEP guidance as the most appropriate responses to assessment outcomes. The KEEPs prescribe 'what works' interventions, which emanate from a body of knowledge and empirical research (mainly) from the US claiming to be able to identify the key ingredients of effective crime prevention and reduction programmes and interventions. The 'what works' movement in youth justice was catalysed by an evaluation of the effectiveness of crime prevention programmes across the US (requested by US Congress) in 1996, which prioritised programmes using 'rigorous and scientifically recognized standards and methodologies' and gave special emphasis to 'factors that relate to juvenile crime … including "risk factors" in the community, schools, and family' (Sherman, Gottfredson, MacKenzie, Eck, Reuter and Bushway 1998). The resulting report, *Preventing Crime: What Works, What Doesn't, What's Promising* (Sherman et al 1998) generated the 'Maryland Scientific Methods Scale' or 'SMS' (based on the earlier work of Cook and Campbell in 1979) to assess the methodological quality of individual crime prevention evaluations according to three methodological criteria: *control* over extraneous (external, unmeasured) variables that might influence relationship between intervention and outcome, *measurement error,* and *statistical power* to detect the effects of a programme (see Hope 2005). The incremental SMS consists of five levels of analysis, escalating in rigour and detail, summarised by Farrington (2000: 14) as:

1. Correlation between a prevention program and a measure of crime at one point in time.
2. Measures of crime before and after the program, with no comparable control condition.
3. Measures of crime before and after the program in experimental and comparable control conditions.
4. Measures of crime before and after the program in multiple experimental and control units,

controlling for other variables that influence crime (e.g. by matching, prediction scores, or statistical controls).

5. Random assignment of units to program and control conditions.

Level five on this scale represents the 'randomised controlled trial' (RCT), the so-called 'gold standard' of evaluation methodology, much favoured by the Home Office and Whitehall. According to Sherman et al (1998), a risk-focused intervention exemplifies 'what works' in youth crime prevention if it is 'reasonably certain' that it prevents crime or reduces risk factors in the social context in which it is evaluated. The intervention must also have findings that are generalisable to similar settings in other places and times, in addition to at least two successful evaluations at level three on the SMS or above. Similarly, programmes were heralded as examples of 'what's promising' if the level of certainty regarding reduction of crime or risk factors was too low to support generalisable conclusions, but there was some empirical basis for predicting that further research could support such conclusions, in addition to at least one successful evaluation at level three. Sherman et al classified 'what doesn't work' as programmes that are reasonably certain to fail to prevent crime or reduce risk factors (or, more accurately, cannot be measured as reducing crime and reducing risk according to the SMS).

The 'what works' movement prescribes a restricted definition of intervention 'effectiveness' from tightly prescribed methodological criteria (Stephenson, Giller and Brown 2007), employing a *positivist* methodology to physically and statistically manipulate (control) aspects of the environment in order to identify constant and predictable causal relationships between interventions and outcomes. The major attraction of this method to youth justice policy makers intent on pursuing a managerialist and reductionist agenda has been its apparent ability to produce data that is replicable, generalisable, defensible and ostensibly value free. However, the 'what works' movement has prospered with little reflection on or acknowledgement of criticisms of its methodology. The 'what works' approach focuses upon interventions (inputs) and reductions in offending (outputs) to the neglect of examining the mechanisms/processes of change (possibly initiated and led by children) that may intervene between the two and the potential influence of context upon implementation and outcomes (see Pawson and Tilley 1998). Instead, 'what works' makes assumptions as to what is going on in the black box between inputs and outputs (typically negative assumptions related to children's inability to resist and negotiate risk factors, concurrent to their ability to choose offending pathways) and 'bleaches out' the complexities of context by treating all potential influences as variables to be controlled (ARCS Ltd 2008). As a result, it is almost impossible to understand 'what works for whom and in what circumstances?' (Pawson and Tilley 1998) and, perhaps more importantly, how and why an intervention works for a specific child. The result at the practice level arguably has been rampant *programme fetishism*: a predilection for quasi-experimental, pseudo-psychological, risk-focused, off-the-shelf programmes that respond to assessed risk located in the individual child. The child is conceived of as a dehumanised 'subject' for experimentation and treatment; the statistical outcome of deterministic interactions between causes (exposure to risk factors) and effects (negative outcomes, particularly offending). The programme fetishism fostered by strict adherence to 'what works' methodology is anathema to a CFOS approach – deindividualising (based on aggregated statistical scores), dehumanising (treating children as a risk to be managed) and prescriptive (prioritising off-the-shelf, decontextualised programmes), with no attempt to account for, among other things, the 'child's' status as deserving of special treatment or the potentialities of engaging children to participate in the design, implementation and evaluation of the relationships and services they experience.

The zenith of managerialist youth justice: the Scaled Approach

The zenith of the government's risk-based managerialist and modernising new youth justice project came on 30 November 2009 with the inception of the Scaled Approach to assessment and intervention. Concerns had been expressed that YOT practice had not been consistent or assiduous enough in linking Asset scores to planned interventions for children (see Baker 2005), in particular, within the follow-up to the *Misspent Youth* report, entitled *Youth Justice 2004* (Audit Commission 2004), which recommended in point 142 that: 'YOTs should make better use of *Asset* to determine the amount as well as the nature of interventions with individuals using a scaled approach.'

Rather than review or replace the assessment and intervention process with a non-risk-led alternative, the government chose to revamp and expand their commitment to risk by introducing the Scaled Approach. The Scaled Approach dictated that every child subject to a Youth Rehabilitation Order (a hybrid, consolidated order replacing the plethora of statutory orders that had gone before it) or a Referral Order (given to children pleading guilty to a first offence in court) was to have the level of their intervention (frequency, intensity and nature) determined by their Asset risk assessment score – with intervention levels categorised in a tripartite manner as low/standard, medium/enhanced or high/intensive (YJB 2009). The Scaled Approach, therefore, involved 'tailoring the intensity of intervention to assessment' (YJB 2009: 4). It constituted a formalised process of linking Asset-based risk assessment with the intensity and nature of intervention (see Case and Haines 2009), coalescing with the 'risk classification' principle of effective practice established by McGuire (1995) – matching intervention to assessed risk of reoffending. The introduction of the Scaled Approach consolidated risk as the primary animator of youth justice policy and practice, albeit a practical and technical animator largely bereft of a robust theoretical foundation or philosophical/principled core. The implementation of the Scaled Approach was subject to a process evaluation from December 2006 to June 2007 in four pilot YOTs in England and Wales, along with four non-Scaled Approach 'comparison' YOTs drawn from each of the YOT 'families' to which the pilot areas belonged (Youth Justice Board (YJB) 2010). The aims of the evaluation were to:

- explore the practice requirements of the risk-based approach to interventions;
- compare the different elements of the risk-based approaches adopted by the four pilot YOTs;
- identify a set of working procedures that can be used to adopt a risk-based approach;
- identify the differences between the pilot and comparison YOTs in tailoring and targeting of interventions.(YJB 2010: 7)

The multi-method process evaluation consisted of analysis of empirical data collected from case management systems and Asset risk assessments. The quantitative statistical data related to 1,133 cases in total, including black minority ethnic and female 'booster' groups. Qualitative data was obtained through interviews with key stakeholders (YOT staff, judges and Youth Court magistrates, Youth Offender Panel members) in the pilot and comparison areas. The evaluation identified a variety of risk-based practice across the pilot areas in terms of risk-level allocation (plotting the risk of reoffending against offence seriousness), pre-sentence report recommendations (the use of risk profiles to guide recommended interventions to court) and intervention planning (for example the extent to which Asset forms were reviewed, the links between assessed risk and intervention). However, there were general similarities in how these process areas were tackled across the pilot YOTs, leading the evaluation team to identify four key process principles for taking the risk-based approach forward: accurate and consistent assessments, intervention plans appropriate to risk, case reviews that monitor and respond to changes in risk, and enforcement of breach (YJB 2010: 14). The evaluation found that the pilot YOTs were significantly more likely than the comparison YOTs to provide risk information (related to risk of reoffending, serious harm, vulnerability) to the courts and Youth Offender Panels and more likely to have a recommendations followed by the courts (although this difference was statistically insignificant!). The evaluation also identified a 'broad and clearly defined consensus among the practitioners in the four pilot YOTs that the risk-based approach results in better outcomes for children'

(YJB 2010: 15). The evaluation report concluded with a series of recommendations for developing the Scaled Approach and rolling it out across the YJS through: the consistent application of any revised guidance, the accurate completion of Asset forms and the rigorous quality assurance of Asset.

Notwithstanding the confident conclusions and recommendations that emanated from the evaluation, the Scaled Approach pilot project contained two striking methodological weaknesses that raise serious doubts over the validity and reliability of its findings. First, the YJB allowed the pilot YOTs to vary their risk-based practice in line with local circumstances, leading to variations in the methods of risk assessment utilised and in the decision making regarding levels of contact with the YOT. This variability in method brings into question the reliability (consistency, replicability) of any conclusions drawn on the basis of such a non-standardised, disparate interpretation and application of risk-based assessment and intervention. Therefore, the outcomes measured across the YOT pilots did not necessarily relate to the same (risk-based) processes in each area. Secondly, the outcomes measures utilised were narrow and no data was collected on outcomes (for example reconviction) or cost effectiveness (for example intervention cost), leading the YJB (2010: 14) to conclude that 'the lack of this information is a constraint in making objective assessments of the variety of practices that were adopted by the YOTs' (see also Sutherland 2009). When these methodological weaknesses are balanced against the strong recommendations for rolling out the Scaled Approach across every YOT in England and Wales, the process evaluation presents as somewhat of a self-fulfilling exercise to legitimate the government's exponentially increasing faith in the efficacy of risk as the concept/tool with which to understand and control children in trouble with the law.

In Focus • Child-friendly practitioner override of the Scaled Approach

In accordance with its ongoing commitment to implementing a rights-based, principled, positive (anti-risk, anti-labelling, anti-interventionist), child-friendly youth justice practice (compare Case and Haines 2004; Safer Swansea Partnership 2008, 2011; Hoffman and MacDonald 2011),

Swansea YOT integrated a policy of discretionary practitioner override of the Scaled Approach following the introduction of the framework at the end of 2009. The practice of practitioner discretion had been highlighted within Scaled Approach guidance as optional and contingent on YOT manager approval (YJB 2009), but the Swansea YOT manager has encouraged practitioners to utilise discretion in all cases as autonomous, standard practice. In order to evaluate the efficacy of this less mechanical and prescriptive implementation of governmental [risk] assessment and intervention policy, researchers from Swansea University Centre for Criminal Justice and Criminology worked with the Swansea YOT information manager to conduct a secondary data analysis exercise (Haines and Case 2012). Data was collected regarding reconviction rates over the period 2010–12 for children working with Swansea YOT and working with a neighbouring YOT area. The neighbouring YOT was classified as a 'Scaled Approach YOT' as it is served as a Scaled Approach pilot area (see Sutherland 2009) and applied the framework assiduously (YJB 2009), with the YOT manager quoted as claiming that 'the approach that the Youth Justice Board (YJB) finally adopted was similar to ours' (YJB and Children and Young People Now (CYP Now) 2009: 5).

Secondary data analysis of reconviction rates for the January–March 2009 cohort of children in both YOT areas (compared to the 2008 baseline figure – in line with the YJB *reoffending* KPI) identified a 45% reduction in reconviction in the 'children first YOT', placing it in the top 5% of YOTs in England and Wales for reductions in reconviction over the measurement period. In stark contrast, the 'Scaled Approach YOT' recorded a 62% increase in reconvictions over the same period, placing it within the 5% of poorest performing YOTs in England and Wales. These preliminary results, albeit gathered over a limited period of time, offer tentative, evidence-based support for a developing model of child-friendly and discretionary assessment and intervention practice, alongside raising issues with the efficacy of a rigid and rigorous adherence to the Scaled Approach risk-based assessment and intervention framework (Haines and Case 2012).

The Scaled Approach: system-first and offender-first managerialism and interventionism

The practice prescriptions of the new youth justice have been criticised for fostering interventionist tendencies (see Muncie 2008b; Goldson 2010) with particular concerns regarding the potential for the Scaled Approach to engender deleterious interventionism, both disproportionate and misguided. Children committing the similar offences or even the same offence (for example co-defendants) could be subjected to *disproportionate interventionism* based on differences in their risk profiles (Bateman 2011). A child could experience excessive or insufficient levels of intervention (in relation to their actual offence), for example due to their assessed risk category. For instance, minor offenders with high-risk scores could be given high/intensive intervention, where serious offenders with low-risk scores could be given a low/standard intervention (see Case and Haines 2009; see also Haines and Case 2012). There is a broader potential for excessive interventionism through use of the Scaled Approach due to the gerrymandering of the risk category thresholds (that is, downward revision) since its introduction, which has inevitably increased the numbers of children subject to enhanced and intensive supervision. This has led critical commentators to observe that 'the link between the *Asset* score and the number of contacts required by the "evidence-base" is sufficiently loose to allow alteration at will' (Bateman 2011: 178), which serves to 'widen the net of influence exerted by the state and the YJS' (Paylor 2011: 31). This disproportionate, excessive interventionism, based on an escalating, hierarchical approach to intervention, can lead to feelings of resentment, and unjust and unfair treatment (lacking in legitimacy) on the part of children, which itself can result in disengagement from the practitioner–child relationship (McNeill 2009), the intervention lacking a positive impact on future behaviour (Tyler 2004) and the subsequent 'technical' breach of the Youth Rehabilitation Order which is underpinned by Scaled Approach interventions (Bateman 2011).

There is a further potential for the Scaled Approach to engender *misguided interventionism* by promoting individualised interventions based on aggregated risk prediction scores/categories, which 'inevitably imposes limits on the accuracy' of these predictions (Bateman 2011: 175). This simultaneous individualised-aggregated approach allocates individual children to interventions based on their membership of a generalised, aggregated population assigned to a broad risk category, producing intervention plans that are not necessarily appropriate or relevant to the lives, social contexts or experiences of individual children. Such an outcome is, in fact, contrary to the intended individualisation and personalisation of interventions. It is also possible that risk-based, scaled interventions are misguided and lack appropriateness and relevance to their recipients due to the privileging of individualised, psychosocial interventions that respond to assessed psychosocial risk factors (for example in the domains of family, school, lifestyle, community and psycho/emotional), such that children are responsibilised for their offending and 'attention is drawn away from structural, social inequalities for which government itself has some responsibility' (Case and Haines 2009: 23).

The interventionism (both disproportionate and misguided) of the Scaled Approach supports accusations that the framework neglects children's rights legislation, which stipulates that 'any reaction to juvenile delinquency shall always be in proportion to the circumstances of both the offenders and the offence' (United Nations 1985, rule 5.1). Potential inequities and injustices could emerge through the application of the Scaled Approach to children experiencing social deprivation, in that these individuals may possess higher Asset scores (indicative of social need as well as criminogenic need) and so can receive more intensive interventions. Therefore, risk-based interventions are 'likely to weigh most heavily upon those children and families living in the most challenging material circumstances' (Jamieson 2005: 196). Specifically, the Scaled Approach 'imposes greater expectations on children least equipped to respond' (Bateman 2011: 180); a perverse situation that Phoenix (2009: 113) suggests represents 'a return to repressive welfarism'. Furthermore, the prescriptive, disproportionate and discriminatory nature of the Scaled Approach intervention bears inherent disregard for the state's power over the individual, due process and children's basic human rights within the youth justice process, because these children are in a weak political position to resist (risk) classification (see O'Mahony 2009; Paylor 2011; see also Gray 2013).

The risk-driven Scaled Approach methodology serves to *individualise* the responsibility for offending by children and for their successful engagement with ameliorative interventions. The Scaled Approach prioritises psychosocial risk factors and fosters individualised understandings of offending behaviour based on children's agency and alleged choice to expose themselves to and/or refuse to resist risk factors. The responsibility (blame) for offending is placed with the child and their inability to resist risk factors, rather than examining broader, far less controllable issues such as socio-structural factors (noticeably absent from Asset), the absence of support mechanisms or the external influence of others (for example criminal justice agencies, politicians, general public) in the construction of youth offending. An inherent contradiction here is that full responsibility is given to a population (children aged 10–17 years), the majority of whom are given precious little other social responsibility in other salient and formative areas of their lives (for example, being attributed with the competence to work, vote, drive a car, own a house, have sex or marry). Children are viewed as lacking the responsibility to fully engage in society and the (adult-centric) decision-making processes that influence their lives, but possessing full responsibility for committing a complex, subjective and socially constructed act that is influenced (at least in part) by factors outside their control.

Paradoxically, the individualising Scaled Approach is structured to *deindividualise* understandings of children by aggregating risk measures across domains (producing a risk profile/score) and then allocating the child to a risk and intervention category based on their total risk score. Intervention is scaled to the likelihood that members of that risk group/category who have previously demonstrated those risk factor characteristics will reoffend (based on a large body of group-based empirical risk research), rather than the likelihood that the individual child will necessarily reoffend – which the artefactual risk factor research base for the Scaled Approach has never examined, let alone established conclusively (see Case and Haines 2009).

Targeting intervention for individuals based on their risk group membership has the potential to result in *disproportionality* because the so-called 'evidence-based' response is derived from broad-brush aggregated evidence, not an individualised, sensitive, contextualised and nuanced analysis of a child's lived experiences. The simultaneous individualisation and deindividualisation within youth justice assessment and intervention has promoted an interventionist governmental agenda that perpetuates understandings of children as risky, passive and in need of adult intervention to prevent further negative behaviour and to encourage individual responsibility for their future behaviour.

The Scaled Approach and the paradox of disengaging engagement

> Engaging young people who offend within their assessment is an essential feature of effective assessment. At the heart of this engagement is a relationship developed through the communication between practitioner and the young person (Mason and Prior for the YJB 2008: 14–15)

> Without successful engagement, interventions or programmes – no matter how well designed – are unlikely to achieve positive outcomes (Prior and Mason 2010: 212)

Children's *engagement* with youth justice practitioners, services and interventions is a much-overlooked relational element of practice. Research that has asserted the need for 'understanding and addressing the fluid dynamics' of children's 'lived experiences' (Farrow, Kelly and Wilkinson 2007: 87) has tended to be practitioner focused, encouraging practitioners to develop softer skills (for example communication and empathy), rather than advocating an approach centred on accessing children's perspectives and experiences of youth justice processes. As others such as Marchant and Kirby (2005: 136) have noted: 'Commentators too often focus on children's competence to participate rather than on adults' competence to support children to make decisions and take action.'

The minimal research that has been conducted across Europe on children's views of engagement with practitioners has typically concentrated on fields outside (but addressing issues connected to) juvenile justice (for example youth work, education, substance use). This small body of research has identified the value children place on relationships based on trust, respect, fairness and voluntarism/choice (see Merton, Payne and Smith 2004; Evans, Pinnock, Beirens and Edwards 2006; ARCS Ltd 2008; Ipsos MORI 2010; Sharpe 2011). It is these features that enable children to make the crucial distinction between actual engagement with intervention and mere participation in intervention (Ipsos MORI 2010); features that are facilitated and enhanced by more holistic and consultative (rather than narrow, prescriptive and risk-focused) assessment models (ARCS Ltd 2008). Indeed, the need to integrate much more emphasis on children's voices in assessment and intervention processes has been identified by the YJB in their recent proposals to reorient the Scaled Approach in response to academic and practitioner criticism (YJB 2011) and has been identified as a significant gap/ priority area by the YJB in Wales *Effective Practice* guidelines for youth justice staff (YJB Cymru 2012). Notwithstanding the lack of children's perspectives in the generation of understandings of engagement, relationships and practices in the field of youth justice, engagement[56] is championed as a bespoke KEEP, *Engaging children who offend* (YJB 2008c). The enforced, court-ordered nature of the practitioner–child relationships that animate the Scaled Approach is anathema to evidence-based notions of effective intervention with children through engaging relationships of voluntarism, trust, respect and equity. Scaled Approach assessment and intervention is 'done to' children by practitioners rather than 'conducted with' children through detailed consultation and participation. Therefore, there is an ironic potential for youth justice processes (for example assessment, supervision, intervention) to actively *disengage* children from participation, commitment and compliance

[56] Although a degree of ambiguity surrounds the precise definition of *engagement*, it is commonly understood across the YJS and communicated to practitioners as relating to children's 'motivation and commitment to involvement in activities' (Mason and Prior, for YJB 2008: 12).

with youth justice practitioners (Case and Haines 2014b). So-called 'engagement' processes singularly fail to engage with the target population for assessment and interventions – children (see Burnett 2007; Prior and Mason 2010). Thus, engagement processes are typically enforced, adult led and prescribed (thus embodying the potential to disengage practitioners also), focused primarily upon the relationship-building skills of the practitioner and their knowledge of child development (see Farrow et al 2007). What is missing is any detailed consideration of the realities and complexities of children's lives, particularly from the perspectives of children themselves (see Case 2006). The voices and qualitative experiences, perceptions, meanings and interpretations of the children in receipt of Scaled Approach processes are largely ignored by adult-centric procedures that produce adult-led understandings of children's lives. The assessment relationship is therefore unbalanced and disengaging (or, at least, unconcerned with engagement); weighted heavily in favour of adults and counter-intuitive to the development of the positive elements that can enhance engagement and promote effective youth justice intervention.

The potential paradox of 'disengaging engagement' (Case and Haines 2014b) could be exacerbated by attempts at engagement within youth justice practice that disengage *practitioners* from the structures, mechanisms and organisations within which they operate (for example the YJS, the YJB, YOTs, the KEEP principles, the Scaled Approach). It is disconcerting that the adults charged with implementing the Scaled Approach (youth justice practitioners) could be disengaged by the enforced and prescriptive nature of the process (unless, of course, they 'buy in' to the Scaled Approach – which some practitioners and YOTs do – see Sutherland 2009; Haines and Case 2012). The Scaled Approach prescribes a technical and heavily quantified procedure that mechanises assessment practice more strictly and broadly than the use of Asset alone. The risk focus of the APIS KEEP and Scaled Approach places practitioners under theoretical and practical duress to pursue restricted reductionist understandings of children's behaviour (Case and Haines 2009) and how best to respond to it – understandings generated by research and theorising conducted by academics, politicians and policy makers rather than the practitioners themselves. A consequence is that practitioner expertise and discretion has been at best undervalued and at worst ignored to the point of the 'deprofessionalization', 'routinization' and 'zombification' of youth justice practice (Pitts 2001). Therefore, it can be argued that a second crucial key stakeholder group within the youth justice process – the YOT practitioner – is relatively neglected when generating understandings of and responses to children's lives – resulting in less valid and appropriate service provision and intervention to reduce and prevent offending by children (see also Puffett 2012). Given this tendency, it is, perhaps, not surprising that there is counter-evidence of an informal mediation, even rejection, of governmental risk-based prescriptions by YOT practitioners who favour the exercising of discretion to 'hold the welfare needs of young people as paramount' (Briggs 2013: 17; see also Sutherland 2009).

Evolving a new 'new youth justice'? AssetPlus

Our critique of the Scaled Approach coheres a growing body of criticism from critical youth justice academics, researchers and practitioners since the framework's inception, particularly centred on its potential for reductionist, disproportionate and disengaging practice. These criticisms, however, have not gone unheeded by the YJB, who (under the leadership of the then Chief Executive, John Drew) initiated a broad consultation exercise in 2010 with key stakeholders (practitioners, policy makers, critical academics, children, parents, victims) with the objective of revising and refining the Scaled Approach based on reviews of: developments in assessment practice, theoretical debates around 'risk' and the perceptions and experiences of practitioners and 'offenders' (Baker 2012).

Current plans are for a new assessment and planning interventions framework for children subject to statutory court orders in the YJS (Referral Order, Youth Rehabilitation Order, Detention and Training Orders) to be known as AssetPlus to replace the Scaled Approach in 2015 (a 'prevention' equivalent, yet to be developed, will be used with children subject to pre-court disposals). Guidance documentation asserts that the new framework will contain a series of enhancements to the current process that go some way to addressing concerns regarding the weaknesses of the extant Scaled Approach (YJB 2013). Thus, AssetPlus promises a more holistic, iterative, contextualised and dynamic assessment and interventions framework, with more emphasis on accessing children's voices, identifying their strengths, assessing interactions between different elements of children's lives, enabling desistance and promoting positive behaviours and outcomes, all of which can facilitate necessarily complex and individualised assessment (no more crude, insensitive 'one size fits all' assessment), greater focus on needs over risks, more scope for practitioner discretion and improved self-assessment tools for children and parents/carers (Baker 2012; YJB 2013).

These proposed enhancements/revisions reflect a culture shift away from the disengaging negative, deficit-based, retrospective risk paradigm and towards more holistic, humane understandings of children's lives that incorporate their dynamic potential for desistance, positive behaviour and constructive contributions to the assessment process, along with the much neglected potential for practitioner expertise to form the foundation of a valid and contextualised assessment and interventions model. AssetPlus challenges (in part at least) traditional conceptions of risk management and early intervention within youth justice practice and reorients these areas towards more holistic, sensitive and positive assessments and interventions with children that are future oriented to meet positive objectives that are generated through meaningful engagement and evidence-based partnership between children and practitioners. In practice, AssetPlus represents an ongoing assessment cycle that spans the entire YJS (from prevention to custody), driven by practitioner completion of a 'Core Record' for each child, consisting of three stages: Information Gathering and Description, Explanations and Conclusions, and Pathways and Planning. A more detailed discussion of the features of the proposed AssetPlus model provides a clearer indication of its structures, processes and foci and how these may differ from those of the Scaled Approach.

The proposed information-gathering and description stage contains four quadrants/sections: Personal, Family and Social

Factors, Offending/Antisocial behaviour, Foundations for change and self-assessment.

- The Personal, Family and Social Factors section will assess the child's current life situation in terms of *family and environmental factors* (for example family history/functioning, wider family networks, living arrangements, housing, social and community/neighbourhood factors, significant life events), *parenting, care and supervision* (for example children's experiences as parents and carers) and the *child's development* (for example mental, emotional and physical health, speech, language and communication needs, lifestyle and behavioural development, substance use and peer associations, relationships and identity, ETE). This section is intended to identify needs, problems and (desistance-promoting) strengths that can help practitioners better understand and explain the offending behaviour without blurring the boundaries between need and the risk of reoffending. The Offending/Antisocial Behaviour section will describe characteristics and patterns of problematic behaviour, including details of *current and previous* offending, *patterns* of offending over time, attitudes to offending, '*other behaviour*' indicative of future offending and a calculation of the *likelihood of reoffending*.
- Foundations for Change will explore facets of the child's life that promote or prevent behavioural change, such as resilience (for example in the face of opportunities to offend), goals, attitudes, engagement and participation. AssetPlus is, therefore, intended to enable practitioners to explore positive factors and willingness to change in detail and to inform intervention plans underpinned by the promotion of strengths and positive pathways out of offending. The Self-assessment section(s) will be completed by both the child and their parents/carers, in order to facilitate their engagement and participation in the assessment and intervention process. Self-assessment is intended to allow these neglected key stakeholder groups to reflect critically on their behaviour, on their *future aspirations* and on what is needed to promote their *desistance* and *positive outcomes*. *Early Practice Change* materials around self-assessment have been circulated by the YJB to give YOTs the option to

> embed AssetPlus processes into their practice prior to full implementation (YJB 2013). The statutory self-assessment tool focuses on factors in children's lives relating to: family, home and relationships, smoking, drinking and drugs, health and how I feel, friends, school, college and work, offending, my future and working with the YOT. Children are asked to rate their strength of agreement (yes, no, sometimes) with a series of statements in each section that are worded to indicate either the presence of *risk* (for example, 'There are problems or arguments at home') or *protection/resilience* ('I know that my family care about me'). Certain sections include an extra open question at the end (for example, 'Who are the most important people in your life?', 'What do your friends think of you?') with restricted space for an extended answer.

The ratings and measures used in each of the sub-sections will not be numerical scores. The move away from numerical ratings eschews the most reductionist elements of Asset, particularly by avoiding the over-simplistic quantification of potentially complex life experiences and circumstance and by ostensibly prioritising a prospective focus on problems, needs and strengths (as opposed to a retrospective and negative risk-based focus) and resilience, desistance, engagement, participation and other positive outcomes (as opposed to the prevention of negative behaviours/outcomes). The move away from the retrospective factorisation of a restricted group of risks and the prevention of negativity are consolidated within a more holistic assessment model containing a more detailed exploration of foundations for change and more emphasis on self-assessment than was possible with Asset. These proposed and purported step changes also reflect a departure from adulterised and adult-centric assessments and the neglect of children's voices and perspectives in the assessment process to place children and their views and aspirations at the centre of youth justice planning and interventions.

Information Gathering and Description data will feed into a practitioner meta-analysis within the Explanations and Conclusions portion of AssetPlus. The explicit intention is for practitioners to utilise the information to develop a more holistic understanding of children's offending behaviour by considering both *contextual information* and temporally sensitive *interactions* between the past and the present, life events, needs, positive factors and the various contexts in which children demonstrate problems (YJB 2013). While consequent explanations of offending by children should be less reductionist and risk driven than those prescribed by Asset due to this broader, less developmentally deterministic explanatory framework and due to less reliance on assessing and factorising risk, the potential for a reductionist element to practitioner explanations remains. It is unclear, for example, how the Information Gathering and Description data will avoid the psychosocial biases and inevitable individualisation of the blame for offending behaviour in its current form, focusing as it does on predominantly psychological and immediate social (family, education, neighbourhood) issues at the neglect of structural, socio-economic and political influences. There is also a creeping re-emergence of quantification (by stealth) in terms of the extent to which different factors will be rated in terms of their assessed ability to predict the *likelihood of reoffending* (both 'indicative' and 'final'), rated on a three-point scale: high, medium or low (YJB 2013). This section, as currently conceived, demonstrates a regression into risk management and its attendant problems, a retreat incongruous with the holistic, prospective and positive evolution beyond risk promised in the opening data-gathering section of AssetPlus.

The final section, Pathways and Planning, is intended to utilise the Explanations and Conclusions information to assist practitioners in designing appropriate interventions to achieve positive outcomes for children (first, as priority), including engagement, participation and positive behaviours, all appropriate to their assessed circumstance, experiences and perceptions (YJB 2013). As such, the concluding section of AssetPlus signals a move away from offence- and offender-focused thinking and practice in the YJS of England and Wales. However, these progressive objectives are in danger of being undermined by explanatory criteria that privilege a reductionist risk focus. Such lack of ambition in the design of AssetPlus, or the preceding reductionist reliance on risk assessment, appears to be exacerbated by proposals to retain the three levels of intervention prescribed by the Scaled Approach – standard, enhanced and intensive (YJB 2013).

The proposed AssetPlus assessment and intervention framework could constitute a major shift in focus away from the measurement of (psychosocial) risk factors and the prevention of offending through risk-focused early intervention, towards a more clearly defined focus on *needs* in personal, family and social domains, *strengths* that promote desistance and change, and *positive* outcomes such as well-being, safety, engagement and participation. However, the proposed explanatory reliance on assessing risk and protective factors (in the self-assessment section) and the risk/likelihood of reoffending as a means of informing a 'one size fits all' scaled intervention appears contradictory to this shift. It can be argued that the proposed changes to the assessment and intervention do not go far enough in reorienting contemporary youth justice towards positive, child-friendly and engaging processes and goals.

The proposals for AssetPlus are largely focused on amending and augmenting current procedures (for example, as the name suggests, risk assessment through Asset will not be abandoned altogether) and reframing adult-led assessment and intervention through an incorporation of more potential influences on children's behaviour and a greater scope for adult practitioners to identify and interpret these influences. While AssetPlus offers a promising improvement on the inherent weaknesses and deleterious elements of the Scaled Approach, it does not offer a comprehensive overhaul of youth justice principles, policies and practices for the benefit of those children who become embroiled in the YJS. There remains very limited scope for the equitable participation of children, beyond vague proposals for 'improved self-assessment' with no accompanying explanation of its potential role or influence in the new assessment process. Indeed, the early practice materials circulated around self-assessment are disappointing – indicative of a residual risk and resilience focus as opposed to any emphasis on strengths and future orientation on promoting positive behaviours and outcomes (protection against and resilience to risk is the absence of a negative, not the presence of a positive – see Chapter Six). AssetPlus is particularly vulnerable to the potential problems outlined. Like the Asset tool, and APIS KEEP, which preceded it, AssetPlus is a technique without an overarching purpose or philosophy (see Haines and Drakeford 1998 for a broader discussion). Tools such as AssetPlus must be animated in the service of a particular objective if they are to achieve coherence in outcomes. The presence of a tool and the absence of a guiding philosophy represent a significant threat to the potential for AssetPlus to reorient youth justice in a more positive direction – and it is to this issue that we turn in the final section of this chapter.

Children First, Offenders Second: systems management through evidence-based partnership

CFOS challenges and overrides the *system first* and *offender first* managerialism of the new youth justice. The model advocates for a *systems management* approach wherein all key decisions regarding children are guided by child-friendly *evidence* generated in partnership between key stakeholders. In particular, decision making is informed by empirical evidence obtained through a four-way partnership between children, youth justice practitioners, policy makers and researchers. Accordingly, *evidence-based partnership* is a central animating feature of CFOS – underpinned by attention to the *relational* aspects of youth justice practice (see Case and Haines 2014b). Child-friendly and child-appropriate evidence emerges from empowering and responsibilising adult practitioners to facilitate constructive, inclusionary, participative, engaging and legitimate relationships between children and adult decision makers (for example YOT workers, police officers, teachers, parents, researchers), including child-friendly research mechanisms implemented through an innovative model known as Reflective Friend Research. Accessing practitioner perspectives is a crucial means of informing the decision-making processes inherent in effective, evidence-based systems management, as is accessing children's perspectives through engagement and participation mechanisms (see later in this chapter; see also Chapter Five).

Engaging with practitioner perspectives

An under-emphasis of the relational aspects of youth justice work reflects an alarming neglect of the voices, perspectives and experiences of children in the YJS (Case 2006), despite cogent empirical evidence that eliciting these perspectives is an effective means of evaluating and developing policy and practice (compare Milbourne 2009; Sharpe 2011; Mycock, Tonge and Jeffrey 2012). Adult practitioner perspectives offer crucial reference points for interpreting children's accounts, as befits their status as co-determinants of the two-way engagement between children and provider (Case and Haines 2014b; Drake et al 2014). To this end, it is essential that these knowledgeable, experienced and dedicated practitioners are given the appropriate level of *discretion* to exercise their professional judgement. However, despite cogent arguments for enhancing practitioner discretion as a means of engaging with staff expertise and facilitating children's engagement in youth justice practices, the managerialism and modernisation of the Crime and Disorder Act 1998 has restricted and 'deprofessionalised' practitioners (Pitts 2001). A raft of performance-monitoring measures and the use of standardised assessments have embedded overly prescriptive, standardised processes across the YJS that elicit automated 'tick box' responses from practitioners (Pitts 2001; see also Case 2010). Consequently, youth justice processes have become system-centric, focused on meeting centralised systemic and organisational performance targets (see Bateman 2011; Case and Haines 2014b) to the explicit detriment of enhancing positive outcomes for children.

The coalition government's recent push towards localism and 'payment by results'[57] has reintroduced the issue of increased practitioner discretion into the youth justice debate. The coalition government's *Breaking the Cycle* Green Paper (MoJ 2010: 37–8) pronounced confidently on a retreat from centralised prescription

[57] An incentivised 'payment by results' measure has yet to be realised in the YJS of England and Wales and remains focused on adults in the wider criminal justice system. If such a system is introduced for work with children in the YJS, a CFOS approach would strongly recommend linking results into future-oriented objectives for the achievements of children, as opposed to the negative-facing reduction of risk and prevention of offending.

and a re-emphasis of practitioner discretion: 'This is a radical and decentralizing reform. We will give providers the freedom to innovate, to increase their discretion to get the job done … Professionals in the public, private, voluntary and community sectors will be given much greater discretion.'

The subsequent government response to the Green Paper toned down these ambitions by removing all reference to 'discretion' (see Drake et al 2014). The following year, a commitment to professional discretion reappeared in the National Standards Trial (an evaluation of the current National Standards with a view to their revision), which mooted the increasing opportunity for professional discretion (in line with the *Breaking the Cycle* recommendations) and increasing local freedoms and flexibilities. However, as discussed in Chapter Three, coalition government changes (precipitated by economic austerity measures) have the potential not just to motivate innovation, but also to induce a dramatic reduction in the range and breadth of service provision and the retrenchment of YOT services (see Yates 2012), taking these in house, rather than working in open, multi-agency partnership structures. The re-emergence of practitioner discretion in coalition thinking as an essential tool for shaping and influencing youth justice has been best evidenced in policy/strategy terms (as yet not in practice) by the introduction of AssetPlus, an assessment and intervention framework based (largely) on professional judgement rather than technical, automated and prescribed guidance. Enhancing practitioner discretion facilitates access to the professional judgement, experience and expertise that can guide and inform systems management in youth justice, engaging and utilising a key (neglected) stakeholder in the youth justice process. However, practitioner discretion should neither be artificially restricted by overly prescriptive centralised guidance, nor left entirely unsupported or unmonitored. One key vehicle to encourage and utilise supported practitioner discretion and expertise in the context of child-friendly, reflective partnership is the Reflective Friend Research model, which we have developed at the local level.

Promoting engagement with practitioners through Reflective Friend Research

The evidence-based practice promoted by the CFOS model is driven by a *partnership* between children (and their families), adult professionals (practitioners, managers, policy makers, politicians) and a much neglected, yet potentially influential, key stakeholder, university-based *researchers* (including undergraduate students on research internships – see Case and Haines in 2015b). The development of child-friendly, promotional, inclusionary and legitimate youth justice policy and practice under CFOS eschews quasi-experimental positivist social science research conducted on inanimate *subjects* and instead pursues more valid and nuanced understandings of the practical realities of the youth justice context through research partnerships with key stakeholders as *participant partners* in the process. A CFOS approach to working with children in the YJS is facilitated by Reflective Friend Research (RFR), a model of social science research that emphasises the *relational* aspects of meaningful, valid and context-specific knowledge development and which facilitates engagement with practitioner expertise and their exercise of discretion (which in turn can be employed to engage children and families). RFR evolves through five central relational processes between the researcher and the 'researched' (see Case and Haines 2014a), the latter of whom are reframed as active research partners:

- **Situated learning** – researchers actively immerse themselves in the everyday contexts of the research partners (for example the practice environments of YOT staff and children attending the YOT, including decision-making structures and processes), working with research partners to co-construct their learning, knowledge and understanding of the practical realities of the YJS. This can involve the co-development of research agendas, explanatory frameworks and the design, implementation and evaluation of youth justice services, disposals, assessments and interventions. As such, key stakeholders (for example children in the YJS, YOT staff) can participate and have their voices heard at all stages of the research process, rather than serving as inanimate, passive subjects and recipients of the research.

- **Research partnerships** – situating research within the everyday contexts of participants can foster the co-construction of knowledge and understanding through equitable and participative research partnerships. These RFR partnerships can resemble 'communities of practice' (see Lave and Wenger 2002; Bredo 2005) to the extent that they enable participants to contribute their expert knowledge, experiences, subjective interpretations and meanings to every aspect of the research (knowledge-generation) process, from initial foci to design to methodology to analysis to the interpretation, dissemination and application of results.
- **Enhanced access** – situated research partnerships can facilitate researcher access to vital facets of the research process, which, in the context of CFOS, can include: research *participants/partners* (for example children, parents/carers, teachers, YOT staff, government ministers, policy makers, other researchers), key data sets locally and nationally (for example performance-monitoring databases, crime and antisocial behaviour statistics, education and social services databases), internal documentation (minutes, policies, (drafts of) local authority and governmental papers) and knowledge-generation processes (meetings, steering groups, committees, advisory panels). This privileged access to a broader range of data sources than is typically possible through the traditional didactic researcher-subject research model of positivism promotes more context-sensitive and detailed knowledge that is faithful to the expert perspectives of research partners.
- **Reflective engagement** – the RFR model utilises reflective and recursive (reciprocal, recurring) feedback loops between all research partners within the partnership (for example regular, embedded feedback given to partners by the researchers, constant dialogue between partners), particularly related to evidence-based decision-making processes. Prioritisation of the relational aspects of applied research is facilitated by situated learning and engenders engagement between research partners in the sense of mutual trust, confidence, openness, respect, interactivity and perceived competence (see also

Cousin and Deepwell 2005). The nature and influence of the 'dense relations of mutual engagement' (Wenger 1998: 74) between researchers and 'researched' parties have been relatively under-explored across empirical social science research (see Iedema et al 2004), yet they underpin and drive the RFR approach to developing knowledge, understanding and evidence through partnership.

- **Critical friendship** – it is crucial that each research partner utilises the RFR processes of situated learning, partnership working, enhanced access and reflective engagement to evaluate and critique the policy, practice and perspectives of their other partners (see also Tuckermann and Ruegg-Sturm 2010). The relational aspect of critical friendship is vital if research partners are to avoid potentially invalidating influences born of friendship, proximity, loyalty, protectiveness and empathy (see Baskerville and Goldblatt 2009); and influences such as bias, subjectivity, lack of independence, self-fulfilling practice and proselytising. It is crucial that the independence of all partners is maintained so that reflective engagement can be used as a tool to enhance the validity and appropriateness of research processes (for example evaluation of practice, explanation of behaviour) and the generation of knowledge and evidence. The situated, reflective nature of RFR enables such critical friendship through regular, reciprocal and open dialogue and feedback between research partners, allowing researchers to raise difficult issues in a non-defensive environment and enabling a focus on the consequent reflexive enhancement of practice.

In Focus • Establishing a YOT–university partnership

A long-term programme of localised, evidence-based programme development through RFR began in 1996 at a meeting to discuss local youth crime prevention policies and practices in Swansea. The meeting was attended by practitioners and managers from the local YOT and Community Safety Department, along with researchers from Swansea University's Centre for Criminal Justice and Criminology (CCJC) – all of whom had previously expressed a commitment to developing preventive practice guided by context-specific, child-friendly evidence. A central driver of the meeting from which RFR evolved had been political attempts to undermine prevention-oriented practice with children in conflict with the law and the youth justice system on the grounds that it was not 'evidence based' or demonstrably 'cost-effective' – key elements of the emerging governmental focus on 'effective practice'. Reflecting in an interview on the local government climate at that time, the then Chief Executive of the newly formed City and County of Swansea explained:

> 'There was a move from some of the politicians to undermine youth work and to say, we're spending all this money, we've got to make cuts in social services and the education budget, why are we spending this kind of money on things that don't seem to make a difference? How do we evaluate things?' (Former City and County of Swansea Chief Executive, interviewed 2010)

During interview in 2012, the Local Authority Community Safety Department Manager (at the time of the original meeting) defined the objective of the approach as developing "a partnership with the University that would give us [Community Safety Department and YOT] that resource to take a more objective look – first of all at the evidence from what we were doing and then secondly the evaluation of what we were doing". The evolving evidence-based partnership approach of RFR animated a local commitment to 'research as inherent and fundamental to project development' (Swansea YOT manager 2012) and to three pivotal principles of CFOS working:

1. *reflective engagement* with researchers and research evidence;
2. belief in a *preventive philosophy* for working with children in conflict with the law and the youth justice system;
3. *consultation with children* (in line with the United Nations Convention on the Rights of the Child (UNCRC)) to encourage their participation and engagement in the generation of child-friendly, child-appropriate evidence that can foster more 'effective' preventive practice.

The YOT/Community Safety Department-CCJC meeting led to a partnership agreement to pursue sources of funding for the development and independent evaluation and ongoing reflective development of a series of local prevention, diversion and social inclusion programmes (beginning with the Promoting Positive Behaviour in Schools programme

– see Chapter Six). The preferred mechanism for this partnership was situated and reflective *relationship building* – practitioners and researchers working collaboratively (with each other and with children and families) to identify and target local issues related to offending by children by situating researchers physically and contextually within the YOT working environments (for example through the allocation of office space), cultures and practices, both formally (for example attending policy and practice development and monitoring meetings, participating in team days, sitting in on assessment interviews, court hearings and family visits with children) and informally (for example relationship building in the YOT staff rooms and offices). Situating researchers within YOT environments, structures and processes provided them with enhanced access to privileged expert contexts and has facilitated the situated learning of both researchers and YOT staff through iterative mechanisms of reflection and critical friendship, such as researchers disseminating and discussing the findings and conclusions of their projects, evaluations and observations with policy makers and practitioners, along with children and families (Case and Haines 2014a).

The RFR model was developed to reflectively evaluate and improve partnership-based systems management/decision making within the local YJS. According to the local YOT manager (interviewed in 2012), "because agencies have been part of the research, things have begun to change." RFR has been employed to develop, evaluate and improve a series of local programmes primarily concerned with diversion (compare Swansea Bureau – see Chapter Five) and the three generations of prevention-promotion work locally (see Chapter Six), founded on evidence-based and engaging partnership between critical (friend) researchers and reflective practitioners, policy makers and children (and families). RFR at the local level has challenged systems-first managerialist approaches to youth justice by prioritising the generation and utilisation of meaningful empirical evidence in partnership with key stakeholders, particularly those parties previously neglected in youth justice research and practice development (that is, children and practitioners).

The RFR model evolves through recursive (reoccurring, reciprocal) and reflective feedback loops between researchers and researched parties. Researchers are integrated within and become part of the decision-making processes subject to research and evaluation, embedding an evidence-based partnership approach to practice evaluation and development. For example, in Swansea:

> 'An action research model developed at an early-stage ... very much looking at using input from the University at a number of levels ... establishing what was happening and why it was happening, and contributing to the process of development to make sure we did the right thing.' (Swansea YOT manager 2012)

Through RFR, situated and critical engagement processes become everyday working practice for researchers and youth justice staff and recursive feedback loops engender a 'mutual learning dynamic' (see Dutton and Dukerich 2006) as a means of enhancing and utilising the evidence produced. The long-term, embedded partnership nature of research relationships imbue them with the tensility and flex to withstand the inherent stress and pressure of everyday working, continued critical friendship and external pressures, resulting in a 'strong connectivity' that leaves partners more amenable and receptive to new ideas and influence (compare Losada and Heaphy 2004). The relational, reflective identity of RFR is underpinned by these research connections, producing new information and understandings for participants as the connections develop (see also Gitell 2003).

It is important to balance our advocacy of the RFR model with a reflective discussion of the nature of the model. In RFR, the researcher is part of the context being described (and ultimately evaluated), rather than functioning as a neutral observer. The situated and participative nature of the researcher role means that the RFR partnership model is vulnerable to accusations of researcher bias and lack of researcher independence. It is possible that situated immersion in practice contexts could exacerbate researcher subjectivity, excessive empathy and a lack of criticality (for example 'going native'), with a mutual respect and trust between partners translating into preferential treatment, misguided loyalty and over-protectiveness (compare Fuller, in Lewis-Beck, Bryman and Liao 2004). However, we would counter that in our experience, critical friendship is the touchstone for RFR. It is possible for the researcher, while not 'independent' in the strictest sense, to develop relationships grounded in reciprocity, trust and confidence, which in turn can enhance the quality of the situated learning, practice developments and research impact at the local level (see, for example, Haines and Case 2012). Within this context, local YOT staff have responded to our criticisms and recommendations constructively, not in a cynical, defensive or guarded manner, but in a reflective, open-minded and appreciative fashion, which prioritises practice improvements for the benefit of local children and families, such that: "Research has been part of a process of enabling practitioners and senior practitioners to be more self-critical about what they do" (Swansea YOT manager 2012).

Promoting engagement through the participation of children: the forgotten perspective

> Children have a right to say what they think should happen, when adults are making decisions that affect them, and to have their opinions taken into account. (UNCRC Article 12)

As discussed, the limited body of engagement research and guidance has privileged the adult perspectives and skills development of practitioners at the expense of children's perspectives, despite successive children's rights conventions advocating that children have the right to be listened to regarding all decisions that affect them (UNCRC Article 12). The neglect of children's voices in youth justice processes and the extent of centralised practice prescriptions has rendered children's subjective experiences 'unknowable' (Phoenix and Kelly 2013). Despite YJB assessment guidance that 'assessors will need to employ individually-oriented interviewing skills which allow them to explore with the young person their own story' (YJB 2008a: 15; see also YJB 2004), the self-assessment portion of Asset (entitled 'What do you think?') has been notoriously incomplete or ignored (see Baker 2005), rendering children in the YJS relatively voiceless and powerless in key decision-making processes (Case 2006). Indeed, following a qualitative analysis of the situated knowledge of children subject to YOT contact, Phoenix and Kelly felt able to reconceptualise the notion of *responsibilisation* as relating to a general lack of engagement by and faith in practitioners, such that children 'came to know there was no one else to help them change their lives (Phoenix and Kelly 2013: 419) and so were compelled to address their issues autonomously and independently (see also Birdwell and Bani 2014).

A central guiding feature of CFOS is that it is *inclusionary* – seeking to engage with (the perspectives of) and encourage the engagement of children by encouraging their meaningful participation (not simply consultation) in the decision-making, assessment and intervention processes of the YJS, rather than visiting these processes upon voiceless, powerless children in adult-centric, (risk) management-led and enforced ways that serve to disengage and exclude them. Therefore, participation can be a vehicle with which to achieve children's inclusion and engagement with youth justice practice, in accordance with its position as a central tenet of the UNCRC (alongside protection and provision) and as 'good practice' in facilitating children's access to justice (UNHCHR 2013). In direct opposition to the adult-centric tenets of much KEEP guidance and the governmental preference for technicised 'what works' intervention with children in the YJS, CFOS emphasise *relationships* as the drivers of engaging, effective practice (see also Creaney and Smith 2014). Children's participation in the YJS has been found to increase levels of engagement (along with compliance) with youth justice disposals, programmes and interventions and to increase their motivation to change their behaviour as a result (Creaney 2014). France and Homel (2006: 305–6) argue that children (unlike adult practitioners) do not privilege programmes and content, but instead value and desire 'a good supportive relationship with an adult who is not judgmental and is able to offer guidance and advocacy … to gain a greater understanding of these processes we need to listen to the voices and perspectives of young people themselves'. However, there has been little empirical study into the nature and effectiveness of child–practitioner engagement in the YJS, despite this relationship sitting at the centre of youth justice practice (Drake et al 2014; McNeill and Maruna 2008; Case and Haines 2014b).

A key vehicle for facilitating children's participation and engagement in the YJS is *practitioner discretion* (discussed in the previous section). Drake et al (2014: 23) advocate: 'maximizing the discretion of youth justice workers to hear and respond to young people's voices, and to "rethink" aspects of practice that impair what can be heard and acted upon'.

Enabling children's engagement with decision-making processes and with the design, implementation and evaluation of youth justice services can facilitate strategic planning, can enhance the meaningful and appropriate decision making of practitioners and services, and can improve the quality of the child–adult relationships that influence intervention effectiveness (see also HMI Probation 2009; Nacro 2011). Indeed, Creaney and Smith (2014: 83; see also Scraton and Haydon 2002; Goldson and Muncie 2006) assert that: '[I]n order to reconcile the lack of user-led engagement of offenders, and experiences of disempowerment, the priority should be, throughout the youth justice system, to involve young people in assessment and decision-making processes.'

In Wales, children's participation in decision making has become a statutory obligation in every local authority area (following the Children Act 2004), with Children and Young People's Partnerships required to facilitate contributions from local children to inform their Children and Young People's Plan. The Welsh government has published guidance on Local Participation Strategies 0–25 to support the statutory status of participation under the Children Act 2004. The Welsh participation agenda has been furthered by the Children and Young Person's Participation Consortium, a multi-agency body established in 2003 to develop children's capacity to participate in decision making and to promote its application in practice. The Consortium works to a definition of participation as the child's 'right to be involved in making decisions, planning and reviewing any action that might affect [them]. Having a voice, having a choice' (Pupil Voice Wales 2014). The Consortium guides the work of the Welsh government's Participation Unit (led by Save the Children), which supports the strategic development of children's participation. Most recently, Nacro Cymru (2009) produced bespoke guidance entitled *Youth Justice and Participation in Wales* to assist YOTs in the use of 'minimal essential components' of participation with children to shape their practice (information, choice, non-discrimination, respect, reciprocity, feedback, practice improvements). The guidance identified a series of challenges and barriers to children's participation and engagement in youth justice processes, notably the enforced, compliance-focused nature of court-ordered disposals, mistrust of adults, communication difficulties and previous unsatisfactory experiences of not being listened to and valued (Nacro Cymru 2009). Several recommendations were offered to address these issues, including empowering children to participate equally in decision-making processes at all stages of their involvement with the YJS – drawing on appropriate consultation methodologies (for example online tools, self-assessment), the provision of information, evidence-based practice and research with children and a commitment to promoting children's rights in order to encourage a 'culture of participation' (Nacro Cymru 2009).

Promoting children's participation in shaping youth justice services is asserted to have multiple potential benefits, particularly improved understanding of youth justice processes and enhanced self-confidence among children, leading to a greater likelihood of engagement and compliance with youth justice provision (see, for example, Charles and Haines, 2014; Hart and Thompson 2009; Nacro Cymru 2009). Children are the experts in their own worlds and should be enabled to communicate their experiences of participation to adults (see Lancaster and Broadbent 2003). However, a significant obstacle to children's participation in decision-making processes emerges upon their entry into the YJS. As discussed, children's capacity to contribute meaningfully to youth justice decision making has been curtailed and neglected by adult-centric, prescriptive practice and an emphasis upon enforcement and compliance, to the detriment of legitimate and engaging partnership relationships between children and practitioners. The neglect of participatory partnership approaches contradicts and contravenes a series of legislative requirements for children's inclusion in the administration and development of youth justice processes, for example:

> [T]he child shall in particular be provided with the opportunity to be heard in any judicial or administrative proceedings affecting the child (UNCRC Article 12)

> [C]hildren and young people should be free to express their views in all matters that affect them and this entitlement should be reflected and implemented at every stage of the criminal justice process (General Comment No 10 Children's Rights in Juvenile Justice, UN Committee on the Rights of the Child in 2007)

At the national level, in Wales, the All Wales Youth Offending Strategy (AWYOS) Delivery Plan commits youth justice practitioners to 'consultation with, and the participation of, children and young people in the youth justice system' (WAG and YJB 2009: 10). As noted, there are significant challenges and barriers to realising (Welsh) social policy aspirations for the child-friendly participation of Welsh children who have offended, largely because they are part of a YJS whose policy and practice is governed by England. For example, the non-negotiable, enforcement- and compliance-led nature of court-ordered disposals can influence and inhibit the extent and nature of the child–practitioner relationship and degree of engagement with the YJS. The imposition of these practice features and barriers to participation by the English-led YJB is a deep-rooted source of policy–practice tension in Wales, a nation that promotes a child-friendly social policy identity in areas outside (non-devolved) youth justice.

Within the YJS, there is a 'duality between the enforcement and enabling functions of the youth justice system' (Hart and Thompson 2009: 4). The enforcement-led elements of disposals and (Scaled Approach) interventions, including their content, timing, duration and location, can actively discourage children's participation in and engagement with the YJS. The control and regulation experienced by children during intervention is counter-intuitive to developing constructive, engaging relationships with adults based on mutual respect, empathy, trust and legitimacy. These potential structural and procedural barriers can be compounded by children's previous negative experiences of youth justice processes, wherein their perceived lack of involvement, failures to take their views into account and their (mis)representation through detrimental labels and stereotypes can precipitate distrust of and lack of faith in the behaviour and intentions of the state, the YJS, YOTs and adult staff (compare Hart and Thompson 2009; Nacro Cymru 2009). It is also possible that the existing socio-structural disadvantages and psychosocial issues (for example mental health, language and communication difficulties) that children in conflict with the law and the youth justice system (disproportionately) experience may result in a lack of confidence and ability to engage and participate in the youth justice services they receive.

In Focus • Facilitating children's participation in decision making

A local research project explored the understandings and perceptions of 'participation' in decision making, using interviews and focus groups with an opportunity sample of 99 children; a mainstream sample of 93 children (aged 11–16 years) drawn from a local secondary school and a 'non-mainstream' sample of six children (aged 11–18 years) from the local YOT and taking part in either a Youth Inclusion Programme or a Resettlement and Aftercare Programme (Charles and Haines 2014). The researchers identified the defining features of effective participation in decision making from the child's perspective, which led them to develop (in partnership with the children from the sample) minimum standards for the measurement of children's participation. The qualitative perspectives of local children highlighted the importance of two child-friendly characteristics of participation in decision making: *intention* and *relationships* (Charles and Haines 2014):

- **Intention** – for local children, their participation in decision making needed to be intentional, rather than by accident, by proxy or through delegation by adults. Children felt that intentional, autonomous participation empowered them to meaningfully communicate what was important and truthful (that is, valid) about their experiences. In this way, intention was seen as distinct from outcomes; challenging adult-centric, system-centric presumption (compare HM Government 2008) that children's participation is positive simply because it produces 'better' outcomes. In this regard, the notion of 'participative quality' was crucial. Children perceived that participation coerced, enforced or hindered by adults was of a lower quality than decisions taken using their own initiative. This correlation between intention and ability to participate was most notable among the non-mainstream, YOT sample, who felt strongly that adults (for example magistrates, YOT staff, social workers, teachers, police) often made decisions *about* them (not *with* them) – apparently in their best interests, yet characterised by bullying and coercion – which had profound implications for their futures. Such an exercise of power and authority is contrary to the spirit of legitimate and equitable participation based on empowering children.

- **Relationships** – reflecting the engagement literature, children felt that adult practitioners overvalued decision making at the expense of the relational aspects of participation. In particular, children valued relationships that they experienced as *enriching* rather than functional (for example to facilitate the delivery of court-ordered intervention). Enriching relationships with practitioners were perceived as the product of inter-dependency and equality of participative power between children and adults. The children involved demonstrated a sophisticated, practical appreciation of the processual reality of participation in their understanding that adults in positions of authority were empowered and obligated to make certain decisions, but these same children stressed that such decisions should take account of their expressed needs, views and experiences.

Having elicited children's perspectives on the nature of existing participation processes, the research sought to develop a measurement tool with which to assess the identified minimum standards for children's participation in decision making (Charles and Haines, 2014). Initially, children were invited to critically review existing participation scales: the Ladder of Participation (Hart 1992), the Diagram of Participation (Treseder 1997) and the Freechild Project Measure for Social Change (UNICEF 2003). Three key features of child-friendly, child-appropriate participation tools were identified; features that are largely neglected by existing instruments. Children suggested that effective participation

> measurement scales should first attend to *language* – ensuring accessibility and clarity, while avoiding obscure, adult-centric terminology and concepts. Secondly, *presentation* of an appropriate nature should be a minimum standard for measuring participation – utilising child-friendly, contextual images and avoiding saturation with complex graphs and charts. Finally, attention must be given to the notion of hierarchy – rejecting understanding of participative hierarchy on a fixed, linear continuum and promoting flexible, context-specific, fluid and sensitive understanding of participation (compare London 2007).

Developing a 'culture of participation' (Hart and Thompson 2009) through the creation of bespoke participatory structures and processes that motivate and enable children to contribute to youth justice decision making (McNeish and Newman 2002; Hallett and Prout 2003) is an essential component of effective youth justice practice, reflecting the child-friendly, child-appropriate, inclusionary and legitimacy foci of CFOS. National Standards for youth justice practice (YJB 2010) demand that all orders children receive should be reviewed at multi-agency panels every three months in order that they remain appropriate to meeting children's needs. Further to this, conceiving of children in conflict with the law and the youth justice system as 'service users' and fully involving them in decision-making processes is asserted as an effective means of addressing children's needs and reducing misunderstandings and disagreements (User Voice 2011), energising new ideas and promoting unique alternatives and solutions (Alderson 2008). However, all too often, the YJS fails to incorporate the views of service users or to acknowledge that children may 'know best' as regards their own lives and how best to respond to their issues. It has been cogently argued by Williamson and Cairns (2005: 1) that 'Principles are one thing; practice is another. Too often the aim of engaging young people is vitiated by existing structures of professional power and cultural attitudes that devalue the opinions and skills of young people.'

Once again, the enforcement–enablement dichotomy is a salient influence. The full and complete integration of children's participation in decision making within youth justice practice is a constant difficulty because YOT practitioners have a statutory obligation to enforce the non-negotiable rules and regulations and to ensure children's compliance with court orders (see UK Children's Commissioners 2008). The enforcement focus of children–practitioner relationships in the YJS can reduce children's capacity, motivation, willingness and confidence to participate and to engage with youth justice services, while also reducing the capacity and willingness of practitioners and organisations to fully include and engage with children.

In Focus • Children's participation in a YOT review system

National Standards in England and Wales (YJB 2010) require that children be continually informed of progress and changes related to their court orders. However, research indicates low participation rates in case planning, intervention design and involvement in decision making (see, for example, Hart and Thompson 2009). A localised research project was conducted by a final-year undergraduate student on a two-month research internship (supervised by a CCJC senior researcher) to explore the extent and nature of participatory practice within Swansea YOT (Lelliott 2013). Situating/embedding the researcher within the YOT on a daily basis was intended to encourage relationship building with practitioners, enhanced access to key data sources (particularly staff) and recursive feedback of and reflective engagement on formative research findings, in line with the RFR model.

The participatory research identified the historical absence of a formal review process involving children in their own case planning within the YOT. Observation of YOT case review meetings and interviews with practitioners found that previous review meetings had been non-participatory and adult-centric, centred around the child's progress on their order, without giving them sufficient opportunity to participate in decision-making processes and intervention planning. However, interviews with eight children (aged 16–18 years) who were attending the YOT as part of Youth Rehabilitation Orders or Intensive Supervision and Surveillance programmes, discovered that children reported a good understanding of the *purpose* of the YOT review system and positive experiences of their *relationship* with their caseworker (Lelliott 2013). Children and staff identified two central barriers to children's participation in review meetings: the formality and complexity of the *language* used in meetings (see also Charles and Haines 2014) and the formality and professional dominance of the *environment* within which the meetings took place (that there were too many professionals present). Using feedback from both children and practitioners, the researcher identified that children's perceptions of being able/enabled to take *ownership* of their court order was a key factor that optimised their ability and confidence to participate in and engage with the review system. The interviews with children also identified the importance of developing positive, trusting relationships with familiar practitioners as increasing children's perceptions of their capacity to participate in both the review meeting and the progression of their court order (see also Hart and Thompson 2009).

The main recommendations for improvements to the review meeting process, presented to the YOT management board and the YOT staff group, were that adult practitioners should address the child more and elicit their views more within meetings, and seek their consent for new people (adults) to join the meeting; that the review environment should be altered to make it more child friendly in terms of containing fewer adult professionals and a less formal layout; and, most importantly, that the review meeting should be led by the child's individual needs, rather than by the uncritical adoption of the standard, single review format (Lelliott 2013). While acknowledging the 'never-ending tension between granting full participatory rights' (Lelliott 2013: 42) and enforcing and requiring compliance with court orders, the research concluded by emphasising the 'importance of the practitioner's role in providing support for young people to participate [in the review system] to the level which suits their individual needs and abilities' (Lelliott 2013: 43) – indicative of a child-friendly, child-appropriate, inclusive approach to children's participation in the YJS.

As an addendum to this, it is significant to note that YOT staff responded very positively to the findings from the research and agreed to change their practice to facilitate enhanced engagement by children in review meetings.

Putting children first in the youth justice system: partnership, practitioners and participation

In this chapter, we have argued that the Crime and Disorder Act 1998 radically reoriented the YJS in England and Wales (already in the midst of a 'punitive turn') towards a risk-based agenda driven by a 'third way' (not welfare, not justice), that operated to control, prescribe and restrict the practice of YOT staff and the ways in which children were understood and treated. The reductionist management of risk and management of practice has marginalised the crucial relational elements of youth justice, particularly engagement between children and practitioners, and marginalised the perspectives of these neglected key stakeholders in youth justice processes such as decision making, intervention planning and programme implementation and evaluation. While there have been some encouraging, tentative signs in the rhetoric surrounding the proposed AssetPlus assessment and intervention framework that children's voices and practitioner discretion and expertise will play more important roles in the youth justice process, initial indications from the AssetPlus Early Practice Change materials are that the framework remains wedded to retrospective (not future-oriented) risk and resilience models of understanding children, which will inevitably individualise offending, responsibilise children and shackle practitioners.

We advocate for a complete and committed move away from risk and negativity into a CFOS approach to understanding and working with children in conflict with the law and the youth justice system – underpinned by systems management, guided by evidence-based partnership and driven by the participation and engagement of children, families and practitioners to generate meaningful, valid, promotional and future-focused practice. Localised research evidence indicates that enhancing practitioner reflection and discretion through the key features of an RFR model (situated learning, enhanced access, reflective engagement, critical friendship) is a promising vehicle for promoting the evidence-based development of youth justice practices and children's participation as a means of enabling their engagement (belief in, commitment to) youth justice (decision-making) processes and relationships. Consequently, *participation* can be used as a tool for reflective practice development and engagement with youth justice interventions, particularly the participation of neglected stakeholders at the forefront of youth justice practice – children, families, practitioners and researchers.

FIVE

Progressive diversion

The previous chapter examined the potential of a Children First, Offenders Second (CFOS) approach to working with children subject to statutory orders in the youth justice system (YJS). In this context, putting children first in the YJS means abandoning the reductionist and disengaging management of risk and practice performance perpetuated by the Scaled Approach assessment and intervention framework and evidenced (to a lesser degree) by the revised AssetPlus framework; replacing this approach with a participation-led model that seeks meaningful engagement with and between children and practitioners, while also working in partnership with policy makers and researchers using a Reflective Friend Research model.

This chapter explores the principles, practices and progression of *division* from formal contact with the YJS. We begin with discussion of the diversionary principles of *minimum necessary intervention*, which is premised on the argument that contact with the formal YJS is iatrogenic and criminalising for children, particularly where this contact is excessive, disproportionate and inappropriate. From there, we explore the zenith of youth justice diversion practice, the 1980s 'decade of diversion', which was animated by the widespread use of cautioning, welfare-focused Intermediate Treatment intervention programmes led by social workers outside the formal YJS and Juvenile Liaison Bureaux situated within the formal system. What follows is a critical overview of the emergence of *interventionist diversion* following the Crime and Disorder Act 1998, which was characterised by a raft of pre-court interventions underpinned by risk management and restorative justice – each with the main objective of reducing first-time entrants into the YJS. We go on to explore how a diversion emphasis has been reignited since 2010 by the UK coalition government, most notably through revised out-of-court disposal processes. We subject these developments to critical scrutiny and discuss whether they have been founded on children-first principles or managerialist, pragmatic and economic concerns. The chapter concludes with a detailed examination of the potential for a progressive and principled CFOS approach to diversion, founded on child-appropriate and inclusionary interventions decided upon through evidence-based partnership between practitioners, children and families, working alongside policy makers and researchers.

Diversion from the formal youth justice system

Diversionary measures have attained a 'strong-hold in Western youth justice systems' (Richards 2014: 124). The practice of diversion of children from referral to and entry into the formal YJS is premised on the argument that system contact (for example arrest, prosecution) and formal intervention are detrimental: undermining informal care networks and exacerbating personal, social and structural problems (including the likelihood/risk of offending) by exerting stigmatising, labelling, harmful and criminogenic effects on children (see Rutherford 2002; see also Lemert 1951). A prominent rationale for diversion in the youth justice field, therefore, is to divert children from the negative consequences of system contact (McAra and McVie 2007: 318):

> In contrast to the precepts of the 'what works' agenda, there is a growing body of research across a range of jurisdictions ... which indicates that contact with the youth justice system and experience of more severe forms of sanctioning, in particular, are as likely to result in enhanced as diminished offending risk. ... Taken to its extremes, this research would suggest (in a manner akin to labelling theory) that contact with the youth justice system is inherently criminogenic.

The emergence of diversion (largely in the guise of cautioning) in the 1980s as a popular principle of youth justice policy and practice (alongside and sometimes preferred to welfare- and justice-based approaches) was motivated by a view of offending as a 'normal' part of adolescence that children grow out of (the 'maturation hypothesis'). This view was based on evidence that most children are likely to grow out of crime without formal intervention (see Rutherford 2002) and research suggesting that services located outside the formal apparatus are much more 'effective' in tackling the root causes of youth crime (Howell, Krisberg, Hawkins and Wilson 1995). Concurrently and relatedly, a de-escalated practice of *minimum necessary intervention* was advocated as a means of avoiding the labelling, criminalising and contaminating of children through system contact (Schur 1973; Smith 2011). Minimum necessary intervention is a variant of the *progressive minimalism* approach, which recommends dealing with low-level offending through diversion from court and informal intervention, while responding to more serious offending through non-stigmatising and non-criminalising community programmes where possible (Lemert 1972). Advocates of minimum necessary intervention do not reject intervention or ignore the problematic nature of offending by children, but instead assert that intervention should not be excessive or superfluous in terms of its nature, intensity and duration. The dual rationales of the maturation hypothesis and avoiding iatrogenic system contact/advocating *minimum necessary intervention* were intended to guard against both disproportionate and misguided interventionism (see related criticisms of the Scaled Approach – Chapter Four).

The diversionary push towards minimum necessary intervention, in the 1980s, was accompanied by the rise to prominence of practitioner-led *new orthodoxy* thinking. At this time, systems management thinking (a technique) was animated by new orthodoxy thinking (a purpose) – on which see Haines and Drakeford (1998). As Chapter One outlines, the *new orthodoxy* model of youth justice (Tutt and Giller 1987; Bottoms et al 1990) aimed to decriminalise children and to divert them from the deleterious effects of the formal YJS and formal intervention through community-based and anti-custody responses guided by *systems management* – targeting key decision-making points regarding children across the YJS (see also Chapter Four). New orthodoxy thinking provided a critique of previous practice, most notably the indiscriminate and intensive nature of certain welfare interventions and the degree to which the (so-called diversionary) interventions that resulted from out-of-court disposals exhibited negative labelling effects on children and an up-tariffing effect. New orthodoxy thinking 'offered a vision for the future' by advocating that youth justice practice should prioritise systems management and focus on key decision-making processes in order to achieve certain principled objectives, including promoting diversion from the YJS, limiting intervention in accordance with offence seriousness and avoiding custody (Haines, in Goldson 2008: 350).

The decade of diversion

The 1980s became the 'decade of diversion' due to the application of minimum necessary intervention principles 'at all stages of the [youth justice] process … [by] … practitioners from statutory and voluntary agencies working at the local level' (Rutherford 2002: 101). During the 1980s heyday of diversionary youth justice, the police were responsible for deciding how to respond to offences committed by children, while social services departments retained a general duty to safeguard and promote the welfare of these children. The 1980s witnessed the increased use of cautioning, achieved (mainly) through inter-agency working, accompanied by patterns of annual declines in the use of custody for children and annual increases in community-based supervision sentences (Allen 1991). A particular form of diversion came to dominate policy and practice in the 1980s, founded on the normalising and anti-interventionist principles of *minimal necessary intervention* and underpinned by what Smith (2011: 178) characterises as: 'A groundswell of support at the level of local practitioners and institutions … a clear sense of a systematic strategy; an acknowledgment of children's distinctive rights … The promotion of child-centered approach.'

A range of responses were made available for use with those children considered to be 'at risk' of offending, the most common of which was Intermediate Treatment (IT) – a generic social work programme that was interventionist in nature, targeting children who had been assessed as being in need of support, whether they had offended or not (see Haines and Drakeford 1998).

Intermediate treatment

A form of social work intervention with children in trouble or need that was intermediate between family work and removal of the child from their family (Case in Goldson 2008), IT was introduced in the Home Office White Paper *Children in Trouble*, which preceded the Children and Young Persons Act 1969. The White Paper asserted that child neglect and offending by children were both products (not symptoms) of deprivation and thus should not be treated and responded to separately. IT became the standard intervention in response to deprivation, often framed as a condition of a court Supervision Order or offered to children on a voluntary basis and typically administered to children assessed as 'in trouble', 'at risk' or 'in need' by a social worker (see Bottoms et al 1990 for a detailed account of IT).

The main objectives of IT programmes were to enable children to reach their full potential and to attain a level of achievement equivalent to children from more secure backgrounds. In order to do this, a wide range of educational, recreational and work-related opportunities were created to address the identified needs of children in conflict with the law and the youth justice system or at risk of being so. This necessitated creating new projects and opportunities and modifying existing resources within the social work and education systems. The content of IT programmes varied between and within local areas and projects, consisting of, among other things, structured and unstructured discussions, social skills development, alternative curriculum education, visits and outward bound adventure training. Due to its varied and ambiguous nature, IT became a catch-all term for a wide range of direct interventions conducted with children by social workers. IT interventions could be either voluntary or compulsory (for example part of a court order) depending on the child's individual circumstances.

Throughout the 1980s IT was also employed across England and Wales as an interventionist alternative to custody for children who had offended, although many areas also retained its broader welfare-based remit and used IT with children who had not offended, but who had been assessed as 'in need' (see Bottoms et al 1990). However, other forces were at work at that time. Academics and practitioners were becoming increasingly critical of the potentially damaging consequences, for children, of transferring welfare concerns into the youth court (Case, in Goldson 2008). These concerns precipitated a back-to-justice movement (see Haines and Drakeford 1998), wherein new ideas about the largely transient and trivial nature of much offending behaviour by children (Rutherford 2002) were gaining ground, while the ability of social workers to diagnose the causes of delinquency and to provide effective treatment was being undermined. Cautioning and diversion from prosecution became official government policy and a practice imperative, championed by youth justice teams (the forerunners of youth offending teams (YOTs)) who wrested IT from generic social work practice.

Juvenile Liaison Bureaux

The other notable diversionary youth justice practice development in the 1980s was the multi-agency Juvenile Liaison Bureau (JLB) model, introduced across England and Wales as a pre-court, multi-agency decision-making body containing representatives from relevant youth justice organisations (for example police, probation, education, social services, youth service). Although varying in precise title and organisational features at the local level, the JLB model cohered around the objective of diverting children away from prosecution (through cautioning, no further action or informal action) and away from the labelling and criminalising influences of contact with the YJS and formal intervention on the basis that most children will grow out of crime without assistance from criminal justice and welfare agencies[58] (Hinks and Smith 1985). The most well-known and intensively researched JLB was established in Northamptonshire.

[58] Although in many local areas, cautioning was accompanied by intervention.

In Focus • Northamptonshire Juvenile Liaison Bureau

The Northamptonshire JLB was subject to a detailed case study analysis by researchers in Bristol University in the late 1980s (Davis, Boucherat and Watson 1989). Northamptonshire JLB implemented a four-stage, tiered, diversionary system for responding to local children who came to their attention through offending behaviour, which consisted of:

- **informal action** – children receive informal advice and warnings from JLB staff, which is the diversionary Bureau's main objective in the majority of cases as it does not result in a criminal conviction or record;
- **police caution** – a more formal measure which the Bureau seeks to avoid, especially for first-time offenders, as it results in a criminal record;
- **bureau involvement** – the JLB interacts with the child to address their behaviour, which can include offence analysis work;
- **prosecution** – a last resort for children with a prolonged record of serious offending, few mitigating circumstances and an inability or unwillingness to engage with offence analysis work.

Case study interviews with staff identified an 'inevitable tension' between diversionary governmental objectives and the professional objectives of the police staff within the Bureau, with police officers articulating a much greater pressure to formalise and respond to low-level crime, largely due to demands related to clear-up rates (Davis et al 1989). However, the staff interviews highlighted a general commitment to, and belief in, diversion as an effective approach to avoiding the negative effects of system contact, reducing reoffending and circumventing the perceived lack of utility of retributive justice and deterrent measures. As such, the Northamptonshire JLB was characterised as 'traditional' diversion based on minimal or non-intervention, as opposed to 'new' diversion requiring rehabilitation and (allegedly) control and punitive measures delivered under the guise of care and treatment (Davis et al 1989). The diversionary Northamptonshire JLB exerted a positive influence on the development of youth justice practice in England and Wales. The programme has been commended as an example of effective multi-agency working in the youth justice arena and 'may have influenced some features of the YOTs established by the Crime and Disorder Act 1998 (Souhami 2007: 25).

Throughout the 1980s and into the early 1990s, cautioning, pro-diversion and alternative-to-custody strategies formed the *new orthodoxy* of youth justice in England and Wales, animated by systems management thinking. As the 1990s progressed, the principles and practices of the new orthodoxy (including IT and JLBs) began to wane in the lexicon of youth justice interventions with children.

From diversion to interventionism

By the mid-1990s and the onset of the 'punitive turn' in youth justice thinking (Muncie 2008b), the political tide was turning against diversion, as critics (Audit Commission 1996) began to equate diversion (often fallaciously) with the policies and practices of *minimum necessary intervention* and *radical non-intervention* (see Haines et al 2013). Diversionary approaches based on 'hands off' minimum necessary intervention were caricatured and castigated as overly liberal and 'soft' on crime and the causes of crime. Even some proponents of *new orthodoxy* thinking and systems management admitted that these approaches could be discordant with the complex realities of the lives of children who offended, which were often blighted by multiple and deep-rooted social disadvantages (Haines et al 2013). This discordance prompted some practitioners to balance the objectives of new orthodoxy thinking with systems management through relatively intensive interventions seeking to minimise the negative consequences and maximise positive outcomes for children (Haines, in Goldson 2008). Concurrently, political parties fought over a punitive, controlling, law-and-order high ground, which was to be animated by an arms race to 'do something' about youth crime in an overtly *interventionist* manner (see Jamieson 2005; Goldson and Muncie 2006). In 1996 the Audit Commission conducted a comprehensive review of youth justice at the behest of the Conservative government. The resultant *Misspent Youth* report (Audit Commission 1996) was highly critical of diversion in its various forms (for example cautioning, out-of-court disposals, alternatives to custody). In particular, *Misspent Youth* characterised cautioning as an ineffective response to youth offending, as 'letting offenders off' and as doing nothing about youth crime; the positive impact of cautioning was largely overlooked (Allen 1991). *Misspent Youth* (Audit Commission 1996: 22) argued that: 'Cautioning works well for first time offenders ... [but] the evidence suggests that, after three occasions, prosecution is more effective in reducing re-offending than a caution.'

The report also asserted that diversion was not actively 'tackling' crime and instead was prioritising children's welfare (Hart 2012). *Misspent Youth* eschewed traditional forms of diversion grounded in *minimum necessary intervention* and *radical non-intervention*, instead recommending that cautions should be accompanied by a package of support, citing as evidence the numerous 'caution plus' schemes (police caution accompanied by voluntary intervention and support) operating in local areas (Audit Commission 1996). The Audit Commission's rejection of traditional diversion and its recommendations for cautioning plus intervention paved the way for the political retrenchment of diversionary practices and a 180° turn towards an interventionist form of diversion and, indeed, interventionism more generally.

The new youth justice of interventionist diversion

In 1997, the incumbent 'New' Labour government in the UK published *No More Excuses: A New Approach to Tackling Youth Crime in England and Wales* (Home Office 1997; see also Chapter Three). When discussing pre-court disposals, the *No More Excuses* White Paper referred to 'nipping offending in the bud' (Home Office 1997: section 5.10) and stated that:

> The trouble with the current cautioning system is that it is too haphazard and that too often a caution does not result in any follow up action, so the opportunity is lost for early intervention to turn youngsters away from crime. While some areas operate voluntary 'caution-plus' schemes, in others there is no backup to try to prevent further crime. Inconsistent, repeated and ineffective cautioning has allowed some children and young people to feel that they can offend with impunity.

The damning indictment of traditional diversion and the pro-interventionist conclusions of the *Misspent Youth* and *No More Excuses* reports provided the impetus for the provisions of the Crime and Disorder Act 1998, which formally legislated into existence a culture of (early) interventionism across the YJS of England and Wales and a form of *interventionist diversion* (see Kelly, Armitage and Phoenix 2014) within the pre-court system. The Crime and Disorder Act introduced several new youth justice measures focused on diverting children away from the formal YJS, often accompanied by some form of early intervention intended to curtail the child's potential (or without intervention, inevitable) criminal career. The main interventionist diversionary approaches introduced cohered around a revised *pre-court disposals* process and an *antisocial behaviour management* agenda (see following section). A more consistent, clear and more restricted pre-court sentencing process (for police implementation) was introduced, with a new requirement to administer Reprimands and Final Warnings as a replacement to the previous system of potentially indefinite police cautioning for first- and second-time offenders (associated in the minds of minsters and others (often erroneously) with *radical non-intervention* – see Goldson 2000; see also Bandalli 2000; Pitts 2003; Haines and O'Mahony 2006).

In a similarly interventionist (but non-diversionary) vein, the Youth Justice and Criminal Evidence Act 1999 introduced the Referral Order to be used with every 10- to 17-year-old pleading guilty and convicted at their first appearance in court (except in cases serious enough to merit a custodial sentence). Children sentenced to a Referral Order were to be required to attend (with their parents/carers and the victim where appropriate) a Youth Offender Panel (also known as a Referral Order Panel) consisting of two volunteers from the local community and a Youth Offender Panel advisor from the YOT. The Youth Offender Panel was required to put in place a 3–12-month contract of reparation and a package of intervention designed to address the causes of the young person's offending in order to reduce or prevent reoffending. These mechanisms for 'nipping crime in the bud' through intervention in the lives of children were the catalyst for the implementation of New Labour's mantra of 'intervention, intervention, intervention' (Case and Haines

2009; see also Goldson 2000; Pitts 2003; Haines and Case 2008). This also marked a shift away from children-first concerns that youth justice systems should 'maximise diversion wherever possible' (McAra and McVie 2010: 202; see also Holman and Zeidenberg 2006) and towards offender- and offence-focused interventionism, premised on the purported efficacy of intervention and support when compared to a 'true diversion' approach of minimum and non-intervention (Jordan and Farrell 2013; see also Richards 2014).

Antisocial behaviour management

> Children have seemingly become the main focus of concern relating to anti-social behaviour in our communities (Howard League for Penal Reform 2007: 1)

The Crime and Disorder Act 1998 introduced the social construct of *antisocial behaviour* as a serious 'problem' to be addressed through criminal justice legislation – the 'disorder' part of the Act. This 'new domain of professional power and knowledge' (Brown 2005: 203) constructed a new category of problem behaviour that blurred the boundaries between civil and criminal law due to its ambiguous and contested definition, variously considered criminal or non-criminal – contingent on context and professional judgement (for example the behavioural categories of littering, noisy neighbours, hanging around the streets, swearing in public, being drunk and disorderly, graffiti). The ambiguous and contingent nature of the category of 'antisocial behaviour' is best illustrated by the subjectivity and variability of its definitions. The Crime and Disorder Act 1998 defines antisocial behaviour as 'Acting in a manner that caused or was likely to cause harassment, alarm of distress to one or more persons not of the same household [as the accused]', indicating a subjectivity to the definition of the behaviour and its actual and predicted effects/outcomes. Similarly, there has been no consensus as to the nature and range of potential 'antisocial' behaviours and their effects in subsequent government publications (for example RDS 2004; Home Office 2005) and ministerial speeches (for example Prime Minister Tony Blair 2005; Home Secretary Theresa May 2012), indicating an ambivalence at the policy level.

What has not been ambiguous about the antisocial behaviour crusade is the increasing projection onto children of public anxiety and fear regarding the problem of 'youth' (see Wood 2004; Millie 2009; Haines and Case 2007), often due to children's use of public space and consequent visibility (Hayden 2007). The Crime and Disorder Act 1998 ushered in a series of new antisocial behaviour management measures aimed at 'antisocial' individuals, with the targeting of children premised on the assumption that antisocial behaviour is an early indicator of an offending trajectory – thus early intervention with 'at risk' antisocial children would 'nip offending in the bud' and protect communities from the blight of antisocial children – variously labelled as 'youths', 'yobs' and 'hoodies' in the UK media and government rhetoric. Two main antisocial behaviour management measures were introduced:

- **Acceptable Behaviour Contracts (ABCs)** – an early intervention with individuals who are perceived to be engaging in antisocial behaviour. The ABC is drawn up and agreed upon by criminal justice agencies (for example YOTs) and the individual, places prohibitions on the individual's activities and on their 'agreed' responses designed to change their behaviour.
- **Antisocial Behaviour Orders[59] (ASBOs) –** a civil order made against an individual child 'demonstrating' antisocial behaviour (referrals made by police or local authorities) placing prohibitions on behaviour. Provision was made to accompany ASBOs with an Individual Support Order offering supportive intervention (for example from a YOT) to the child to address the issues related to their behaviour. Breach of an ASBO was, however, a criminal offence – illustrating a classic criminalisation process whereby a child can receive a

[59] Although ASBOs were introduced primarily as a housing measure to enable local authorities to deal with 'nuisance neighbours', they rapidly became disproportionately focused on children, driven in large part by neoliberal responsibilising and criminalising governmental discourses such as the 'Respect' agenda, with its accompanying 'Action Plan' and 'Taskforce'.

criminal conviction and experience increased system contact for breaching an order given for 'non-criminal' behaviour.

The Antisocial Behaviour Act 2003 extended the antisocial behaviour management measures of the Crime and Disorder Act 1998. Building on a government White Paper entitled *Respect and Responsibility: Taking a Stand Against Antisocial Behaviour* (HM Government 2003), which made recommendations to allow the government to provide local authorities and the police with wider and more flexible powers to address nuisance crime and low-level incivility. The resulting Antisocial Behaviour Act 2003 widened the use of ASBOs to allow local authorities, registered social landlords and the British Transport Police to apply for them. In addition, Police and Community Support Officers were empowered to issue Dispersal Orders to any group of two or more people, within a designated area, whose behaviour they believed likely to cause harassment, alarm or distress to members of the public. The Act also broadened the availability of Parenting Orders to parents of children who had truanted or been excluded from school (rather than restricted to parents of a child who had offended) and created a statutory basis for Parenting Contracts, wherein parents had to agree to comply with the requirements of the order (HM Government 2003). The broadening of antisocial behaviour powers expanded the net-widening and interventionist influence of the YJS by drawing in children who had not offended and subjecting them to formal intervention (for example ASBOs, notices to disperse, Parenting Orders) which, if breached, constituted a criminal offence – archetypal criminalisation of childhood behaviour in preference to the normalisation of offending behaviour (see Millie, Jacobson, McDonald and Hough 2005).

Local authority areas in England and Wales have typically implemented the governmental antisocial behaviour management measures with children using a tiered/staged system, often coordinated by a bespoke local Antisocial Behaviour Unit (ASBU) (of varying construction and title). The tiered system begins with a *warning letter* to the child and their family (following referral of the child by police or a local authority agency), followed by a second warning letter and/or a *home visit* by an ASBU officer, police officer or YOT worker, followed by the imposition of an ABC and (sometimes as a last resort – see Wilding 2007) application to the court for an ASBO. Tiered antisocial behaviour management practice was officially supported in Home Office guidance recommending that 'these interventions should be used incrementally as independent reports have shown that this is what works' (Home Office 2008: 11; see also National Audit Office 2008).

In practice, most local authority areas chose to animate government policy through a hierarchical, *tiered* approach, with warning letters and home visits employed as precautionary, pre-emptive and diversionary measures that sought to address the underlying causes of antisocial behaviour and to avoid more punitive, regulatory antisocial behaviour management measures such as ABCs and ASBOs. Crawford, for example, has questioned the effectiveness of a hierarchical, tiered response to antisocial behaviour, likening the process to an escalator 'where each subsequent intervention is more serious than the first … movement is always upwards' (Crawford 2009: 825), which serves to 'intensify forms of intervention and hasten punishment' (Crawford 2009: 812). The antisocial behaviour management 'escalator' has been criticised, notably for presenting a veneer of voluntarism, engagement and ownership by children who participate in antisocial behaviour processes, when in practice the threat of legal sanctions for non-compliance (that is, criminalisation and net widening rather than diversion) and coercion into a contract with the state has been inherent in tiered approaches (see MacKenzie 2008; see also Home Office 2008).

Other local authority areas, however, notably Manchester, embraced (and, to a certain extent, proselytised) the 'anti-social behaviour crusade' (Millie et al 2005; Squires and Stephen 2005; Burney 2009) – actively seeking to maximise the use of ASBOs and to flex the range of powers (including for breach) that the Act allowed. A particularly salient issue, therefore, is how local authority areas have chosen to implement approaches to antisocial behaviour by children and with what objectives. Some local areas have animated the escalator through punitive, zero-tolerance, criminalising and net-widening approaches that sweep up vast numbers of children and process them through the tiered system as quickly and forcefully as possible. The most notorious local example in England and Wales is Greater Manchester, dubbed the 'ASBO capital of the UK', which has administered more ASBOs to children aged 10 to 17 years than any other area, including London – an alarming 773 over the period 1999–2012 (MoJ 2013). Commenting on this situation in 2004, Prime Minister Tony Blair heralded the Greater Manchester approach as 'trail-blazing', noting that 'Manchester, of course, doesn't have a worse problem than others on antisocial behaviour. It has just been more determined to root it out' (Blair, *Manchester Evening News*, 28 October 2004). Subsequently, the leader of the Greater Manchester ASBU, dubbed 'Mr ASBO', was seconded as an adviser to the government's antisocial behaviour strategy unit and was awarded an MBE for his work tackling antisocial behaviour by children. In stark contrast, during the same period, the Chief Constable of South Wales labelled the use of ASBOs with children as 'a sign of failure' (Chief Constable Barbara Wilding, Wales Online, 4 October 2007). Accordingly, Wilding instigated a force-wide policy of using ASBOs with children only as a 'last resort', asserting that many complaints regarding the 'antisocial behaviour' of children were actually based on 'normal' childhood behaviour. Generally speaking, however, ASBOs have not been employed as a last resort with children in England and Wales – far from it. From April 1999 to the end of 2009, for example, 7,248 ASBOs were issued to 10- to 17-year-olds, with their use increasing by 178% over this 10-year period (Home Office 2011).

The coalition government has clearly stated their opposition to what they view as the protracted, bureaucratic and expensive nature of existing tiered approaches to antisocial behaviour management. Within the report *More Effective Responses to Antisocial Behaviour* (Home Office 2011), the government outlined a new 'pyramid' of antisocial behaviour interventions, starting with restorative justice, followed by warning letters, then ABCs, rehabilitative and restorative out-of-court disposals, and Crime Prevention Injunctions to replace ASBOs. The coalition's ambitions to phase out the use of ASBOs have been realised in annual statistics (MoJ 2013) regarding their use with children in 2011 (decreasing 30%, from 536 to 375) and 2012 (decreasing

27%, from 375 to 273). The *More Effective Responses to Antisocial Behaviour* report's recommendations for informal and restorative antisocial behaviour interventions are not presented in any degree of detail and there is no discussion of the future role (or even existence) of Youth Inclusion Programmes or Youth Inclusion and Support Panels (see Chapter Six) within early intervention practice. However, what is clearly documented is that, despite an endorsement of existing provision (warning letters, ABCs), the tiered pyramid model is not meant to be a tiered escalator, but rather 'practitioners need to choose the approach most appropriate for the behaviour in question and do not need to start from the bottom' (Home Office 2011: 13), indicating the introduction of a degree of practitioner discretion in line with the coalition's emerging localism and practitioner-focused agendas for the delivery of youth justice.

In Focus • Antisocial behaviour management as early intervention in Swansea

A local approach to the nationally adopted tiered management of antisocial behaviour by children has developed within a context of CFOS, entitlements-based youth justice practice focused on maximising children's engagement and promoting positive behaviour (see Case 2004; Swansea Youth Action Network 2010; see also Chapters Three and Chapter Four). Local antisocial behaviour practice has been founded on multi-agency partnership working characterised by a shared commitment to a common (CFOS) rights-based philosophy that has enabled agencies to work across traditional departmental boundaries. Stable leadership within key stakeholder agencies has enabled a consistency of approach locally to antisocial behaviour by children and the development of solid inter-agency relationships (Hoffman and MacDonald 2011; see also Chapter Six). Processes for dealing with antisocial behaviour by children have developed reflexively through the systematic collection, evaluation and integration of independent research evidence, such as the series of detailed interviews with Swansea ASBU[60] and YOT staff conducted by researchers from Swansea University School of Law (Hoffman and McDonald 2011) and the secondary data analysis and qualitative

[60] The ASBU has been subsumed into the local YOT and consists of two YOT antisocial behaviour officers.

interviews with key stakeholders conducted by Swansea University Centre for Criminal Justice and Criminology (Haines, Case, Charles and Davies 2012).

Annual statistical returns have reflected the local commitment to *diversion* from the tiered antisocial behaviour management system, indicative of a local youth justice practice culture of *minimum necessary intervention*. From 2006 to 2012, the annual use of stage one warning letters has decreased by 84% (from 1377 to 217), stage two letters/visits have decreased by 84% (from 158 to 26), stage three ABCs have decreased by 70% (from 10 to three – although the percentage measure is skewed by the very low numbers of children each year) and only three ASBOs have been administered (Swansea YOT ASB Department 2014). This *de-escalation* of antisocial behaviour management responses has been identified by key stakeholders in interviews with researchers (Hoffman and MacDonald 2011). Practitioners perceive the tiered processes as flexible (rather than mechanical) and discretionary (rather than prescriptive), enabling them to exercise their professional judgement and skills to address the underlying causes of antisocial behaviour and thus to avoid escalating and criminalising responses to children's behaviour. Alongside the local commitment to diversion and de-escalation, a number of other positive characteristics of Swansea's antisocial behaviour management approach were identified by practitioners during interview (see Hoffman and MacDonald 2011), including:

- **Consistency and avoiding net widening** – the tiered approach was thought to enable a consistent and diversionary response to antisocial behaviour by children due to the ASBU having oversight of the allocation of children to antisocial behaviour or criminal processes. The potential problem of the police choosing to deal with incidents as criminal without referral to the ASBU has now been addressed through the creation of the diversionary Swansea Bureau (see this chapter: ' Case study: Children First, Offenders Second diversion through the Bureau model').
- **Constructive multi-agency partnership working** – key stakeholders believed that antisocial behaviour management locally was characterised by effective partnership working underpinned by collective responsibility, shared commitment to (children-first) principled practice, needs-led service provision and the pooling of

expertise. However, issues were raised regarding the lack of participation by certain agencies (notably the Education Department) in the antisocial behaviour partnership process and decision making, along with concerns regarding certain agencies' unwillingness to share information, and the paucity of appropriate structures/procedures within which to locate and disseminate antisocial behaviour information.

- **Voluntarism, engagement and compliance** – interviewees reported that participating children had the tiered approach fully explained to them in the spirit of engagement, transparency, honesty and fairness. Participation in the process, however, was perceived as akin to Field's 'qualified voluntarism in relationships with children' (Field in Hoffman and MacDonald 2011: 164). Practitioners asserted that children (at stage three/ABC in particular) had the consequences of non-compliance explained to them fully and this contributed (at least in part) to their compliance with requirements and encouraged their desistance from antisocial behaviour and engagement with management processes (Hoffman and Macdonald 2011).

Swansea's interpretation and execution of the tiered approach to antisocial behaviour management reflects the degree to which the localised responses to children's antisocial behaviour (Home Office 2011) and offending (Home Office 2011) sought by the coalition government can produce 'spaces for reworking, reinterpretation and avoidance of national and international directives and/or particular socio-political pressures' (Muncie 2011: 52). In Swansea's case, practitioners have mediated national (Westminster government) policy to enable practice to be informed by Welsh government (rights-based) policy towards children (Hoffman and Macdonald 2011) and to fulfil more diversionary objectives, rather than overtly interventionist and regulatory goals.

Interventionist diversion: the obsession with first-time entrants

Following the implementation of the new (diversionary) interventionist measures flowing from the Crime and Disorder Act 1998, concerns began to be expressed regarding the increasing numbers of children processed through the courts following one or two minor offences, who then risked being 'up-tariffed' through subsequent community sentences (NAYJ

2013). Although the new measures were designed to reduce the inconsistency in the use of pre-court outcomes, what they actually did (some argued) was to precipitate the labelling, stigmatisation and criminalisation of children for low-level offences due to their excessive use of (risk-based) targeting (see Creaney and Smith 2014; Morgan 2007). This situation was exacerbated by changes to police practice, notably the introduction in 2002 of a Sanction Detection target for the police to increase the proportion of Offences Brought to Justice (Home Office 2002). The former chair of the YJB, Professor Rod Morgan, has argued vehemently that the Sanction Detection/Offences Brought to Justice target placed considerable and unhelpful pressure on police performance. He portrayed the police as systematically targeting children and everyday youthful behaviour in order to meet these targets, characterising this criminalising practice as 'picking the low hanging fruit' (Morgan 2007) and citing it as a justification for ultimately resigning his YJB position. Indeed, when the Sanction Detection target was amended in April 2008 and thereafter abolished, first-time entrant (FTE) numbers immediately began to decrease, with Morgan (in Children and Young People Now 2012) claiming that: 'All the evidence pointed to the fact that the police were no longer earning Home Office brownie points for criminalising children and young people, not that there was any change in youth behaviour.'

In response to criticisms of its interventionist agenda on both practical and ethical grounds, the Labour government introduced new performance measures for YOTs in 2002 (the precursors to the key performance indicators) in order to target a reduction in the number of children entering the formal YJS. Statistics were collected on the number of direct entrants – those children with no previous pre-court orders or court orders/convictions, and the number of first timers – those children with only one previous Reprimand and/or Final Warning (YJB 2003). These measures were the forerunners to the FTE key performance indicator (KPI), which was introduced in 2005.

The diversionary emphasis of the FTE measure was consolidated by the piloting of additional new measures to divert children away from the formal YJS, rather than diverting them from offending behaviour per se (see Richards 2014), although these measures retained the governmental predilection for early intervention (see Chapter Six) and managerialist interventionism. New diversionary interventions included the following:

- **Penalty Notice for Disorder 2003** – a statutory measure enabling the police to issue penalty notices (constituting a £30/£40 fixed penalty) to anyone committing one of 24 low-level offences. The Penalty Notice for Disorder (PND) measure was extended (from an exclusive focus on adults) to children aged 16–17 years in the Antisocial Behaviour Act 2003 (officially introduced in January 2004). All children receiving a PND were thus excluded from official crime statistics and not formally classed as FTEs. The trend in the number of PNDs given to children was one of annual increases (October–September) since their introduction in 2004/05 (10,575) to 2005/06 (17,791, a 68% increase) to 2006/07 (20,630, a 16% increase). Indeed, a large part of Morgan's rationale for resigning as Chair of the YJB was that the police's excessive use of PNDs was (ironically) criminalising children without their entry into the formal YJS, thus artificially reducing annual numbers of FTEs into the YJS and erroneously suggesting that the YJS was operating in a less punitive and more effective way (Morgan 2007). Since the Sanction Detection/Offences Brought to Justice target was abolished in 2008, annual PND numbers have decreased in 2007/08 (15,417, a 25% decrease), 2008/09 (12,757, a 17% decrease), 2009/10 (8,371, a 34% decrease), 2010/11 (6,607, a 21% decrease), 2011/12 (4,021, a 39% decrease) and 2012/13 (1,410, a 65% decrease). This trend is broadly similar to that for FTEs into the YJS and reflects the changes in police behaviour in response to the Sanction Detection/Offences Brought to Justice target (MoJ 2012)
- **Youth Conditional Caution 2008** – a statutory out-of-court disposal aimed at reducing the number of children taken to court for low-level offending, while also balancing the views of the victim and addressing the behavioural needs of the young person. The measure is available for children aged 16–17 years who have no previous convictions, who admit

guilt and who agree to the caution. The Youth Conditional Caution (YCC) was introduced by the Criminal Justice and Immigration Act 2008. Conditions can be attached to the measure, including rehabilitation, reparation, attendance requirements and/or a fine. The YCC was piloted from 2010 to 2011 in five police force areas in England and Wales, but no results are currently available.

- **Youth Restorative Disposal 2008** – a police-administered, non-statutory, informal, response introduced following the Youth Crime Action Plan 2008 for children aged 10–17 years committing a low-level offence who had not received a previous Reprimand, Final Warning or YCC. The measure was a joint development between the YJB, the Association of Chief Police Officers, the Department for Education and the Ministry of Justice. Piloted in eight police force areas in England and Wales from April 2008 to September 2009, the Youth Restorative Disposal (YRD) is intended as a quick and effective means of dealing with low-level youth offending and antisocial behaviour, based on the principle that early intervention can prevent/reduce youth offending (YJB 2010). The evaluation of the YRD pilot scheme identified initial support from key stakeholders (police and YOT staff), who viewed the measure as a more effective use of their time (compared to formal disposals) and as a valuable opportunity for staff to provide early support and intervention for children at risk of offending in a timely manner (YJB 2011). However, concerns remain over whether YRDs have been fully integrated within broader strategic approaches in local authority areas, rather than being employed as standalone, one-off initiatives (YJB 2011), whether YOT staff have been properly integrated into the YRD process or marginalised by police (for example, informed only after a YRD has been issued) and whether the speed of the YRD process eschews a considered, evidenced approach that guarantees children due process (NAYJ 2013).
- **Youth Justice Liaison and Diversion 2008** – a scheme piloted by the Centre for Mental Health from 2008, with the objectives of identifying children with mental and emotional health or other vulnerabilities when they first came into

contact with the YJS and fast-tracking them into support services, in order to divert them from the formal YJS and to reduce reconviction (Centre for Mental Health 2009). An evaluation of the six pilot sites ran from 2009 to 2012 (Haineset al 2012). The evaluation concluded that children referred to the scheme had multiple, interrelated complex needs, including social, psychological and mental health issues. Data indicated that the scheme had demonstrated some initial success in referring children in need of further intervention to appropriate services or providing them with a brief intervention. However, only two out of the six pilot schemes had succeeded in systematically influencing decisions relating to charge (for example promoting diversion) on a consistent and demonstrable basis.

- **Deter Young Offenders 2009** – a management framework (Home Office and MOJ 2009) replacing the Prevent and Deter strand of the Prolific and Other Priority Offenders (POPOS) programme. The YJB requires that a Deter Young Offenders (DYO) initiative must be in place in every local authority in England and Wales, to be managed by the local YOT and the local Criminal Justice Board. The objective of the DYO framework is to reduce reoffending among those children in each locality who are considered to have the highest risk of reoffending (as measured through Asset and using the Scaled Approach process – see Chapter Four). Official guidance for DYO frameworks (YJB 2009) requires each DYO management board in each local authority area to use the Scaled Approach to identify a cohort of persistent and/or high-risk offenders (no more than 10% of the YOT's total case load), to assess this group regularly and to support them in accessing deterrent/crime reduction services (for example education, training and employment, substance use intervention, mental health provision). Accordingly, the DYO management framework consists of the Scaled Approach, management meetings, Criminal Justice Simple, Speedy, Summary[61] and access to wider children services.

- **Triage 2009** – the Triage model was established under the Youth Crime Action Plan 2008 and began officially in 2009 in 69 local authority areas. Triage is a partnership between the police, YOT and the Crown Prosecution Service targeted at children who have committed low-level offences. The scheme enables YOTs to assess children at the point of arrest (in custody suites) with a view to diverting them from the formal justice system into alternative pre-court disposals (Home Office and MOJ 2009), thus avoiding criminalisation and processing children more quickly through the system (Haines et al 2013). Similar to the Scaled Approach, children are processed by Triage at three levels, depending on their offence seriousness – *diversion* (low offence seriousness), *intervention* and *fast track* into the YJS (for the 'most serious' cases). The central aim of Triage, therefore, is to divert children away from the formal YJS by categorising them as at 'low risk' of reoffending and their offending as 'low-level', then providing (risk-based) preventive and restorative intervention to address offending behaviour and to re-engage the child with mainstream services. The utility of Triage was highly commended by the Independent Commission on Youth Crime and Antisocial Behaviour (ICYCAB), which perceived 'merit in extending triage procedures to children and children who are being considered for a reprimand or final warning' (ICYCAB 2010: 61). An evaluation of Triage (Institute for Criminal Policy Research, for the Home Office 2012) reported positively on its impact on the working relationship between police and the YOTs. However, the same evaluation identified significant shortfalls and local variability in the quality, consistency and availability of local monitoring data, such that it was not possible to properly evaluate or demonstrate the disposal's effectiveness.

[61] A cross-agency programme aiming to deal with and manage Magistrates' Court cases more efficiently, with the key objectives of reducing the number of hearings and reducing the time taken from hearing to disposal.

In contrast to the 1980s ethos of diversion and minimum necessary intervention, the Crime and Disorder Act 1998 had made the case for a prevention/reduction approach grounded in the rehabilitative influence of formal intervention and system contact (as opposed to viewing such contact as deleterious and stigmatising). The expanding scope of interventionism, therefore, ran counter to academic arguments and empirical evidence that contact with youth justice agencies can be iatrogenic and stigmatising (see McAra and McVie 2007). The post-Crime and Disorder Act 1998 measures were intended to complement the FTE KPI, indicative of a 'considerable liberalization in the treatment of "young offenders"' (Smith 2014: 109) through a reduction in formal processing across the YJS and the emergence of a dual focus on diversion and crime prevention and/or reduction (practices that are not synonymous, as we discuss in Chapter Six), with both foci wedded to interventionist measures seeking to reduce and manage FTEs – an increasingly important managerialist KPI. Formal, 'new' youth justice intervention, founded on risk-based 'what works' and Scaled Approach principles, has been criticised as disproportionate and precipitating the labelling and marginalisation of children in trouble with the law (see Chapter Four; see also Haines and Drakeford 1998; Goldson and Muncie 2006; Bateman 2011). However, the Crime and Disorder Act 1998 introduction of antisocial behaviour management measures and new out-of-court disposals (Reprimands, Final Warnings) did not mean diversion from intervention, nor even support for minimum necessary intervention. The out-of-court disposals in particular animated the government's belief in the use of intervention as a means of diversion from the formal YJS (for example reducing FTEs) and diversion from future or further offending (see also Kelly, Armitage and Phoenix 2014; Richards 2014).

Figure 5.1 illustrates a general trend of annual decreases in FTE figures since the introduction of the FTE KPI. Following a slight 3% increase from 2005/06 (107,187 children) to 2006/07 (110,188 children), FTE numbers decreased by 9% in 2007/08 (100,105 children), by 20% in 2008/09 (79,851 children), by 23% in 2009/10 (61,422 children), by 26% in 2010/11 (45,519

Figure 5.1: Annual FTEs into the YJS in England and Wales 2005–13 (May–April)

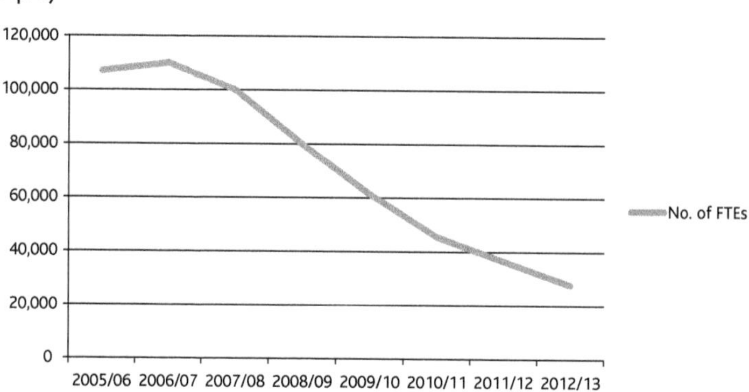

children), by 19% in 2011/12 (36,677 children) and by a further 24% in 2012/13 (27,854 children).

Annual statistical outcomes relating to the reduction of FTEs mirror similar trends in the decreasing numbers of children being processed across the YJS (for example arrest rates, pre-court disposals) in recent years (House of Commons Justice Committee 2013; MoJ, Home Office and YJB 2013). While annual reductions in FTEs have been encouraging, there remains a lack of robust evidence that reductions in FTEs have been caused or even influenced by diversionary youth justice practice. Arguments persist that FTE reductions are, in large part, artefacts of changing police practices. For example, it has been alleged that the (now abolished) Sanction Detection/Offences Brought to Justice target incentivised the police 'to secure formal recordable disposals rather than dealing with minor offences informally' (MoJ and YJB 2013: 22), while following its abolition 'out-of-court disposals are being used over-zealously by the police' (Magistrates' Association, quoted in House of Commons Justice Committee 2013: 20). However, a coherent and comprehensive explanation of the reductions in FTEs has yet to be developed. There are undoubtedly a number of causes and explanations for this trend, including falling numbers of identified offenders each year,[62]

[62] However, this trend is a continuation of annual decreases in the numbers of children identified as having offended that precedes the FTE obsession of 2008 onwards (Smith 2014).

changes in the processing of children and a shift towards various forms of diversionary intervention, but the extent to which the trend is a product of youth justice policy changes is moot.

According to Phoenix, Kelly and Armitage (in Carlile 2014: 9):

> ... whilst a professional wisdom is being developed that diversion has reduced First Time Entrants (FTEs) (i.e. that diversionary practices have prevented young people coming into the youth court), there is no robust evidence on the ground that contemporary practices of diversion are responsible for the reduction in FTEs, in part because of the diversity, variability and complexity of what is being practised.

As a result of the lack of an overarching philosophy of practice for the YJS, there have been significant local variations in the mediation of policy across England and Wales. These local differences have been compounded by the variable adoption, adaptation and implementation of new practice models such as Triage, which has been animated 'in a variety of shapes and sizes ... to meet local needs' (Institute for Criminal Policy Research 2012: 7; see also Sutherland's 2009 conclusion regarding the implementation of the Scaled Approach).

Interventionist diversion: principled or pragmatic?

There has been a significant change in the direction of youth justice interventions and disposals since the coalition government assumed power in the UK in May 2010, heralding what Creaney and Smith (2014: 83) have dubbed 'a new age of diversion'. The incumbent UK government has been heavily critical of the current YJS and its inexorable commitment to an 'hierarchical' and 'escalating' approach to intervention (particularly through out-of-court disposals), expanded and protracted by the introduction of Reprimands, Final Warnings and a plethora of community sentences (since consolidated into a generic Youth Rehabilitation Order in 2009) and antisocial behaviour management measures (see Chapter Six). The nature of the coalition critique has been, therefore, one geared towards financial pragmatism and cost cutting in an era of economic crisis and its resultant austerity measures, rather than necessarily a principled attack on the ill-treatment of children. The net-widening practices and outcomes of the foregoing interventionist diversion measures have been lambasted from a practical perspective as overly expensive and a waste of police time (that is, a bureaucratic burden) rather than for their systems management failings (for example the manner in which they engender excessive, disproportionate and inappropriate decision making regarding children) or for their criminalising impact on children through, for example, labelling and up-tariffing.

The *Breaking the Cycle* Green Paper (MoJ 2010) signalled a shift in policy direction for youth justice in England and Wales to a more nuanced approach where individual circumstances could be taken into account (NAYJ 2013), notably through the diversionary potential offered by out-of-court disposals. The Green Paper (MoJ 2010: 68) asserted that: 'Under the current system of out of court disposals, young offenders are automatically escalated to a more intensive disposal, regardless of the circumstances or severity of their offence.'

Through *Breaking the Cycle*, the government signalled its intention to simplify the current out-of-court disposal framework, rendering it more flexible (for example ending the automatic escalation element) and giving more discretion to youth justice staff (for example police, YOT workers, prosecutors). At the same time, however, the coalition government has retained faith in the diversionary initiatives piloted at the national level under its predecessors (mostly following the Youth Crime Action Plan 2008), such as the YCC, the YRD, the Youth Justice Liaison and Diversion scheme and the Triage model, along with promoting promising local programmes such as Durham Pre-Reprimand Disposal[63] and Swansea Bureau (see later). There is clearly some

[63] A partnership between County Durham YOT and Durham Constabulary (which began in 2007), employing home visit assessments and needs-focused interventions with children aged 10–18 (expanded from 10- to 13-year-olds to 10- to 17-year-olds in 2008 and to 18-year-olds in 2009) who have committed a low-level offence. The objectives of the scheme are to improve outcomes for children, to protect their futures and to reduce FTEs. Early results (2007–10) indicate a 98% completion rate, 50% fewer children reoffending compared to those given Reprimands and a 71% reduction in FTEs (C4EO 2014).

variation between these diversionary schemes in terms of their nature and priorities, with some (for example Triage) seemingly geared towards reducing the workload and time taken in processing children in the formal YJS and pursuing a minimum necessary intervention approach (see Haines et al 2013), others (for example YRD) appear more oriented towards reparative and restorative activity, while others (for example Swansea Bureau) are more committed to addressing the support needs of children (Creaney and Smith 2014).

The recommended changes to the out-of-court disposal system were animated by the Legal Aid Sentencing and Punishment of Offenders Act 2012 (LASPO), which abolished the existing (inflexible, escalatory) out-of-court disposal process of Reprimands, Final Warnings and PNDs and replaced them with a more flexible and discretionary system consisting of: no further action, community resolution, Youth Caution and YCC (expanded to 10–17s under the Act). The LASPO Act 2102 therefore provided space for 'dialogue around costly, net widening, criminalising, counterproductive, and damaging institutional practices' (Yates, 2012: 5). Subsequent guidance given to YOTs regarding the implementation of the new out-of-court system alongside existing diversionary measures (MoJ and YJB 2013) recommended that their assessments of children focus on: *risk* (of reoffending, of self-harm, to the general public), *appropriateness* (of the intervention and of the agency seeking to meet the child's needs) and *engagement* (the child's attitude to interventions, their motivation to participate, the likelihood of family support). The revised pre-court processes are to be underpinned by the AssetPlus assessment and intervention framework (see Chapter Four), with the 'statutory' self-assessment tools for children and families modified into 'prevention' tools for pre-court use by simply removing the term 'offending' from the statutory tool! (YJB 2013).

The coalition's new pre-court system seeks to utilise an interventionist form of diversion to avoid the criminalisation of children through system contact. However, this intent raises the dilemma of exactly how to offer support through (diversionary) intervention without the child acquiring a criminal label through risk-based assessments. It could be argued that, in fact, the revised system offers little to improve children's access to the range of non-offending-based services that could benefit them, while the emphasis on restorative approaches could unintentionally compound the child's negative identity (NAYJ 2013) and embroil them within the very interventionist system they are ostensibly being protected from. Furthermore, there remains a significant potential for practical ambiguities, confusion and conflict across the emerging system, which demands urgent resolution. The status of existing diversionary schemes is unclear, with a pervading lack of clarity over local arrangements to determine how these schemes will fit into the new system of out-of-court disposals. For example, Triage affords a proactive role for outside agencies to support the police in their decision making, but this role has not been formally incorporated into the new pre-court system (NAYJ 2013). Furthermore, the precise or desired relationship between police and YOT staff in delivering diversionary programmes remains unclear, as does any potential role for children or parents/carers in diversionary processes (Haines et al 2013).

Recent developments indicate the re-emergence of a governmental commitment to moving away from restricted, criminalising, punitive and controlling justice-based approaches and towards diversionary measures underpinned by rehabilitation, restoration and practitioner discretion. However, that is not to say that this 'new age of diversion' is the principled, needs-led, holistic and universal model that the political rhetoric of *Breaking the Cycle* and the LASPO Act 2012 may lay claim to. Instead, the government's priority for diversionary schemes appears to be a form of expedited or 'fast track' justice, rather than a considered, consultative and evidenced diversionary approach (Haines et al 2013) – the likely product of economic austerity measures such as the 'pragmatic retrenchment' of universal services and the 'marketisation' (through payment by results incentivisation) of targeted youth justice services (see Creaney and Smith 2014; Cromby and Willis 2014). Therefore, the coalition government's diversionary commitment may represent more of a practical drive for cost-effectiveness (following a re-examination of costly and counterproductive institutional practices – see Yates 2012), a 'minimum (cheapest) intervention' (Smith 2014: 110), rather than a principled or progressive commitment to reorienting how children who offend are perceived and responded to.

The re-emergence of diversion as a central driver of youth justice practice in England and Wales (also internationally, such as in Australia – see Richards 2014), reflects the centrality given to diversion in children's rights conventions. The UN Guidelines for the Prevention of Juvenile Delinquency (the 'Riyadh Guidelines') assert that 'Law enforcement and other relevant personnel … should be familiar with and use, to the maximum extent possible, programs and referral possibilities for the diversion of young people from the justice system' (United Nations 1990: paragraph 58). Similarly, the UN Standard Minimum Rules for the Administration of Juvenile Justice (the 'Beijing Rules') recommend 'dealing with juvenile offenders without formal trial … [and] without recourse to formal hearings' (United Nations 1985: paragraph 11.1–11.2). However, an international debate has emerged regarding the appropriate rationale and objectives for youth justice diversion in practice, beyond the need to meet children's rights. Citing the iatrogenic nature of formal system contact as the key rationale for diversion has received extensive international support (see Holman and Zeidenberg 2006; Wallace and Jacobsen 2012; Jordan and Farrell 2013), but dissenting voices persist. Sceptics question the veracity and breadth of the evidence to support the 'hands off' and 'true diversion' approach, which seeks to avoid the labelling, stigmatising and criminogenic effects of system contact, even arguing that limiting (supportive) intervention could actually increase offending and system contact in the future as children are left to fend for themselves (see Weatherburn, McGrath and Bartels 2012; see also Richards 2014). Furthermore, other diversionary rationales exist, grounded in, among other things, welfarist approaches to meeting children's needs within and (particularly) outside the YJS, along with restorative justice goals. The trajectory and foci of government diversion policy in England and Wales have illustrated these multiple objectives and rationales, oscillating between the desire to avoid iatrogenic system contact, welfarist and restorative ideologies and advocacy of interventionist forms of diversion. Diversionary practice within international youth justice systems is experiencing something of an identity crisis, with opinion divided as to what children should be *diverted from* (for example the YJS, court, custody, offending behaviour) and *diverted to* (for example youth justice versus external supports and interventions, the ability to access their rights, non-intervention), although a general consensus appears to exist regarding the ultimate goal of diversion to prevent offending (see Jordan and Farrell 2013). These concerns will be addressed as we move into a discussion of what a CFOS approach to diversion should look like.

Progressive Children First, Offenders Second diversion

So what would a principled and progressive CFOS model of diversion look like? First and foremost, a CFOS approach to diversion would be holistic and inclusionary, applied to all children, not simply those deemed to have committed low-level offences and those at an early stage in the system (for example, FTEs). It would seek to normalise offending, treating it as an everyday behaviour that exists as only one element of children's complex and multifaceted lives – thus warranting a whole-child approach. It would also pursue the engagement of key stakeholders in the process to maximise the child-appropriate nature of interventions and their potential to promote positive behaviour. Subsequent decision making would take place in evidence-based partnership with children and their families, thus underpinning diversionary objectives with systems management processes and adherence to children's rights to participate and be heard regarding issues and decisions that affect them. In this way, CFOS diversion would seek to divert children *from* system contact, formal youth justice processes (court, custody), offending behaviour and obtaining a criminal record, while diverting children *to* youth justice and non-youth justice interventions and supports. Thus, CFOS maintains that any intervention must be child appropriate and at the minimum necessary level, contrary to contemporary interventionist diversion, which does not prioritise diversion from system contact (see Kelly, Armitage and Phoenix 2014). The potential for just such a principled, informal, non-criminalising, engaging and holistic diversionary model that addresses both the causes of offending and individual needs without recourse to formalised, systemic intervention(ism) is offered by the localised Bureau model (see ICYCAB 2010; NAYJ 2013; see also Haines, Case, Charles and Davies 2013).

Case study: Children First, Offenders Second diversion through the Bureau model

The deleterious effects of youth justice intervention have been addressed through a localised approach to working with children and that is grounded in the children-first principles of diversion, promoting positive behaviour, social inclusion and access to entitlements/rights (see Chapter One). The Swansea Bureau was established in May 2009 as a partnership between Swansea YOT and the local division of South Wales Police, which has developed a contemporary interpretation of the Juvenile Liaison Bureau system by blending the promising features of previous and current diversionary schemes (for example Northamptonshire JLB, Triage, the Scottish Children's Hearings system[64]):

> We pinched pieces from all over the place ... We looked at some work, which was done in Northamptonshire ... We looked at the Scottish

[64] Welfarist- and care-based responses to children who offend have been preferred in Scotland since the Kilbrandon Report (Kilbrandon Committee 1964) and the introduction of the 'Children's Hearings' system following the Social Work (Scotland) Act 1968 (with the system subsequently incorporated into the Children (Scotland) Act 1995). Since 1971, children in Scotland under the age of 16 (in some cases under 18) who commit an offence (except for a serious offence such as murder or life-threatening assault) are referred to the Scottish 'Reporter' by police, social workers, education staff or health professionals (and in some cases by parents and even the child themself). The Reporter investigates the child's circumstances and behaviour before deciding on the next steps to be taken: no action, referral to the local authority (typically a social worker) or referral to the Children's Hearing. Where the latter is chosen, a Children's Hearing Panel is convened, consisting of the child, their parents/carers and three volunteer lay members of the public who have been trained to advise on suitable supervisory measures. The Hearing's recommendations must prioritise the welfare and best interests of the child, but should also consider other circumstances, including the offending behaviour. The structure and format of the Children's Hearing system resonate, therefore, with more restorative and community-based youth justice measures in England and Wales such as the Family Group Conference and the Youth Offender Panel (MoJ 2012). See also Miles and Raynor (2014) for research into the operation of the Parish Hall system in Jersey.

> reporter system. We looked at some processes in Europe, which are much more family orientated ... We sort of melted all three of those elements to shape it into a system, which we think suit the needs of children in Wales. (Swansea YOT Manager 2010)

The partners identified the need to work together in order to change the existing police bail system to divert children from the formal YJS, to enable the identification of the underlying cause of offending and to promote pathways to positive behaviour using comprehensive assessment and by facilitating access to a range of local services. 'The Bureau was intended to do a lot of things, but mainly to change the way that we work with children at the lower end of offending. If we fail the children at that end, then we are storing up problems for the future.' (Senior Police Officer, South Wales Police 2010)

The dual diversionary objectives of Swansea Bureau were, therefore, to divert local children from the formal YJS and from future offending behaviour, with the official aims agreed as:

- to divert children out of the formal processes of the Criminal Justice System;
- to provide a diversionary program that tackles the underlying causes of youth offending by providing mechanisms to promote prosocial and positive behaviour;
- to treat young offenders as children first (Hoffman and Macdonald 2011).

The Bureau began life as an intervention targeted on FTEs who had committed a low-level offence (Offence Gravity Score 1–3 on the ACPO Scale[65]). It is founded on a five-stage process:

1. **Arrest and bail** – following arrest, children admitting to an offence that has a gravity score below 4 have the Bureau process explained to them by a custody sergeant and are

[65] The Association of Chief Police Officers' system to assess the gravity/seriousness of offence, with Gravity Score 4 being the most serious (for example murder, aggravated burglary, kidnapping, GBH/wounding with intent).

bailed (with no formal charge) to participate in the Bureau clinic two weeks later. South Wales Police notify the Bureau coordinator (a South Wales Police officer seconded to Swansea YOT) via an arrest/bail form and the South Wales Police computer system, with this notification triggering stages two and three of the process.

2. **Assessment of the child and their family** – over the course of two weeks (the 'Golden Fortnight'), the Bureau co-ordinator requests information on the child and their family from a range of agencies (for example police, YOT, local social services, secondary schools). This information is collated by the YOT pre-court officer, who meets with the child to discuss and assess the circumstances and underlying causes of their offending, and suggests appropriate actions in response (reparative, rehabilitative, prosocial). This assessment informs a report to the Bureau Panel, which contains a recommendation for either a non-criminal disposal (NCD) (the priority of the Bureau) or formal processing, alongside a bespoke support package.
3. **Assessment of victim's needs** – the YOT victim support officer meets with the victim to solicit their views on appropriate reparative actions and to link them to independent follow-up support. The victim's views are then incorporated into the Bureau report.
4. **Bureau Panel** – the multi-agency Panel (Bureau co-ordinator, police sergeant, a specially trained Referral Order Panel member) convenes to discuss the report and to agree an appropriate response: NCD, police Reprimand, Final Warning or prosecution.
5. **Bureau Clinic** – the child and their parent/carer/representative meets with the Bureau co-ordinator and police sergeant to agree a mutually beneficial outcome.

The Swansea Bureau has been subject to an ongoing evaluation by Swansea University Centre for Criminal Justice and Criminology (CCJC) since its inception in 2009 (Haines, Case, Charles and Davies 2013). The evaluation team implemented a mixed methodology of quantitative data analysis of Bureau statistics and qualitative interviews with key stakeholders to evaluate professional perceptions of Bureau processes. The researchers have worked in evidence-based partnership with the YOT information manager to obtain 10 years of annual data (May–April) on local pre-court decision making in relation to all FTEs into the YJS pre-Bureau (since 2004/05, when reliable record records became available) and following its inception (up to and including 2013/14). Figure 5.2 illustrates the extent and nature of annual pre-court *decision making* for and *disposals* given to FTEs since reliable record keeping began and up until the pre-court process revisions of the LASPO Act 2012.[66] As discussed in Chapters Four and Five, prior to the LASPO Act 2012, decisions for FTEs were restricted to NCD, Reprimand, Final Warning and prosecution (Referral Order, community sentence/Youth Rehabilitation Order, custody).

Prior to the inception of the Bureau, there was a general trend of decreasing numbers of FTEs locally each year (although FTEs increased in 2007/08). Trends in decision making for FTEs were similarly inconsistent in terms of annual numbers of each disposal given and their use as a proportion/percentage of all decisions:

- The number and percentage of *Reprimands* increased in 2005/06 (from 241 to 273, from 66% to 70%), decreased in 2006/07 (from 273 to 192, from 70% to 64%), increased in 2007/08 (from 192 to 256, from 64% to 72%) and decreased in 2008/09 (from 256 to 197, from 72% to 68%). The use of *Final Warnings* reflected a similar alternating trend, but in the opposite direction (decrease-increase-decrease-increase). The number and percentage of Final Warnings decreased in 2005/06 (from 59 to 55, from 16% to 14%), increased in 2006/07 (from 55 to 69, from 14% to 23%), decreased in 2007/08 (from 69 to 49, from 23% to 14%) and decreased (in number) and increased (in proportion) in 2008/09 (from 49 to 45, from 14% to 16%). The use of *prosecutions* displayed no discernible trend – decreasing in 2005/06 (from 65 to 60, from 18% to 15%), then remaining consistently 14% of all disposals used each year,

[66] In April 2013, following the LASPO Act 2012, Bureau eligibility was extended to all local children and all offence levels, beyond its original remit of only working with FTEs who had committed a low-level offence.

Figure 5.2: Decision making for NCDs/FTEs in Swansea 2004–13 (May–April) – percentage of all disposals

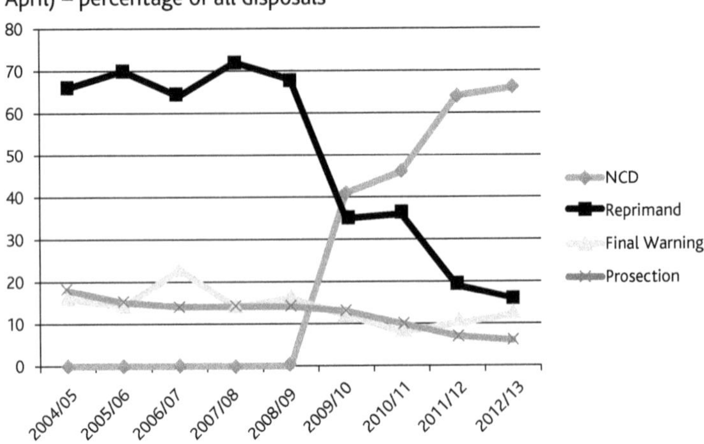

despite their numbers decreasing again in 2006/07 (from 60 to 41), increasing in 2007/08 (from 41 to 51) and decreasing in 2008/09 (from 51 to 47).

Following the introduction of the Bureau, numbers of FTEs (whether NCDs are included in or excluded from the total figure) have decreased annually – a downward trend that has continued in 2013/14 following the LASPO Act 2012 revisions to the pre-court process (see earlier in this chapter). Trends in decision making have been generally consistent in terms of the increased use of NCDs each year, both in number[67] and as a proportion of all decisions. There was an equivalent decrease in the annual use of prosecutions (in number and as a proportion of all decisions), although both figures increased in 2013/14.[68]

While post-Bureau trends have been inconsistent in terms of the use of Reprimands and Final Warnings, the use of these pre-court disposals has in general terms decreased dramatically (from

[67] There was a small decrease of seven in 2012/13 and a further decrease of seven post-LASPO Act in 2013/14 when NCDs became community resolutions.

[68] This increase was the result of 'motoring offences', which are currently not eligible for Bureau intervention and must be brought before the court and subject to prosecution – unlike with adults, where such offences can qualify for out-of-court 'penalty points'. The Swansea YOT manager is in discussion with the South Wales Police and Crime Commissioner to address this anomaly in Bureau eligibility.

2008/09 to 2012/13), with Reprimands decreasing in total by 82% and Final Warnings decreasing in total by 42%. This trend in decreasing pre-court decision making has continued in 2013/14 through the use of 49 pre-court disposals (46 Youth Cautions, three YCCs), a decrease from the 62 pre-court disposals (36 Reprimands, 26 Final Warnings) used in 2012/13. The general trends of *increasing use of NCDs* and *decreasing use of pre-court processes and prosecution* reflects an increased local commitment to diversion from both the pre-court processes and the formal YJS.

The evaluation team has also analysed *reconviction* rates (strictly speaking, *conviction* rates for those children given pre-court disposals) for FTEs over the measurement period – enabling a comparison of pre- and post-Bureau outcomes (see Figure 5.3).

Figure 5.3: Reconviction rate for NCDs/FTEs in Swansea 2004–13 (May–April) – number and percentage of each disposal

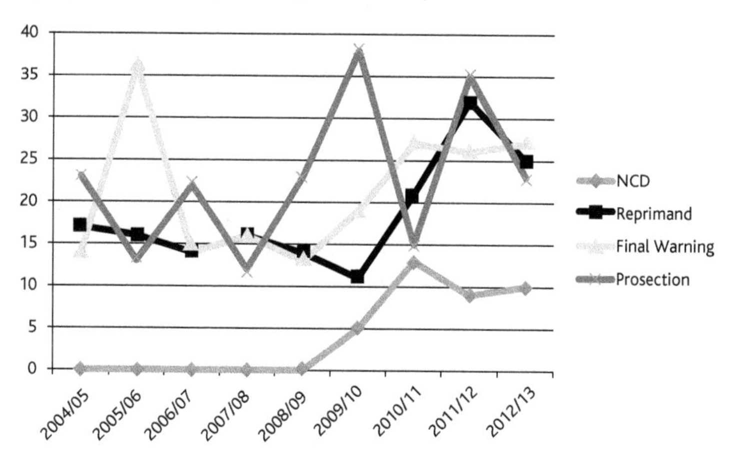

Figure 5.3 demonstrates that the annual numbers of children receiving pre-court disposals or prosecuted who are subsequently reconvicted have decreased appreciably in the post-Bureau years. Although these decreases are not necessarily reflected in the percentage statistics relating to the proportion (%) of children reconvicted having received a particular disposal, it should be noted that percentage statistics are skewed by very low numbers of children in each cell. What is clear from the 2004–13 data, however, is that NCDs result in the lowest rates

of reconviction on average (although the caveat of low cell numbers skewing the data remains), followed by Reprimands, then Final Warnings, then prosecution. While low 'n' statistics for post-Bureau reconviction suggest that caution should be exercised in interpreting this data, the research could find no obvious differences between the children in terms of the way that they had been processed by the YJS compared to those in receipt of an NCD – suggesting that the lower reconviction rates for children receiving an NCD are (at least in part) a product of the nature of the disposal.

Thematic analysis of the qualitative interview data from the Bureau evaluation identified widespread belief among key stakeholders in the positive influence of animating CFOS principles through Bureau mechanisms. The *child-friendly*, diversionary and inclusionary nature of the Bureau was articulated by a senior officer from South Wales Police: 'If we believe in children, we shouldn't criminalise them. Instead, we should try to support them, invest in them, and see them as our future. The Bureau gives us a chance to do that.'

The Bureau focus on *inclusion, engagement* and *participation* is indicative of the delegation of decisions to children and families where appropriate (according with the 'good practice' principles of Harding and Becroft 2013). These foci were supported by a Bureau co-ordinator, who asserted that:

> 'Our Bureau gives kids the chance to get their view across. If they think we haven't taken account of something they can tell us. They can also say if they think we are wrong. I think sometimes they are shocked that we listen to them. But, their views are so important. After all, the Bureau is about them and their lives.'

There was further reflection by a South Wales police sergeant on the effects of engagement, specifically engaging parents through Bureau processes, suggesting the operation of elements of *evidence-based partnership* and *legitimacy* are underpinning Bureau practice: "You find even the ones, the parents who have been through the mill themselves, the last thing they want is for their kids to go through the same. [They] don't want their kids going down that line. They do try."Annual statistical returns (KPIs) demonstrate that the Bureau has exerted a positive impact locally on decision making and (reconviction) outcomes for children. Qualitative data has extrapolated these findings by offering explanations for the decision-making changes and positive outcomes that are congruent with the CFOS principles of inclusion, engagement, participation, partnership and legitimacy.

It has been estimated that the positive outcomes achieved since the implementation of the Bureau have produced 'an annual saving to the public purse of over £2.8 million in Swansea' (City and County of Swansea Cabinet 2013: 110). The Bureau model embodies a minimum necessary, child-appropriate form of interventionist diversion, with proven outcomes of diverting children from system contact and from (future and further) offending behaviour. The approach provides a localised exampled of 'good practice, prioritising principles both of *diversion from* the justice system and of *diversion towards* other forms of intervention to enhance young people's well-being' (Smith 2014: 119). Swansea Bureau has achieved national recognition since its inception: cited as effective diversionary and rights-based practice by the Youth Justice Working Group (Centre for Social Justice 2012), the Independent Commission on Youth Crime and Antisocial Behaviour (ICYCAB 2011), the Ministry of Justice *Effective Practice Library* (MoJ 2014) and the YJB Cymru *Effective Practice Compendium* (YJB Cymru 2012). The apparent faith placed in the efficacy and appropriateness of the Bureau model by YJB Cymru as a means of animating the revised pre-court processes introduced by the LASPO Act 2012 indicates a growing national (Welsh) commitment to articulating CFOS principles in substantive and evidenced diversionary youth justice practice. Reflecting on the early and significant successes of Swansea Bureau, YJB Cymru (the YJB for Wales) has begun a process of rolling out the Bureau model across all YOTs in Wales. At the time of writing, locally mediated versions of the Bureau model are currently in place in 12 out of 18 Welsh YOTs:[69] Bridgend,

[69] A process of YOT reconfiguration and amalgamation has been proposed in Wales that will reduce the number of Welsh YOTs.

Caerphilly and Blaenau Gwent, Gwynedd and Ynys Mon, Carmarthenshire, Merthyr, Monmouthshire Torfaen, Neath Port Talbot, Newport, Rhondda Cynon Taf, Powys, Pembrokeshire and Swansea. The Triage model continues to operate in two YOTs: Cardiff and the Vale of Glamorgan (email communication from YJB Cymru, 2014), while the remaining YOTs have neither model. Early indications are that the roll-out of Bureau is having a similar impact in other YOT areas as it has done in Swansea.

From principles to practice to progress

This chapter has explored the principles, practices and progression of diversion in England and Wales since the peak of its popularity in the 1980s. The Crime and Disorder Act 1998 introduced a governmental preference for *interventionist diversion* over the use of cautioning, Intermediate Treatment and Juvenile Liaison Bureaux that characterised the 1980s 'decade of diversion'. This interventionist diversion emerged from the 1990s 'punitive turn' in youth justice and betrayed a managerialist and 'bifurcated' mindset, wherein diversionary intervention was considered by Smith (2011: 179) as 'only being applicable in practice to those at early stages of the process and in relation to minor offences ... [rather than] ... a principle which infuses all aspects of intervention'.

The result has been a predilection among successive governments for interventionist diversionary measures that (in part at least) seek to avoid the iatrogenic nature of system contact for children by diverting children towards antisocial behaviour management measures, pre-court decision-making and disposals. These pre-court processes have been animated by the government's system-first (not children-first) obsession with the reduction of FTEs. In direct contrast, the Bureau model has delivered a CFOS approach to diversionary practice that is holistic, child friendly and available to *all* children at *all* stages of the youth justice process, child appropriate in nature (more so than minimum necessary intervention per se), constituting diversion from the formal YJS and into external support services where appropriate. The Bureau embodies systems-management thinking in that it slows down the justice process, informing its child-friendly decisions through holistic assessment, by engaging key stakeholders in youth justice processes (children, families, practitioners) and by prioritising evidence-based partnership in pre-court decision-making processes. Importantly, the development of this CFOS approach to diversion has been underpinned by the generation of research and engagement outcomes between key stakeholders functioning as critical friends.

SIX

Progressive prevention-promotion

The previous chapter set out the principles, practices and progression of the use of *diversion* within the youth justice arena. We identified ambiguities surrounding the preferred objectives of diversion (for example avoiding contact with the formal youth justice system (YJS), preventing offending, restorative justice, meeting individual needs by facilitating access to youth justice and external services) and highlighted an insidious movement away from the principle of *minimum necessary intervention* with children and towards a contemporary form of *interventionist diversion* with a restricted group of children – first-time entrants (FTEs) into the YJS who have committed low-level offences. Although recent revisions to the pre-court process have sought to curb the potentially criminalising and net-widening excesses of previous diversionary practice, these developments have been primarily motivated by economic and pragmatic concerns, rather than by a move towards the more principled and (child-) appropriate treatment of children who come to the attention of the YJS in England and Wales. The chapter concluded with a detailed examination of the Bureau model of pre-court diversionary decision making, which served as a potential Children First, Offenders Second (CFOS) approach to inclusionary, engaging, legitimate and evidence-based diversion *from* the YJS and offending behaviour and diversion *to* youth justice and external support services.

In this chapter, we explore the concept of *prevention* as it has been understood and applied within the field of youth justice since being established as the primary duty of the YJS by the Crime and Disorder Act 1998. We discuss how the 'new youth justice' that emerged from the Crime and Disorder Act prioritised reduction and early intervention objectives, such that much activity classed as 'prevention' since then has, in fact, been targeted on the reduction of existing risk (factors) and existing behaviours (for example officially recorded offending) by using risk-focused early intervention into the developmental trajectories of the same risk factors and so-called negative behaviours. We discuss how, consequently, youth justice prevention has animated the negative-facing, interventionist, net-widening tendencies of the risk factor prevention paradigm (RFPP), which is anathema to the principled and promotional objectives of CFOS. We outline a six-stage prevention-promotion constellation that situates targeted reduction and early intervention at one end and more progressive forms of universal prevention and (targeted and universal) *promotion* at the other. A progressive form of prevention is explored in relation to the developing youth justice policy context in Wales, detailed in two key documents: the All Wales Youth Offending Strategy (AWYOS) (which asserts that 'prevention is better than cure') and *Youth Crime Prevention in Wales: Strategic Guidance*. From there, a progressive form of 'prevention-promotion' (as we call it) is discussed, which has begun to promote positive behaviours and outcomes and the protective and enabling factors that may encourage them. This progression is illustrated using three examples: the Positive Youth Development movement in the US, the evaluation of the Welsh government's Extending Entitlement strategy and the case study example of the generational development of prevention-promotion in Swansea. We conclude with a discussion of what a CFOS model of prevention-promotion could look like, drawing upon a localised example of the approach, the Positive Promotion Project, to illustrate the practical application of the model beyond aspirational theoretical frameworks and policy rhetoric that are ultimately undermined by strict adherence to the targeting of risk factors.

Prevention! Prevention. Prevention?

> [I]t shall be the principal aim of the youth justice system to prevent offending (including re-offending) by children (Crime and Disorder Act 1998, section 37)

The UK government rationale for giving prevention pride of place in their 'new youth justice' policy was the belief that many children 'at risk' of offending or engaged in petty first-time offending were not receiving any intervention, or were 'getting away with it' so needed to be held accountable for their behaviour and have their problems addressed by adult-led intervention. The mantra of 'prevention, prevention, prevention' was, therefore, closely allied to an associated mantra: 'intervention, intervention, intervention' (see Case and Haines 2009). Governmental perceptions of appropriate intervention to 'prevent' offending by children have cohered mainly around *early intervention* manifested in practice by the targeting of risk factors for further offending, premised on three central tenets: the earlier the intervention the better, targeted intervention is preferable to universal intervention and the coercive engagement of children is crucial (Blyth and Solomon 2009).

Government prevention policy in the UK since the Crime and Disorder Act 1998 has privileged a particular form of 'prevention' that is *targeted* on children demonstrating exposure to *risk factors* purportedly linked to future offending and reoffending. Prevention policy and practice has cohered around the targeting of specific populations/groups of children identified as being 'at risk' of offending due to their demonstrable (assessed) exposure to a range of 'psychosocial' risk factors for offending and other problem behaviours (for example antisocial behaviour, substance use, serious harm to self and others) located in their personal and immediate social lives (for example in the family, school, neighbourhood, lifestyle). This risk-led agenda is evident across the childcare and health fields in England and Wales more generally, with risk-focused social policy for children proliferating since the Labour government assumed power in 1997. Social policies and practices were introduced to target and reduce the problems of children allegedly 'at risk of a range of negative behaviours and outcomes beyond the remit of the YJS (see France and Utting 2005; Turnbull and Spence 2011), including social exclusion, academic underachievement and disaffection, psychological and physical ill-health, teenage pregnancy, unemployment and poverty (compare *Bridging the Gap* – Social Exclusion Unit 1999; *PAT 12:Young People* – Social

Exclusion Unit 2000; *Every Child Matters* – DfES 2004; *Youth Matters* – DfES 2005).

Targeted crime prevention policy for children in England and Wales contrasts with the prioritisation of universal social policy for children (focused on family, education and community) by approaches employed as a vehicle of crime prevention in other European countries (Allen 2009). Youth justice prevention policy and practice in England and Wales has pursued a risk-led agenda to its fullest in order to meet the dual objectives of preventing offending by children who have been identified by official agencies as on the cusp of offending and preventing *re*offending by existing offenders within the YJS – both objectives being more accurately understood as *reduction* goals due to seeking the reduction of established risk and the reduction of existing problem behaviours (see Case and Haines 2015b). There has been a notable paucity of 'pure', non-targeted and *universal* (made available to all children) prevention policy within and outwith the formal YJS addressing children's needs or universal rights/entitlements to support from adults and the state. Instead, the UK government has prioritised the developmental form of crime prevention, which utilises 'interventions designed to prevent the development of criminal potential in individuals, especially targeting risk and protective factors' (Tonry and Farrington 1995: 2–3).

Risk-focused developmental crime prevention is inherently *interventionist*, neglecting theoretical and empirical evidence that offending and antisocial behaviour are 'adolescence-limited' behaviours (Moffitt 1993) that most children will mature out of (Rutherford 2002) and despite the research evidence that this normalising, maturation hypothesis was a central conclusion of the father of the RFPP (see later in this chapter), the *500 Criminal Careers* study (Glueck and Glueck 1930; see also Case and Haines 2009). As asserted by McAra and McVie (2007: 337): '[T]argeted early intervention strategies, far from diminishing the number of offence referrals, are likely to widen the net of potential recipients even further. Greater numbers of children will be identified as at risk and any early hearing involvement will result in constant recycling into the system.'

Academic protestations from sociologists and criminologists have held that controlling and regulatory formal intervention/ system contact is iatrogenic (McAra and McVie 2007 – see Chapter Five), exacerbating offending (and a range of other negative outcomes) by children due to, among other things, assigning the label of 'offender' to a child, which has a detrimental effect on self-image and leads to self-stereotyping behaviour, negative societal reactions, negative social interactions and restricted life opportunities (see Becker 1963; Lemert 1972). As asserted in the Riyadh Guidelines (1990: para 5f): '[L]abelling a young person as deviant, delinquent or pre-delinquent often contributes to the development of a consistent pattern of undesirable behaviour … formal agencies of social control should only be utilized as a means of last resort.'

Goldson (in Blyth and Solomon 2009) takes issue with targeted early intervention in the youth justice and child welfare fields on no fewer than four fronts: *theoretical* (it leads to labelling), *conceptual* (it precipitates detrimental individualisation and responsibilisation), *practical* (it lacks a robust evidence base) and *ethical* (it is a breach of children's rights to intervene on the basis of what they 'might do' rather than what they 'have done' – see also Case and Haines, in Goldson and Muncie 2015). However, notwithstanding these arguments and despite evidence of successful diversionary youth justice practice in the 1980s (see Chapter Five) the Labour government's 'new youth justice' (Goldson 2000) was underpinned by excessive (risk-led, early) interventionism. In 2006 Prime Minister Tony Blair (31 August 2006) stated confidently that his government 'had to intervene much earlier to prevent problems developing when children are older … If we are not prepared to predict and intervene far more early … the kids a few years down the line are going to be a menace to society and actually a threat to themselves.'

The emerging New Labour policy of prevention through early intervention was couched in the language of welfare (for example meeting children's needs) and (targeted) prevention (for example reducing risk to the child and the public, 'nipping crime in the bud'). As Munro (2007: 41) explains: 'At first sight, a policy of prevention and early intervention … looks beguilingly altruistic. It has many persuasive attractions: it could reduce the amount of distress or harm experienced by the child [and] problems may be easier to tackle while they are still at a low level.'

The reality, however, was quite different. Labour's interventionism was inherently managerialist and controlling/regulatory of children's behaviour, widening the net cast by the YJS to encompass ever younger age groups committing a broader spectrum of youthful behaviours (notably antisocial behaviour), while eschewing 'pure', universal prevention and diversionary principles and practices. The 'new youth justice' approach to prevention through targeted early intervention is illustrated by the practice development that emerged from the Crime and Disorder Act 1998:

- Youth Inclusion Programmes (2000) – established in 2000, Youth Inclusion Programmes (YIPs) were bespoke preventative programmes for 8- to 17-year-olds living in the most socially deprived and high-crime neighbourhoods in England and Wales, with three key objectives:
  - to engage with those children considered to be most at risk of offending and reoffending;
  - to address the risk and protective factors identified by Onset assessments;
  - to prevent and reduce offending through intervention with individuals, families and communities. (YIP Managers Guidance, YJB 2006)

Each YIP worked with children referred by local agencies (for example YOTs, schools) who had been identified by Onset[70] risk assessment as the 'top 50' most 'at risk' of offending in that neighbourhood. Through their risk focus, YIPs targeted the reduction of offending by children, along with the reduction of arrest rates, truancy and school exclusion. Once the child had

[70] Onset was introduced in April 2003 as a referral, assessment and intervention process for use with 8- to 13-year-olds identified by key stakeholders as at risk of offending. The risk-assessment tool broadly corresponds to Asset, containing the main risk sections/domains (living and family arrangements, education, neighbourhood and friends, substance misuse, emotional and mental health, perception of self and others, thinking, behaviour and attitudes, positive factors, vulnerability and risk of harm), which are rated by practitioners as a risk (yes/no) for the onset of offending in the current life of the child.

been identified as 'at risk', YIPs offered risk-focused 'preventive' (reductive) provision such as education and training, sporting opportunities, mentoring, drugs interventions and detached and outreach youth work[71] (see Morgan Harris Burrows 2003). Evaluation of the YIP scheme concluded that YIP staff did not clearly understand the rationale for, or potential impact of, risk-focused intervention. The evaluation further concluded that YIP projects lacked consistent, universal application, lacked an internal coherence (for example, several YIPs were merely a collection of diverse projects) and lacked adequate technical, political, institutional and practical resources (Morgan Harris Burrows 2003). However, the main recommendation of the evaluation was for further research into 'how interventions should be best targeted, tailored and sequenced to address known risk factors' (Morgan Harris Burrows 2003: 14). We have provided a more detailed discussion of YIPs and their associated evaluations in our book *Understanding Youth Offending: Risk Factor Research, Policy and Practice* (see Case and Haines 2009).

- **Youth Inclusion and Support Panels (2003)** – introduced in April 2003 in 13 pilot areas across England and Wales, Youth Inclusion and Support Panels (YISPs) are multi-agency panels of representatives from agencies working with children, typically the statutory agencies of police, probation, health and local authority (for example YOT, education, social services), which aim to prevent offending by 8- to 13-year-olds (or 14- to 18-year-olds in the YISP+ scheme). Children are identified as 'at risk' using Onset and are referred to the YISP for intervention. As explained by the independent evaluators of the pilot YISPs, the Newcastle Centre for Family Studies and Newcastle University (Walker et al 2007: ix): '[U]sing

[71] There are clear overlaps between YIPs and the Home Office Positive Futures youth crime prevention programme (Catch 22 2014) delivered by 91 projects in deprived communities across England and Wales until funding ceased at the end of March 2013 (although over 60% of projects have secured ongoing funding from Police and Crime Commissioners and other local partners). Positive Futures targeted 10- to 19-year-olds considered 'at risk' of offending and substance use through skills-based and prosocial interventions encouraging active and responsible citizenship, such as volunteering, mentoring, sports and artistic activities (Catch 22 2014).

> a matrix of the risk and protective factors which may lead children into, or protect them from, crime, the YISPs were tasked with constructing a personally tailored package of support and interventions… to facilitate the kind of provision which will prevent the child moving further towards crime.'

The evaluators identified serious gaps in available assessment data across the pilot YISPs (only 229/403 of cases (57%) contained what was rated as 'complete' assessment data that could be subject to evaluation), although they still felt able to proffer certain quantitative conclusions, particularly that children demonstrating high levels of assessed risk at referral were more likely to benefit from risk reductions through YISP participation, especially if they were at the older end of the 8- to 13-year-old remit. YISP practitioners interviewed by the evaluators identified a consistent risk focus underpinning referrals to the scheme, notably around risk factors related to education, neighbourhood, lifestyle and emotional/mental health. Interviews with parents of participating children asked about any improvements in the child's behaviour that could be explained by the factors in the Onset risk domains (that is, a self-fulfilling, restricted explanatory exercise) and concluded (unsurprisingly and inevitably) certain risk-related behavioural improvements following referral to the YISP (for example improved attitudes and behaviour at home and in school, reduced offending and antisocial behaviour). However, the evaluators also concluded that these improvements did not necessarily persist once YISP involvement had ended. The evaluators made the tentative conclusion that YISP activities (for example constructive leisure programmes, skills development, training and mentoring, increased parental support) could create supportive and constructive contexts for children's behaviour to improve within (Walker et al 2007: 23), such that the interventions:

> may not themselves have had an impact on the children … [but] some of the changes in circumstances may well have been facilitated by the fact that the child had been referred to the YISP and members of the multi-agency panel had been able to commit resources to affecting change in the family's life.

- **Prolific and Other Priority Offenders Strategy (2004)** – in 2004, the Youth Justice Board (YJB) published the Prolific and Other Priority Offenders Strategy, otherwise known as POPOS (YJB 2004). The strategy was divided into three strands: Prevent and Deter (to prevent offending and to prevent the escalation of offending), Catch and Convict (to actively seek to arrest and sentence offenders) and Rehabilitate and Resettle (to intervene in the lives of offenders to reduce reoffending). In their guidance to YOTs, the YJB explained the purpose of the Prevent and Deter element of the strategy (replaced in 2009 by the Deter Young Offenders (DYO) management framework – see Chapter Five) as the use of prevention 'to tackle the risk factors that may drive their [children's] offending behaviour', but through an early intervention approach of 'identifying and targeting those most at risk of offending with appropriate intervention programmes' (YJB 2004: 7). A review of the first five years of POPOS recommended that local authority areas should review their Prevent and Deter programmes in the light of their recent conversion to DYO schemes (including recommendations to fully utilise the risk-based Scaled Approach as the key vehicle to identify children for the scheme) and that areas should maximise the engagement of local children's trusts and services (with no mention of engaging children themselves) in meeting children's needs (Home Office and MoJ 2009).
- **Youth Crime Action Plan (2008)** – in their final piece of significant youth justice legislation before relinquishing power, the Youth Crime Action Plan (YCAP), the Labour government committed to 'cutting the number of children entering the criminal justice system for the first time by preventing youth offending' (Home Office 2008: 9). The twin objectives to achieve this aim were to identify (target) and work with children 'at greater risk of offending' and to offer children 'positive and engaging activities' (Home Office 2008: 27). The YCAP highlighted the work of children's trusts (a development confined to England), multi-agency Crime and Disorder Reduction Partnerships (called Community Safety Partnerships in Wales) and cooperation between YOTs,

police, schools and third sector organisations (such as voluntary agencies and charities) in addressing psychosocial risk factors, particularly psychological (for example temperament, attention deficit hyperactivity disorder, low IQ) and family based (for example low maternal IQ, maltreatment, parents convicted of a crime *known* to be associated with offending by children). Alongside these extant multi-agency risk-focused interventions, the YCAP committed the YOT in each local authority area and others to the expansion of a range of parenting support services (for example Sure Start Children's Centres, Parent Support Advisers, Parenting Early Intervention Projects, Family Intervention Projects) and risk-based and prosocial interventions (for example Full-Service Extended Schools, Positive Activities for Children Grants, the Youth Opportunity Fund), all designed to prevent offending through enhanced levels of formal and informal intervention in the lives of 'at risk' children and their families. The underpinning ethos of this interventionist agenda, however, was largely one of responsibilisation, driven by a perception of children and their parents as troublesome, risky, irresponsible and feckless in the absence of intensive and coercive levels of formal 'support'

The prevention policy and practice developments of the Labour government within and beyond the Crime and Disorder Act 1998 are clear examples of risk-focused targeted early intervention practice seeking reduction goals, rather than prevention per se. While the measures all aim to prevent offending (in the sense of first-time and officially recorded offending) by children, they prioritise the reduction of extant measured risk factors and extant measured problem behaviours and outcomes in the child's life, rather than the prevention of these issues emerging in the first place. This agenda was articulated in the YJB publication, *Towards a Youth Crime Prevention Strategy* (Ashford 2007), which privileged risk-based, targeted crime prevention on the basis that:

> Mainstream or universal services alone are not able to deliver the corporate aims of the youth justice service and there is clear evidence that services are still failing to reach the most socially excluded who

> are particularly exposed to the risk (and absence of protective) factors associated with offending … targeted and sustained early prevention programmes are needed. (Ashford 2007: 4)

The prevention of offending by children in England and Wales under the Labour government (1997–2010) was animated by *neoliberal correctionalism* – seeking to 'correct' and reduce the 'problem' of offending by (adults) targeting perceived deficiencies in the individual (child), including the choice ('agency') to offend and/or to not attempt to resist risk, for which the child is held responsible (*neoliberal* prevention). This agenda labels children as 'offenders', as 'risky' or 'at risk' of offending ('pre-offenders'), pursuing offender-first and offence-first youth justice prevention that is retributive, punitive, coercive, interventionist and which, it has been argued, can have deleterious consequences for children, such as criminalisation and deviancy amplification (compare McAra and McVie 2007; Goldson 2008; O'Mahony 2009; Bateman 2011; Paylor 2011). Furthermore, tailoring prevention projects around the risks presented and experienced by children 'can serve to consolidate negative representations of the risk posed by young people (or "define deviance up") and give credence to the notions of choice and intractability that underpin punitive policies. Meanwhile, alternative justifications for youth provision are silenced' (Kelly 2012: 101). By linking prevention inextricably to risk and negative behaviours and outcomes, the neo-correctionalist and neoliberal Labour approach to prevention fosters reductionist, regressive and repressive preventive youth justice that individualises explanations for behaviours and outcomes, responsibilises children (and their families) for these behaviours and outcomes. Neo-correctionalist, neoliberal prevention, therefore, eschews more progressive models that facilitate children's strengths, potentialities and capacity for prosocial and positive behaviours and outcomes through their consultation, participation, engagement and enablement (by adults) to access universal entitlements and rights.

In Focus • The risk factor prevention paradigm – anathema to Children First, Offenders Second

It is evident that much of what the UK government has espoused as 'prevention' in youth justice terms following the Crime and Disorder Act 1998 can be more accurately defined as *targeted early intervention* – with this targeting and intervention focused on assessed 'risk factors' for offending and reoffending. Indeed, the objective of targeted early intervention has been primarily *reduction* rather than prevention, specifically the reduction of (the risk of) negative behaviours and outcomes such as reconviction, reoffending, serious offending, persistent offending, antisocial behaviour, substance use, social exclusion, teenage pregnancy, educational disaffection, poor physical and/or psychological health, and serious harm to self and others (Case and Haines, in Goldson and Muncie 2015). The prioritisation of targeted early intervention as the means with which to achieve reduction goals has been underpinned and driven by the Risk Factor Prevention Paradigm (Hawkins and Catalano 1992), itself derived from the public health model of responding to risk. Farrington (2007: 606) has articulated the RFPP as a user-friendly vehicle: 'The basic idea ... is very simple: Identify the key risk factors for offending and implement prevention methods designed to counteract them. There is often a related attempt to identify key protective factors against offending and to implement prevention methods designed to enhance them.'

Following Farrington, youth justice practice targeting the 'prevention' offending behaviour by children in England and Wales (indeed across much of Europe – see Görgen, Evenepoel, Kraus and Taef 2013) has its practical and technical foundations in the RFPP, whether it be targeted risk assessment through Onset and Asset, interventions with children considered to be 'at risk' of offending for the first-time (for example YIPs, YISPs), the Scaled Approach assessment and intervention framework used with children in the formal YJS or significant elements of the new AssetPlus model (see Chapter Four).

We have been heavily critical of the methodological and evidential weaknesses of the RFPP. This critique is detailed at great length elsewhere (Case and Haines 2009; see also Case 2006, 2007; Haines and Case 2008; Case 2009) and so we do not wish to revisit it here. However, this is an opportune point at which to critically evaluate the RFPP in relation to progressive and ethical CFOS principles. The RFPP is not guided by principles; it is a practical, technical, managerialist and adult-centric framework that reduces children to a quantifiable risk factor score/statistic to be targeted through adult-led risk-focused intervention. The technicised, automated manner in which YOT practitioners are obliged to animate the RFPP (see Pitts 2001; Case 2009; see also Chapter Four) is *reductionist*, child *un*friendly and child *in*appropriate in the extreme. Children are reduced to a dehumanised bundle of risks with little contribution to make in understanding and shaping their own lives; practitioners are reduced to deprofessionalised automatons ('handmaidens of the status quo' – Piven and Cloward 1982) deprived of the capacity to utilise their experience, expertise and discretion; the child–practitioner relationship is reduced to a time-restricted, technical exercise where the view of neither party is particularly valued. Such reductionism begets the disengagement of the two key stakeholders in the youth justice assessment and intervention process – children and practitioners (see Case and Haines 2014b). The overriding neglect of the perspectives and expertise of children and practitioners in terms of understanding and responding to children's lives, experiences and behaviours fosters artificial, invalid methods, findings and outcomes/recommendations from assessment that do not necessarily reflect children's lived realities; not to mention the practice realities of YOT staff and their views of 'what works' in their own experience and with that specific child. This is exclusionary prevention, not the *inclusionary*, participatory and engaging prevention work inextricably linked to the child-friendly and child-appropriate processes and outcomes of CFOS.

Neither can such detached, prescriptive, risk-focused relationships between children and practitioners be seen as *evidence-based partnership* – the extent and nature of the 'evidence' is reduced and prescribed by the risk-assessment instruments used and their associated privileged interventions proclaimed as 'what works' (leading to programme fetishism – see Chapter Two), while any 'partnership' is restricted to the 'efficient' and 'reliable' completion of the prescriptive, pre-emptive tick-box risk-assessment instruments that drive assessment and shape intervention. The enforced nature of the child–practitioner relationship is problematic enough when desiring the engagement and participation of the child (see Chapter Four for a fuller discussion of these issues), yet the RFPP compounds this enforced nature by placing pressure on the child and practitioner to ensure the success of any interventions recommended by the assessment process, regardless of disengagement and invalidity issues (Case and Haines 2014b).

It could be argued that, in accordance with CFOS principles, the RFPP responsibilises some adults (practitioners) to facilitate children's access to and engagement with interventions and supportive services. However, the foundation of the RFPP is one of responsibilising children for their offending (or the problems associated with it), for their own exposure to risk factors and for their (in)ability to extricate themselves from their own problematic circumstances without adult intervention. Furthermore, the seemingly indisputable requirement for adult-led intervention fostered by the RFPP promotes net widening and interventionism, whether it be through the use of Onset risk assessment (to underpin YISPs and YIPs) when a child is considered 'at risk' before entry to the pre-court or formal court systems or the use of Asset risk assessment at the pre-court stage (for example, to inform community resolutions, Youth Cautions and Youth Conditional Cautions) or the use of the Scaled Approach across the formal YJS. Consequently, the RFPP runs counter to CFOS principles of child-friendly diversion, with its inherent interventionism anathema to any child-friendly *diversion* ethos. The interventionist inherent net widening and targeting by the RFPP inevitably leads to the formal YJS working with increasing numbers of children targeted for an increasing range of behaviours (some constituting offending, some simply considered 'problematic', such as certain antisocial behaviours) at increasingly younger ages (for example, incorporating children as young as eight and nine years old within YIPs and YISPs, despite the age of criminal responsibility being 10 years in England and Wales). By individualising the so-called 'causes' of children's offending and by responsibilising children and practitioners to treat and cure the 'problem' of offending behaviour and associated 'problems' through restricted, prescribed and risk-focused assessment and intervention frameworks grounded in the RFPP, the 'state' (government in this case) is not *working with* key stakeholders, but instead *doing to* children by compelling practitioners to enforce a reductionist, negative-facing and criminalising paradigm that runs counter to the CFOS philosophies of practice.

Coalition prevention: more of the same?

The governmental push for targeted early intervention (couched as prevention) over diversion and universal prevention as the most appropriate and 'effective' (practically and financially) response to the behaviour of children who come to the attention of the YJS and associated agencies (for example social services, health, education) has shown no signs of abating since the demise of the Labour government. In 2011 the UK coalition government's Under-Secretary of State for Prisons and Youth Justice, Crispin Blunt, asserted that most existing prevention programmes in England and Wales actually 'target' children on the cusp of offending, justifying the need for more investment in early intervention (Children and Young People (CYP) Now 2011). In October 2012 Prime Minister David Cameron confidently asserted that 'prevention is the cheapest and most effective way to deal with crime. Everything else is simply picking up the pieces of failure that has gone before' (Cameron 2012, speech to the Centre for Social Justice). However, an offender-first and offence-first, reduction-based prevention agenda has emerged from the coalition government and has been articulated in their early youth justice policy and practice legislation:

- ***Breaking the Cycle: Effective Punishment, Rehabilitation and Sentencing of Offenders* (2010)** – the *Breaking the Cycle* Green Paper advocated for more emphasis on prevention work in the YJS. However, the coalition set out an early interventionist prevention (reduction) agenda committed to the notion that 'intervening early in the lives of children at risk ... [is] our best chance to break the cycle of crime' (MoJ 2010: 68). *Breaking the Cycle* therefore consolidated the existing risk-based, targeted early intervention trajectory of the 'new youth justice' and also consolidated the foregoing YCAP agenda of *responsibilisation* (tempered by supportive intent) – responsibilising children through the use of restorative justice as an 'informal intervention' to enable children to 'face up to the consequence of their crime, provide reparation and prevent further offending' (MoJ 2010: 68) and 'responsibilising parents who refuse to face up to their responsibilities' (MoJ

2010: 68) by enforcing more Parenting Orders alongside providing more parenting skills support. *Breaking the Cycle* also contained the recommendation to incentivise successful prevention activity locally through a 'payment by results' model, which introduces the potential for the (unprincipled, anti-CFOS) manipulation of practice and outcomes to achieve performance targets (similar to Morgan's accusations that the police overused the Penalty Notice for Disorder disposal to artificially reduce first-time entrant (FTE) figures).

- ***Prevention Matters: How Sustained Investment in Prevention Programmes Has Reduced Youth Offending* (2009)** – the *Prevention Matters* publication details the youth justice work conducted over the past 10 years aimed at 'preventing children and young people from becoming involved in crime' (YJB and CYP Now 2009: 2). Using local case study examples and testimony from children who have desisted from offending, the publication champions 'a robust raft of targeted interventions' (YJB and CYP Now 2009: 2), notably YIPs, YISPs, Safer Schools Partnerships and parenting programmes, which have purportedly demonstrated success and cost-effectiveness in reducing annual numbers of children entering the YJS (that is, FTEs – previously heralded as a *diversionary* objective – see Chapter Five), reducing reoffending rates and reducing custody levels. By espousing and conflating multiple objectives and outcomes (diversion, reduction, prevention), *Prevention Matters* paints a confused picture of prevention activity – using the term 'prevention' as a catch-all for a range of governmental pre-court and court practice;
- **Independent Commission on Youth Crime and Antisocial Behaviour (2011)** – as discussed in more detail elsewhere in this book (see, for example, Chapters Three and Five), the 'blueprint for reform' of the YJS provided by the Independent Commission on Youth Crime and Antisocial Behaviour (ICYCAB 2011) heavily criticised the 'new youth justice' of the previous Labour government for its 'adultifying' tendencies (treating children as adults) and for targeting and criminalising children. A recommended reform principle was an increased emphasis on *prevention*. However, the ICYCAB remained wedded to risk-based targeted early intervention

and responsibilisation over broader considerations of the universal prevention and children's rights agendas (Case 2011), articulated by its assertion that 'an understanding of "risk" and "protective" (or "promotive") factors provides a valuable basis for planning and implementing prevention strategies' (ICYCAB 2010: 39).

- **Early Intervention Grant (2011)** – the coalition government's commitment to early intervention as prevention was formalised in 2010 by the establishment of an Independent Commission on Early Intervention, tasked with identifying best practice models of early intervention which 'ensure that children at greatest risk of multiple disadvantage get the best start in life ... to help fulfil their potential and break the cycle of underachievement' (Department for Education website, August 2010). The Commission's recommendations for effective early intervention practice were supported by the Department for Education's Early Intervention Grant, a new funding stream (in England only – education is a devolved policy area in Wales) to subsidise local authority provision of early intervention and preventive services and to replace funding streams for existing early intervention initiatives (for example Sure Start Children's Centres, Youth Opportunities Fund, YCAP, Children's Fund, Positive Activities for Children). The government allocated £2,222 million to the scheme in 2011-–12, rising to £2,307 million in 2012–13, but spending on the initiative decreased to £1,709 million in 2013–14 and £1,600 million in 2014–15, largely due to service funding cuts during the period of economic austerity. While the Early Intervention Grant can provide funding for universal programmes and activities for children and their families, it has been used mainly for the funding of targeted services for those in need of intensive support (for example Sure Start, targeted support for families with multiple problems, targeted mental health provision in schools). However, National Audit Office reports have drawn attention to difficulties in implementing these schemes and their propensity to produce poor outcomes (see NAO 2008).
- **Legal Aid, Sentencing and Punishment of Offenders Act 2012** – as discussed in detail in Chapter Five, the Legal Aid and Sentencing and Punishment of Offenders Act 2012

> (LASPO) offered clear indications of the new government's intentions to improve the YJS, most specifically through a new pre-court disposals process created to replace the previous punitive and inflexible systemic responses and usher in non-criminalising, systems-management-led, diversionary responses. Explicit discussion of 'prevention' was limited in the LASPO Act, but the reorientation of pre-court processes suggests a tentative progression from risk-led targeted early intervention (at least for first-time offenders) and towards the prevention of entry into the formal YJS.

The coalition government has continued along a path of criminalisation and interventionism when it comes to the prevention of offending by children, with an unflinching commitment to the neo-correctionalist, neoliberal targeting of particular children (and their families) and risk factors and prioritising the reduction of existing and emerging problem behaviours in children's lives. This offender-first approach has privileged the child's status as an 'offender' in possession of, and presenting, risk and consequently problematises rather than normalises offending and other childhood behaviours. However, government investment in both (targeted) prevention and universal services has been significantly diminished in recent times (Cleary and Smith 2014). Therefore, recent moves towards *interventionist diversion* as prevention (see Chapter Five) and a move towards a more child-friendly AssetPlus assessment and intervention framework (see Chapter Four) may not imply that government thinking regarding the prevention of offending by children is becoming more flexible and child focused (despite much legislation and policy thus far reinforcing the risk-based trajectory of prevention since the Crime and Disorder Act 1998). Indeed, others argue that policy and practice changes have been driven by economic concerns (for example to prevent the costly processing of children in the YJS) and to rationalise service provision and resource allocation in the context of budget cuts (see, for example, Peters 1986; Yates 2012; Smith 2014).

The prevention-promotion constellation

The notion of prevention with children in the youth justice field has been at best ambiguous and at worst misrepresented since the Crime and Disorder Act 1998. Much alleged prevention activity has been targeted early intervention with crime reduction objectives, reflecting a governmental predilection for the practical efficacy of the RFPP (see previous In Focus box); a predilection that has been reflected in prevention work with children outside the YJS, for example in relation to health and social care, youth work and childcare, wherein children have been held 'individually responsible for their current, or potential future, negative outcomes and, therefore, subject to some form of preventative intervention based upon their perceived future risk' (Turnbull and Spence 2011: 943). Indeed, much prevention work with children in England and Wales can be situated at the (targeted) centre of a tiered 'hierarchy' of intervention (compare Paylor, Measham and Asher 2012; Early Intervention Foundation 2014; Robinson 2014) – moving from primary prevention through universal, mainstream services (for example schools, work-based training, information services, doctors) to secondary prevention through targeted early intervention (for example YIP, YISP, Triage, Bureau, antisocial behaviour management, harm reduction programmes) to tertiary prevention through specialist, intensive services (for example court-ordered YOT provision, drug treatment, secure accommodation, special educational needs service).

It is possible to argue, however, that targeted reduction and early intervention services packaged as prevention are distinctly English phenomena that occupy specific positions along a discernible, six-stage prevention-promotion constellation of the principles, policies and practices for working with children that works from universal and targeted *promotion* (mapping onto universal, mainstream services) to *universal prevention* and *targeted early intervention* (mapping onto targeted services) to *targeted reduction* (mapping onto specialist, intensive services):

1. the *universal promotion* of characteristics and circumstances (for example exposure to 'enabling factors' linked to enhanced access to rights/entitlements – Haines and Case 2009) that promote positive behaviours and outcomes (for example competencies, strengths) (for example the CFOS model – Case and Haines 2011; Haines and Case 2012; Case and Haines, 2015a);the *targeted promotion* of characteristics and circumstances (for example ability to access rights/entitlements) that promote positive behaviours and outcomes (for example competencies, strengths) (for example 'Positive Youth Development' – Catalano, Berglund, Ryan, Lonczak and Hawkins 2004; *Positive Futures* – Catch 22 2014; Promoting Prevention – Haines and Case 2005);
2. the *universal prevention* of negative behaviours and outcomes for all children (for example the AWYOS – WAG and YJB 2004);
3. the *targeted early intervention* into the established behavioural trajectories of children identified as 'at risk' of negative behaviours and outcomes (for example *Youth Inclusion and Support Panels* – Walker et al 2007; *Youth Inclusion Programmes* – Morgan Harris Burrows 2003) and experiencing critical transitions that may trigger negative behaviours and outcomes (Early Intervention Foundation 2014);
4. the *targeted reduction of risk* (factors) of negative behaviours and outcomes for (convicted) children within the YJS (for example the Scaled Approach to assessment and intervention – Sutherland 2009; YJB 2010);
5. the *targeted reduction* of established negative behaviours and outcomes for (convicted) children within the YJS (for example Offending Behaviour Programmes – YJB 2003b).

Each of these approaches can be discerned within contemporary youth justice prevention and social policy for children in England and Wales (and internationally) and each represent different and distinct approaches (see Case and Haines 2015b). Rather than viewing the necessity for contact with the YJS (a specialist, intensive service) as the total failure of the targeted and universal services that precede the system, a CFOS approach to youth justice prevention seeks to work with and retain children at the promotional, universal, mainstream levels of intervention where possible, in accordance with the principles of social inclusion, diversion, facilitating access to entitlements and promoting positive behaviour and outcomes (see also Creaney and Smith 2014; Robinson 2014). The degree to which such principles have been pursued and achieved is explored in the following sections.

In Focus • Prevention and the vexed question of measurement

The inability of the YJS to extricate itself from focusing on the *reduction* of existing problems (for example exposure to risk factors) and negative behaviours (for example offending, antisocial behaviour), combined with *early intervention* to 'prevent' their reoccurrence, escalation and persistence, could be an inevitable by-product of the managerialist pull towards *measurement*. Performance measurement and management pervades the YJS (see Chapter Four). The definition of *prevention*, the first of 13 performance measures (the precursors to key performance indicators (KPIs)) was 'to reduce the involvement ... of young people who are "usually resident" in the Yot area, who receive a "substantive outcome" for ... vehicle crime ... domestic burglary ... robbery' (YJB 2012: 56). Therefore, the original prevention performance measure for practitioners was clearly based on reduction. Indeed, the KPIs that have replaced the 13 performance measures (see Chapter Four) prioritise reduction (and to a lesser extent, diversion) – the reduction of FTEs, reoffending and custody, with no mention or measure of *prevention*.

The inherent difficulty with pursuing prevention as the primary duty of the YJS is that it relies on producing *evidence of absence* – the absence of risk and the absence of negative behaviours. This has encouraged systemic responses focused on the initial measurement of demonstrable, pre-existing problems and behaviours so that subsequent measurement following system contact can evidence their reduction or cessation. The immediate issue here is, at what point can we confidently claim that a problem or behaviour has ceased (that is, been prevented)? When do we stop measuring for its absence? What is needed, therefore, is the further development of measurable positive outcomes and behaviours to enable YOT practitioners to prioritise the *promotion* of what children need, what they want, what they should have and what they are entitled to. This issue is discussed further in this chapter in the context of Positive Youth Development, enabling factors and the positive outcome measure of 'perceived level of access to entitlements' (PLATE).

Progressive prevention in Wales?

A growing movement of academics, politicians, policymakers, policy advisers and progressive practitioners has begun to identify and assert significant divergences between England and Wales in relation to their approaches to prevention (at least in policy terms) with children within and outside the YJS (see, for example, Edwards and Hughes 2009; Haines 2009b; Morgan 2009; Drakeford 2010). Social policy making for children in post-devolution Wales has adopted a more explicit and principled focus on meeting the requirements of the United Nations Convention on the Rights of the Child (UNCRC) than has been the case in England. Both the *Seven Core Aims* and Extending Entitlement have pursued a distinctive social and legislative identity for Wales by prioritising social justice, progressive universalism (for example in relation to service availability/access and delivery), equality of outcome, engagement, participation and access to rights/entitlements for children, whereas England has pursued a more opportunities- and responsibilities-focused strategy (see Chapter Two for a more detailed explanation of the CFOS themes and Chapter Three for in-depth discussion of policy divergences; see also Haines 2009; Drakeford 2010). Consequently, there are substantive differences and tensions between England and Wales in terms of their respective strategies/policies for children as they relate to prevention, which have been manifested in an influential youth justice policy proclamation emerging from post-devolution Wales – the AWYOS (WAG and YJB 2004).

All Wales Youth Offending Strategy: progressive prevention?

The AWYOS is the 'national framework for the prevention of youth offending and re-offending among children in Wales … underpinned by the UN Convention on the Rights of the Child' (WAG and YJB 2004: 1; see also Chapter Seven). It espouses the key principle that 'prevention is better than cure' (WAG and YJB 2004: 3) by articulating a strategy focused on children's *welfare* and *rights* (in accordance with Welsh social policy for children – see Chapter Three) and, most notably, the treatment of children who offend as 'children first and offenders second' (WAG and YJB 2004: 3). However, these progressive elements of prevention are presented alongside the overarching goal of the targeted, risk-based prevention of offending (in accordance with youth justice policy for England and Wales). The AWYOS attempts to accommodate and reconcile the disparate and distinctive philosophical positions of the Welsh and English governments, which results in a mishmash and uneasy conflation (even conflict and contradiction) between the respective approaches, illustrated by the strategy's approach to animating the prevention agenda. The AWYOS (WAG and YJB 2004: 3; see also Haines 2009b) asserts that:

> A balance between the interests of the child or young person and the interests of the wider community and potential victims can be maintained through early intervention, restorative justice measures, appropriate punishment and supported rehabilitation [English government/YJB sentiment]. Promoting the welfare of children reduces the risk of offending and re-offending and in doing so protects the public. The strategy therefore promotes the principle that children should be treated as children first and offenders second [Welsh government sentiment].

The commitment to children's welfare and rights (or 'entitlements' under the Extending Entitlement strategy – see later in this chapter; see also Chapter Three) places the AWYOS approach to prevention at stage three on the prevention-promotion constellation (the universal prevention of negative behaviour and outcomes) and as such implies that a more progressive, 'children first' prevention agenda is emerging in Wales. These children-first overtones are consolidated by the doctrine of universal entitlement to services, support and guidance set out in Extending Entitlement. These entitlements must be made available to *all* children, including those who have offended or who are at risk of offending. In order to achieve its objectives, the AWYOS endorses a 'holistic approach' to delivering entitlements and meeting the needs of children in the YJS. However, these principled objectives are to be pursued using early intervention addressing the risk factors that are encompassed by many youth justice-related policy areas that are devolved to Wales (for example education, social services, health), suggesting a restricted and individualised conception of prevention more akin to stages four to six on the prevention-promotion constellation. Furthermore, the preventive aim of the AWYOS is underpinned by a responsibilising emphasis (drawn from English policy) on restorative justice elements – responsibility (holding children to account for their offending), restoration (allowing children to make amends for their offending) and reintegration (providing support, assistance and guidance to reintegrate children into their communities following offending). Therefore, the AWYOS outlines a confused and contradictory practice model for prevention in Wales, simultaneously underpinned by a rights/entitlements-based, children-first *policy* perspective, alongside more interventionist and punitive *practice* recommendations – reflecting the uneasy conflation of both distinctively Welsh and distinctively English approaches. The tangible philosophical tensions between the two policy-making bodies that collaborated in the production of the AWYOS (the Welsh Assembly Government and the YJB) are not resolved in the original strategy document, particularly in relation to prevention (although see discussion of the revised strategy in Chapter Seven).

Youth Crime Prevention in Wales: Strategic Guidance: progressive prevention?

The *Youth Crime Prevention in Wales: Strategic Guidance* document was the collaborative 'prevention-focused' follow-up to the AWYOS (WAG and YJB 2008). The document provides strategic guidance to key stakeholder agencies delivering youth justice in Wales, predominantly to fulfil the preventive (more accurately, diversionary) aim of reducing the number of FTEs into the YJS in Wales. *Youth Crime Prevention in Wales* favours targeted early intervention as prevention through its recommendations that local partnerships with an interest in prevention (for example Community Safety Partnership, Children's Framework

Partnership) 'target individual children identified as being on the cusp of offending, involved in antisocial behaviour or subject to a number of risk factors' (WAG and YJB 2008: 5).

The Strategic Guidance document outlines a three-tiered Welsh approach to prevention, which embodies targeted and risk-focused objectives:

1. **diversionary intervention** – targeted on 'high-risk' neighbourhoods and groups over-represented in the YJS;
2. **targeted prevention intervention** – targeted on 'at risk' children on the cusp of offending;
3. **early intervention** – targeted on children in the early stages of involvement with the YJS (for example subject to pre-court disposals and Referral Orders).

The guidance is firmly grounded in the tenets of the RFPP, presented as corresponding with 'a growing body of practice that deploys resources on a risk-led basis' (WAG and YJB 2008: 5) and asserting that 'decreasing risks and bolstering protective factors is the responsibility of all ... it is unlikely that a YOT in isolation will be able to achieve a significant reduction in first-time entrants' (WAG and YJB 2008: 9). However, a concurrent focus on meeting children's rights and entitlements can be discerned within the AWYOS – a commitment to enabling children in trouble with the law to access their rights and entitlements as set out in the UNCRC, the *Seven Core Aims* and Extending Entitlement. This commitment is animated by an important statement of Welsh values (WAG and YJB 2008: 4), namely that: '[T]he best way to protect children from the risk factors associated with offending behaviour is to secure access to universal entitlements.'

The central recommendation of *Youth Crime Prevention in Wales* is that Welsh YOTs should be enabled (by partner agencies) to participate and integrate more effectively in local arrangements for children such as Community Safety Partnerships, Children's Partnerships and Children's Framework Plans. However, the guidance also expresses the reservations of YOT Managers Cymru (the collaborative body of Welsh YOT managers) regarding the multifaceted, uncoordinated and confused youth justice prevention landscape in Wales, characterised by 'different strategies that are often complementary but sometimes contradictory' and 'a plethora of partnerships', which result in 'partnership silos ... poor communication and duplication of effort ... [and] a confused environment in terms of expectations' (WAG and YJB 2008: 9). The guidance concludes that targeted prevention in Wales has been and should continue to be 'philosophically and structurally citizen-centred' due to situating children at the heart of the process. However, it goes on re-emphasise the need to target risk factors by 'weaving a golden thread' through the initiatives, agendas and structures identified within the document. The Welsh strategy's emphasis on individual (risk-based) targeted projects rather than universal programmes is a product of the neoliberalism emanating from England. The neoliberal responsibilisation doctrine of the UK government's 'new youth justice' privileges short-term, stand-alone, targeted project-based responses to children's behaviour such that the funding offered to Wales does not permit or encourage entitlements-based, universal approaches; neither does the restricted, reductionist, risk-focused evidence base generated in England on which the development of youth justice in Wales has to rely for guidance.

Both the AWYOS and Youth Crime Prevention in Wales have moved the prevention agenda forward into more positive territory by advocating for universal prevention services (stage three prevention-promotion) coordinated by multi-agency partnerships, rather than restricting prevention to the youth justice arena and the responsibility of YOTs. Both documents attempt to articulate the distinctive social policy-making identity of Wales by promoting universalism, welfare and children's rights. However, this Welsh policy ethos has been tempered, even undermined, by the apparent desire to reconcile CFOS principles with the risk-based (RFPP) policy and practice requirements emanating from the UK, which lead inexorably to targeted, early interventionist and reductionist approaches with the potential to label, exclude, punish and criminalise the very children whom Welsh practitioners are seeking to put first and support in positive ways.

Progressive promotion: protective factors and enabling factors for positive outcomes

Contemporary youth justice prevention practice with children 'at risk' of developing problem behaviours has shown encouraging signs of moving into the territory of *promotion* (stages one and two on the prevention-promotion constellation) through specific international and localised programmes that have explored the potential for *protective factors* (derived from the RFPP) to facilitate a range of bespoke positive outcome measures. This positive movement is best illustrated through three case study examples: Promoting Positive Behaviour in Schools and Promoting Prevention (Swansea), Positive Youth Development (the US) and Extending Entitlement (Wales).

Case study: CFOS prevention-promotion in Swansea

The case study of Swansea provides an important illustration of how a localised CFOS prevention approach to youth justice can evolve through inclusionary, legitimate, evidence-based partnership. Since 1996, three generations of prevention-promotion practice have developed locally, driven by a commitment to animating the principles of CFOS in the youth justice field – a commitment that pre-dates the AWYOS. Each prevention-promotion programme has built on its predecessor and has been evaluated by Swansea University Centre for Criminal Justice and Criminology (CCJS), which has in turn worked closely with local agencies to support them through the reflective, intellectual journey of policy and practice development. The first two generations of prevention-promotion, Promoting Positive Behaviour in Schools (first-generation prevention-promotion in schools) and Promoting Prevention (second-generation prevention-promotion in schools, the YOT and the community) offer cogent examples of the evolution of a reflective, evidence-based promotional CFOS approach to working with children; an approach that pre-dates and informs Welsh prevention policy. The most recent evolution of this local approach, the Positive Promotion Project (third-generation needs-led prevention-promotion in all areas of the child's life), will be discussed in the final section of this chapter.

Promoting Positive Behaviour in Schools (1996–99)

The first-generation Promoting Positive Behaviour in Schools (PPB) initiative was introduced in 1996 and piloted in three local secondary schools. The programme was created to prevent secondary school exclusion, which had been identified as a growing local problem by the YOT (then youth justice team) and the education department following data analysis indicating positive correlations between those children who had been excluded and those coming to the attention of the YJS. The finding that many of the same children were being excluded and dealt with by the YJS indicated that the same circumstances, experiences and personal and social problems were likely to be influencing both negative outcomes. A multi-agency working group was convened to explore the issue (Working Group on School Exclusions and Disruptive Pupils 1995) and their discussions produced a recommendation for a multi-agency initiative to address the problem. A multi-agency PPB steering group was formed, consisting of representatives from the youth justice team, the local authority education department, the special educational needs service and the pilot schools. The steering group managed the creation and extension of child-friendly preventive service provision (see Haines and Case 2003): whole school behaviour codes (developed in consultation with children), Family Group Conferencing (FGC) and Action Planning Panels (APP) (working with children to identify and implement positive solutions to disaffection and disruptive behaviour in school), a youth access initiative (alternative educational provision for disaffected children) and a community service volunteers scheme (in-school mentoring and out-of-school befriending by young adults). The rationale for this provision was that unmet needs and problems in and out of school could be contributing towards behaviour leading to school exclusion, so if these needs and problems could be identified then they could be targeted through intervention and schools could be enabled to support and maintain children in full-time education.

The evaluation of PPB assessed the programme's rationale (Haines, Jones and Isles 2001) using a four-part methodology of questionnaire, interviews, focus groups and systems analysis, which accessed children, parents and key stakeholder staff.

- **Youth social audit questionnaire** – pupils in the pilot schools completed a questionnaire consisting of 13 sections relating to potential problem areas in their lives: health, self-image, money and living conditions, social activities, relationships with boys/girls, other social relationships, isolation, morality, home and family, curriculum and teaching, school and education, crime, the future. Each section contained five items/statements with which pupils expressed their strength of attitude/agreement on a five-point Likert scale (from 'a problem that is not troubling you at all' to 'a problem that is troublingly you very much'). An opportunity sample of 162 pupils in school years 10 and 11 (aged 14–16 years) was divided into an experimental group (50 pupils who had been excluded, either fixed-term or permanently) and a control group (124 pupils never excluded). Analyses identified the most problematic areas across the whole sample (in terms of mean score) as: the future, curriculum and teaching, self-image, school and education and social activities. Although children from both groups expressed similar concerns about their needs and problems in their lives, the experimental group of excluded pupils demonstrated higher levels of perceived problems in 10 of the 13 sections (the exceptions being relationships with boys/girls, other social relationships and isolation), which offered tentative indications that these school and social problems were contributing to school exclusion (Haines and Case 2003)
- **Focus groups with school staff** – the attitudes of staff in each pilot school to discipline and behaviour management in their institution were elicited, with the rationale that commonly held punitive and disciplinary-based beliefs about responding to pupil misbehaviour were contributing to school exclusion rates. Focus groups (comprised of teachers, senior

and middle managers, school governors and ancillary staff) expressed negative attitudes towards difficult and disruptive pupils and support for punitive disciplinary procedures (for example in-school sanctions, fixed-term and permanent exclusions), but positive attitudes towards the general pupil population and towards more children-first positive practice (for example whole-school behaviour codes, rewarding positive behaviour). Many staff believed that disaffected pupils were experiencing school-based and social problems that teachers and schools were ill-equipped to deal with in the absence of support from external agencies; validating the development of the multi-agency, multiple intervention PPB programme, which balances targeted and universal prevention provision.

- **Systems analysis of PPB implementation** – the PPB model was underpinned by a systems-management perspective that efforts and resources should be targeted upon key decision-making points within the school exclusion process. Systems analysis (informed by staff consultation and documentary analysis) identified that pre-PPB disciplinary structures varied significantly between schools based on pupil population size and the internal organisation of the school. However, the number of clear structural similarities were identified, notably that school staff had broadly similar options for dealing with difficult or disruptive pupils (for example similar punitive referral, sanction and exclusion mechanisms), typically exercised through a hierarchy of decision making (for example more severe sanctions were only available to senior staff members) within a closed disciplinary structure (with little recourse to external support or resources) driven by a pivotal staff member (see Haines et al 2001). The PPB system was perceived as open, participative and inclusionary (rather than hierarchical) in its decision making, offering a wide range of flexible options and services focused on problem solving designed to enhance engagement with, and to meet the needs of, the pupil, their family and the school. The systems analysis identified attenuated links between PPB structures and those in the three pilot schools, with a consequent 'lack of obvious direct service provision and benefits accruing to the schools and the key staff within the schools' (Haines et al 2001: 8).

- **Family Group Conferencing and Action Planning Panel questionnaires** – user involvement and satisfaction was assessed on the basis that engagement with and commitment to such processes were seen to be a key indicator of successful long-term outcomes (see Haines et al 2001). Separate questionnaires relating to FGC and the APP were completed by pupils, family members, school representatives and the FGC convener. The majority of participants (pupils, family and staff) felt positive about their FGC experiences and found the process to be effective in sorting out problems and reaching satisfactory agreements for action. In addition, most participants (children and family members) felt involved and engaged in the process in terms of being able to have their voices heard, take part in discussions, ask questions and contribute to the resolution of problems, which was considered to be an encouraging sign of longer-term success of the process. The APP was also viewed positively by participants: considered to be working well and fulfilling its function, providing clear and up-to-date information regarding the child, and adopting a children-first approach focused on problem solving and meeting the needs of the child. The purpose of the APP was well understood, as were the roles of individuals and agencies within the process. Participants generally agreed that the meetings were constructive and that their views were listened to and appreciated by other participants. APP questionnaire responses clearly indicated commitment, engagement and confidence in a constructive and positive process.

The PPB research identified several crucial issues locally, which were being addressed by the different elements of the PPB initiative, most notably:

- **unmet needs** – children in local secondary schools demonstrated high levels of unmet needs, particularly those children who had experienced exclusion from school (in line with the initial conclusions of the Working Group on School Exclusions and Disruptive Pupils);

- **support for schools –** local secondary schools required (and recognised their need for) support from external agencies in dealing with these problems (foregrounding the *Youth Crime Prevention in Wales* recommendation some 12 years later);
- **multi-agency partnership working** – schools and local agencies were willing to cooperate constructively to target resources more effectively and to influence (systems management) decision-making processes regarding secondary school exclusions.

Although the long-term impact of PPB on children's lives, levels of secondary school exclusion and school processes could not be determined within the time limited evaluation (1996–99), the evaluation was able to test the underlying assumptions of the initiative and to assess the early implementation of the PPB system (see Haines et al 2001). PPB offered an early evidence-based example of universal prevention (stage three prevention-promotion) and targeted promotion (stage two) for all secondary schoolchildren, including those experiencing educational disaffection and exclusion, which are viewed as outcomes closely associated with offending. The PPB programme itself was transient, a product of the political priorities for short-term funding of targeted projects (for example Youth Access Initiative, YAI) over long-term, mainstreamed, universal services (see Haines 1997). However, PPB "philosophies have been mainstreamed across secondary schools locally" (Swansea YOT manager, 2014) – manifested in access to universal services as standard practice, consultation with children via schools councils (for example prioritising the generation of whole-school behaviour codes), the pursuit of Rights Respecting Schools status in all institutions (see later in this chapter – the Positive Promotion Project) and close working relationships with the YOT (for example through the YOT subsuming the FGC initiative within YISP provision). PPB services were grounded in the nascent CFOS principles of inclusion, engagement, promotion (rewarding positive behaviour) and systems management (of disciplinary and reward procedures). Crucially, PPB's prevention-promotion activity was framed in a 'whole child', holistic manner, with adult practitioners responsibilised to facilitate children's access to external support services that responded to their expressed needs and problems, with little suggestion of a need to base this supportive intervention in the prescriptions of the RFPP.

Promoting Prevention (1999–2004)

The Crime and Disorder Act 1998 placed a primary duty upon all those working within the YJS to prevent offending by children. In Swansea, a multi-agency YOT working group was formed in 1998 to produce an action plan to deliver this preventive approach (in anticipation of the inception of YOTs in April 2000). The action plan became known as Promoting Prevention. A successful application was made to the crime prevention arm of the YJB Development Fund[72] was completed by the working group in March 1999, within which the principles and objectives of Promoting Prevention were formalised as establishing wide ownership and participation locally (by key stakeholders and children) in a 'youth crime prevention strategy'. This was to be pursued by reinforcing universal rights to services and information for children in Swansea (in accordance with the UNCRC 1989) and delivering universal and targeted services and information to those in need. Therefore, Promoting Prevention was developed as a socially, educationally (compare PPB) and economically inclusive approach to preventing offending by children. In October 1999 all agencies represented on the YOT steering and working groups were invited to provide representatives (at operational

[72] Following recommendations in the Crime and Disorder Act and in order to meet a key objective to commission research and provide grants for developing best practice, the YJB 'Development Fund' was established. In spring 1999 the Development Fund solicited applications from YOTs (in partnership with other statutory and voluntary agencies) to provide services to 'young offenders' and their families, with the overall aim of preventing or reducing youth offending. In addition to a national evaluation of each programme, the YJB required every local project to be independently evaluated (Ghate and Ramella 2002).

management level) to the Promoting Prevention steering group,[73] which was formalised in April 2000, contemporaneous with the introduction of the YOT.

The Promoting Prevention steering group began to develop a package of corporate and strategic interventions that partners had identified as appropriate means of preventing and reducing offending by children following a review of risk factor research (reflecting PPB's faith in the efficacy of the RFPP), although interventions were largely systems based rather than individualised (reflecting a children-first faith in systems management and non-stigmatising practice). The key psychosocial (individualised) risk factors identified for targeting by intervention were: school exclusion, truancy and pupil disaffection (all products of the development and evaluation of PPB), lack of training and employment opportunities, drug and alcohol misuse and social exclusion (see, for example, MORI 2003). Extant provision locally (notably YOT interventions and the PPB programme) was fused with interventions specially created to address perceived shortfalls in local provision and funded by and/or adopted from partner agencies (for example, the local health authority seconded a clinical psychiatric nurse to the YOT), particularly around mentoring and alternative curriculum:

- **Community Service Volunteers 'on line' mentoring scheme** – in-school support to staff and pupils and an out-of-school befriending service for pupils led by young adult mentors, where such services could prevent in-school problems (for example school exclusion, disaffection).
- **Involve 'Just Us' mentoring scheme** – adult volunteers of all ages (not limited to young adults) working with children identified by schools and the YOT as educationally and socially disaffected, on the basis that developing a positive relationship

[73] Reflecting local Community Safety Partnership membership, Promoting Prevention became a multi-agency partnership between statutory agencies (local authority – mainly YOT, education, social services and youth services, police, probation, health), along with two mentoring/befriending organisations (Community Service Volunteers, Involve), two vocational support and training agencies (Guiding Hand Association, Careers Business Company), a charity (Prison? Me? No Way!) and the independent evaluators (Swansea University CCJC).

with an adult can address problematic issues. Just Us offered in-school support to staff and pupils, and an out-of-school befriending service.

- **City and County of Swansea Training Centre** – offers a variety of youth provision as an alternative to formal education for disaffected children who have been excluded from school or who are assessed as at risk of exclusion. For example, children may be referred by schools or the YOT to the (PPB) YAI, which provides them with life skills, training and employment opportunities, as well as education (for example vocational training through local colleges).
- **Guiding Hand Association** – a registered local charity providing vocational, educational, recreational and social skills courses/programmes to educationally and socially excluded, disaffected and disadvantaged children. Established as a collection of motor maintenance projects, the Guiding Hand Association addresses many categories of need among children, including empathy, support, friendship and skills development.
- **Careers Business Company** – an independent organisation offering careers guidance and information for children and adults. Careers Business works closely with other Promoting Prevention partners to engage all children (including those who are disaffected and disengaged) in training and employment.
- **Prison? Me? No Way!** – a road show dealing with issues surrounding crime and its consequences, particularly imprisonment, which is delivered to local school pupils, disaffected children, real victims of crime, serving prisoners, prison officers, police and judges. The road show utilises drama, live sound and vision satellite links, pop music, drug agencies and prisoner testimonies. Trained facilitators visit over 2,000 pupils per year in the catchment area of Swansea prison.

The *inclusion* and *engagement* of local agencies and staff within the multi-agency Promoting Prevention partnership were pivotal to the inception and successful evolution of the programme. The driving forces behind the early stages of Promoting Prevention were the managers of the local YOT and Community

Safety Department. They adopted a strategic, persistent and opportunistic approach to co-opting and engaging partner agencies locally, cohered around regular mail/email contact, presentations and informal discussions within meetings – focused on the benefits of participation in the programme for the agency targeted. As the Community Safety Department Manager explained:

> 'We arranged to go and meet them, talked to them, brought them in, discussed how they might help, how it might work. Nothing may have happened for several years, but we'd made the contact, we'd got the plan, we kept in touch, and at some stage the right moment was reached to involve them. It was about building relationships, building a knowledge of one another, until we got to the point where we could come together and deliver something' (Local Authority Community Safety Department Manager 1999–2002, interviewed in 2011)

The multi-agency, multiple intervention Promoting Prevention initiative constituted the second generation of local prevention as it expanded the educational, in-school focus of PPB into the community, to incorporate offending and related problem behaviours and outcomes (for example antisocial behaviour, substance use) under the purview of the YOT, while integrating PPB initiatives and newly created initiatives driven and shaped by the CFOS principles of universalism, inclusion, rights/entitlements and promoting positive behaviour.

The initiative was evaluated from 2000 to 2004 (Case 2004; Case and Haines 2004; Haines and Case 2005) – an evaluation that was funded as a requirement of the original YJB Development Fund grant and match-funded by the Promoting Prevention partner agencies. The two-part evaluation consisted of a *systems analysis* (based on the systems management model) of the structures and processes of Promoting Prevention (for example organisations, interventions, committees, documents, individuals) and a *children's questionnaire* assessing self-reported problem behaviours and levels of risk and need among different groups of children locally. The key objectives of the evaluation were to elucidate the extent, nature and operation of Promoting Prevention and the degree to which interventions were addressing the expressed risks and needs experienced by local children (see Case 2004; Case and Haines 2005).

Systems analysis of Promoting Prevention

Semi-structured interviews were conducted with a snowball sample of 35 local key stakeholder practitioners from Promoting Prevention partner agencies in order to scope the extent and nature of interventions within the programme, to map their interrelationships and broader programme structures and to gain an understanding of the nature and operation of the initiative. Steering group members reported that the exploration and explication of the full complexity of Promoting Prevention's constituent multi-agency and multiple intervention structures, processes and relationships had proven extremely beneficial for partner agencies seeking to locate their position and clarify their role and contributed to effective programme delivery within the partnership structure (see also Crawford 2002).

Systems analysis identified a number of salient issues related to the nature and operation of Promoting Prevention, particularly in terms of the partnership model adopted, how the programme was coordinated, the informality of partnership working and inequalities within the partnership structure. Although Promoting Prevention espoused a corporate model of partnership with no specific lead agency and joint responsibility for partnership coordination, decision making and implementation (see also Liddle and Gelsthorpe 1994), the initiative clearly adhered to a local authority partnership model (see Morgan 1991), dominated by the YOT. The YOT manager was identified as the driving force behind the partnership and it was noted that his professional background (social work) was highly influential upon the 'children first' principles guiding many of the interventions, such as the inclusionary, participatory emphasis of PPB programmes (for example FGC, APP) and the promotional, needs- (not risk-) led emphasis of newly created and co-opted initiatives (for example the mentoring schemes, Guiding Hand

Association, Careers Business Company). Concerns were raised that the influence of the YOT manager upon the construction, content, coordination and direction of Promoting Prevention meant that programme development and sustainability were potentially 'over-reliant upon a single charismatic, motivational individual' as opposed to being predicated on a representative partnership structure. However, mechanisms had been set in train to devolve the coordination and (policy/practice) foci of the different elements of Promoting Prevention to designated groups and individuals (for example, responsibility for the preventive agenda was devolved to the YOT education youth worker and community issues were devolved to the Community Safety Department manager), thus building sustainability into the Promoting Prevention structure.

Key stakeholders felt that the programme had enhanced and embedded partnership working around youth justice issues locally, engendering a culture shift away from certain agencies claiming ownership of crime-related issues and towards 'a commitment to multi-agency working practices' that 'fostered strong inter-departmental relationships and a willingness amongst partners to make the scheme a success' (Parent and Pupil Support Unit Manager, Education Department, in Case 2004). Beyond the local authority, external partners advocated Promoting Prevention's ability to enable 'collaboration and partnership working in an effort to undermine the previously antiquated system of isolated agencies in Swansea, where progress and resource sharing was dependent upon the personalities of senior management' (Assistant Chief Probation Officer, West Glamorgan Probation Service, in Case 2004). However, effective cooperation and partnership working were not necessarily consistent within Promoting Prevention, with certain partners' (for example health, probation, careers) findings that the flexible, dynamic and informal nature of the partnership precipitated ambiguities over their identity and role within a prevention-oriented programme. That said, due to Promoting Prevention expanding the prevention focus locally beyond offending issues by prioritising social inclusion, children's rights (thus pre-dating both Extending Entitlement and the AWYOS) and the promotion of positive behaviour, disparate agencies found it easier to cohere around broader, shared thematic objectives: 'Although at first it was difficult to see how [my] organisation could contribute to crime prevention activity, we quickly realised that we could have a valuable input due to our shared commitment to social inclusion and the universal rights of all children' (Health Service representative, in Case 2004)

Promoting Prevention children's questionnaire

In order to evaluate Promoting Prevention's objectives of preventing and reducing offending by children by addressing their expressed needs (conceptualised and understood as risk factors by the Promoting Prevention working group, in line with their support for the RFPP), a questionnaire was devised to:

- assess whether self-reported offending (a measure with the potential to access the 'dark figure' of unreported and unrecorded crime) had decreased since the inception of Promoting Prevention;
- identify the key risk factors for offending by local children for targeting by Promoting Prevention provision. The findings were intended to enable evaluation of whether Promoting Prevention structures, processes and interventions (identified through systems analyses) were addressing the risk factors for offending identified by local children. Offending was measured using the UK version of the International Self-Reported Delinquency instrument (Graham and Bowling 1995) – an inventory of 14 offence types which participants reported having committed/not committed in the past 12 months ('active offending'). Exposure to risk was measured using an adaptation of the Asset risk assessment instrument (YJB 2000) and the Communities that Care Youth Survey (Beinert, Anderson, Lee and Utting 2002) – with participants expressing their strength of agreement on a five-point Likert scale (strongly agree to strongly disagree) with a range of risk statements situated within psychosocial risk domains (family, school, neighbourhood, lifestyle, personal). The questionnaire was administered interactively via computer self-interviewing, a methodology that has demonstrated

> numerous advantages over traditional paper-based surveys in relation to enhancing the validity of researching sensitive issues with children – including addressing low literacy levels, enhancing comprehension and completeness, and reducing response bias (see, for example, Banks and Laurie 2000; Case and Haines 2004).

The questionnaire was administered in 2002 and 2003 to an opportunity sample of 1,278 children in school years 7–10 (aged 11–15 years, with year 11 unavailable due to exam commitments), with an even distribution of gender and age group across a self-selected sample of six local secondary schools. All schools provided at least one class from each school year group. One in three children (30%) reported active offending[74] The most prevalent self-reported offences were criminal damage, shoplifting and public fighting (all reported by 29% of the whole sample). Every offence on the inventory was reported by a higher percentage of boys than girls and a higher percentage of 14- to 15-year-olds than any other age group.[75] Inferential statistical analysis through logistic regression was employed to identify statistical relationships/associations between the presence/absence of active offending and levels of exposure to self-reported risk by the sample as a whole and by the sub-groups within it. In terms of risk domain, the following 'risk factors' were identified as having a significant statistical relationship with self-reported active offending:

- **family** – sibling drug use (whole sample), parental criminality (whole sample), parental drug use (12- to 13-year-olds only) and unclear parental rules (13- to 14-year-olds only);
- **school** – poor relationship with teachers (whole sample), being a bully (females only), academic underachievement (11- to 12-year-olds only);

[74] The evaluation team chose not to analyse the 'ever offending' measure because it was considered to be an historical behaviour from which the child could have desisted (that is not all 'ever' offenders were 'active' offenders who had committed an offence in the previous year), so any identified associations with risk could be statistical artefact.

[75] With the exception of theft from school/work (a higher percentage of 12- to 13-year-olds and 13- to 14-year-olds reported this) and trespass with intent of theft and pickpocketing (higher percentage of 13- to 14-year-olds).

- **neighbourhood/community** – availability of drugs (whole sample, lack of attachment to neighbourhood (13- to 14-year-olds only);
- **lifestyle** – antisocial behaviour (whole sample), antisocial peers (whole sample), substance use problems (males only), criminal peers (females and 12- to 13-year-olds only), positive attitudes to drugs (13- to 14-year-olds only), lack of participation in positive activities (14- to 15-year-olds only);
- **personal** – rule breaking attitudes (whole sample), risk-taking behaviour and sensation seeking (whole sample), impulsivity (males only), self-harming behaviour (females only), inability to defer gratification (males and 13- to 14-year-olds only), stress (12- to 13-year-olds only), feeling sad/miserable (13- to 14-year-olds only) (Case 2004; see also Haines and Case 2005; Case and Haines 2004).

The risk factors identified by the children's questionnaire as statistically associated with (not causal of) self-reported offending indicated that much extant Promoting Prevention provision had been focused appropriately on the risks and problems that were relevant to local children, particularly those related to school (addressed through PPB and alternative curriculum), personal and lifestyle (addressed by YOT staff, for example the newly seconded YOT clinical psychiatric nurse). The evaluation recommended that more attention be paid to family-related risks and needs (beyond existing YOT work with parents and links to social service agencies) and particularly to neighbourhood/community issues, which children identified as broader and more socio-structural than much (second-generation) Promoting Prevention provision sought to address through its focus on psychosocial, individualised risk factors (Case 2004).

Caveat • A critical reflection on risk factor research and the risk factor prevention paradigm

It should be noted that quantitative (artefactual) risk factor research has been restricted in its efficacy due to prioritising the reductionist quantification ('factorisation') of complex psychosocial elements of children's lives and understanding these factors in an holistic, uncritical and deterministic manner as somehow predictive or causal of (rather than simply correlated with) broad, over-generalised outcome measures such as offending (Case and Haines 2009). Risk factor research has been further weakened by grounding explanations of youth offending in group-level risk factors, an 'aggregation' process that weakens conclusions because they are not representative of or necessarily applicable to any individual group member (see Goldson 2005). Several of these criticisms are, to some extent, applicable to the Promoting Prevention individual study (for example factorisation, aggregation, broad outcome measures), although some clearly are not (for example, statistical associations are interpreted as correlational, not causal). We have written at length on these criticisms (Case 2006, 2007; Haines and Case 2008; Case and Haines 2009) as they apply to risk factor research generally and to the conclusions from it that have underpinned the RFPP. Part of our position here, however, is that where we have utilised traditional risk factor research methodologies and analyses, this has been done on a less generalised basis, with risk measured within smaller sub-groups (for example age groups) and with an openness to the possibility of non-risk-related findings producing results which challenge the negative, risk hegemony. Our view is that aggregated risk factor data should only be utilised to illuminate broader social policy questions, thus leaving youth justice practitioners free to decide how to address identified variables and implement interventions. Therefore, while the Promoting Prevention questionnaire identified a series of risk variables linked to offending, none are claimed as explanatory or indicative at the individual level (particularly as the study design was cross-sectional). The questionnaire sought to identify factors correlated with, rather than explanatory of, offending and did not conceive of these variables as necessarily generalisable to other populations of children (particularly as the sample was opportunity in nature), but rather as indicators to guide the development of social policy, professional assessment and intervention in the local context.

Promoting Prevention was a second-generation prevention-promotion approach that expanded the scope and remit of local prevention practice beyond the school and into the community. Like PPB before it, the Promoting Prevention programme was funded centrally as a short-term project with targeted prevention objectives and aspects of its bespoke provision have since ceased to be funded (for example the Involve 'Just Us' scheme, Guiding Hand Association), although provision co-opted through original partner agencies persists (for example YOT interventions, Prison? Me? No Way!, local authority schemes such as vocational education through the Training Centre, Careers Business Company – now Careers Wales Swansea). To a degree, Promoting Prevention regressed the promotional emphasis of PPB through its negative objectives (preventing and reducing offending) and its employment of the negative-facing, retrospective RFPP to address these objectives. The overriding focus on offending behaviour, risk factors and a YOT dominance of systems (management) situated Promoting Prevention within existing (punitive, risk-centric) youth justice structures, processes and objectives. However, since the inception of the programme, local agencies (led by the YOT) and local structures (for example the Safer Swansea Community Safety Partnership) have reflected critically on Promoting Prevention (through an ongoing Reflective Friend Research relationship with the Swansea University Centre for Criminal Justice and Criminology (CCJC)) and have sought to progress its non-traditional (youth justice) CFOS principles across local mainstream practices with all children, including those in conflict with the law and the youth justice system. The most notable subsequent development of these principles (for example diversion, inclusion, normalisation, responsibilising adults) has been the Swansea Bureau diversion programme (see Chapter Five), although other CFOS extensions of Promoting Prevention can also be discerned locally (for example adult-facilitated universal access to vocational education and careers advice, Rights Respecting Schools).

Two generations of progressive prevention-promotion in Swansea

The PPB and Promoting Prevention programmes have been founded on the consultation, inclusion and engagement of user groups/key stakeholders (children, families, staff) and the concurrent generation of information through evidence-based partnership, which has been fed back into, and applied reflexively by, the coordinating partnerships. PPB and Promoting

Prevention were heralded as best practice examples by the *Promising Approaches* review of youth crime prevention initiatives (Utting 1999) and by the Extending Entitlement youth inclusion policies (National Assembly Policy Unit 2002), in addition to Promoting Prevention being highly commended in the British Community Safety Awards in both 2002 and 2003. The subsequent mainstreaming of the guiding philosophies and constituent interventions of PPB and Promoting Prevention across all local secondary schools since the evaluations were completed is indicative of a growing local commitment across agencies to CFOS principles and ways of working with children to pursue rights-based preventive goals.

Prevention and early intervention policy and practice locally have been the long-term drivers for perceiving and responding to the circumstances and behaviours of local children on an holistic level that goes beyond a narrow offending context. Crucially, prevention and early intervention locally have developed reflexively in response to empirical evidence generated through regular internal data collection and through embedded evaluation processes drawing on the expertise of researchers, who function as critical friends and research partners with local stakeholders (see Reflective Friend Research – Chapter Four). A portfolio of evaluation outcomes locally have evidenced the extent to which Swansea has been able to animate (often pre-dating and pre-empting) the prosocial, rights-based and CFOS policy rhetoric of the Welsh government approach to prevention that has been intended to set Wales apart from the more punitive, responsibilising and adulterising approach to children adopted in England. Prevention locally has evolved through a reflective intellectual and empirical journey that has broadened the scope of prevention provision beyond the school, into the YOT and further out into the community. The objectives and principles of 'prevention' have themselves broadened into a prevention-promotion model that moves beyond the simple prevention (through targeted intervention) of negative behaviours, negative outcomes and their associated risk factors (traditional youth justice prevention approaches anchored to stages four to six of the prevention-promotion constellation) and into the promotion of positive behaviours and outcomes for children.

Case study: Positive Youth Development

The Positive Youth Development[76] movement emerged in the US in the early 21st century with the aim of highlighting the characteristics of children that were associated with their positive development; a challenge to the negative focus on risk and avoiding problems that had dominated prevention research to that point (Catalano, Berglund, Ryan, Lonczak and Hawkins 2004). Positive Youth Development evolved from the Social Development Model (Hawkins and Weis 1985), which itself underpinned both the RFPP and the Communities that Care intervention programme (see Beinert et al 2002). The Social Development Model 'organizes a broad range of risk and protective factors into a model specifying causal hypotheses to capture key elements of socialization' (Hawkins et al 2003: 279). The objectives of the model were to identify the risk factors associated with negative behaviour by children and also to extend traditional risk factor research by exploring the protective factors that facilitated children's positive social development and ability to navigate exposure to risk, with a particular focus on:

- *involvement and interaction* – with family, school, peer group, workplace, intimate relationships;
- *skills* – social, academic, work-related;
- *bonding* – commitment and attachment to parents, school, peers, intimates;
- *belief* – in moral order and antisocial opportunities;
- *exogenous variables* – socio-structural position, socio-economic deprivation, external/adult constraints on behaviour and agency, individual/psychological factors.

The Social Development Model foci demonstrate clear overlap with those of Social Control Theory (Hirschi 1969), but with an extension into risk and protective factor territory with the addition of the exogenous variables category. The Positive Youth Development model extended these foci still further through

[76] Positive Youth Development has spawned a US positive youth justice model (see Butts, Bazemore and Meroe 2010).

a deliberate 'shift in approach' that sought to prioritise positive development and to explore a purported 'common aetiology' for the risk and protective factors linked to negative and positive behaviours and outcomes. A meta-analysis of Positive Youth Development programmes (Catalano et al 2004) confirmed this common aetiology by concluding that the same individual, family, school and community factors often predicted both positive outcomes (for example academic success) and negative outcomes (for example delinquency) for children, indicating a potential for intervention programmes to simultaneously create positive developmental pathways and prevent the occurrence of problems (akin to the tenets of the RFPP). Although a clear and consensual definition of 'Positive Youth Development' was not discernible from the programmes evaluated, in general, the programmes aimed to foster, strengthen and promote similar positive behaviours and outcomes, notably: social, emotional, cognitive behavioural and moral competencies, self-efficacy, self-determination, clear and positive identity, opportunities for (rewarded) participation in positive activities, bonding, resilience, belief in the future and prosocial norms and standards for behaviour[77] (Catalano et al 2004).

The Positive Youth Development movement constituted a huge conceptual shift in thinking about how to deliver prevention work with children. The focus of its research and prevention programmes expanded beyond the risk-based targeting of deficits in the individual into a 'whole child' examination of a broader range of interactional, contextual and socio-structural influences. The exploration of a common aetiology (of risk and protective factors) for positive and negative outcomes expanded research and programme foci by introducing the potential for protective factors to exert promotional and prosocial influences, rather than simply protecting the child against negativity and risk. However,

[77] There are similarities here with the adult-focused Good Lives Model (Ward and Maruna, 2007; Ward, Yates and Willis 2011), a strengths-based rehabilitation theory that aims to equip clients with internal and external resources to live a 'good' or 'better', socially acceptable and personally meaningful life. The Good Lives Model targets criminogenic needs (risk factors) as internal or external barriers against living a good life, which are addressed within a broader strengths-based framework and need-focused approach that motivates 'offenders' to desist.

the evaluation of Positive Youth Development programmes demonstrated that the movement was restricted by an inability and/or unwillingness to break free from the shackles of the RFPP. Despite its good intentions, Positive Youth Development (like the Social Development Model before it) has been more concerned with preventing and reducing problems than with promoting development, seeming to assume that Positive Youth Development occurs naturally in the absence of problems (Pittman et al 2003). As Pittman and Fleming (1991: 3) assert, 'problem-free is not fully prepared' – so preventing, reducing and 'fixing' problems is not the same as promoting positivity and preparing children for the future. This prevention and reduction emphasis is illustrated by the lack of consensus over the nature of the positive behaviours and outcomes that the Positive Youth Development model should pursue and a lack of standardised and agreed ways in which to measure them.

The purported 'common aetiology' of risk and protective factors fails to convince on methodological and evidential grounds (see Case and Haines 2009 for a more detailed discussion). There is a paucity of cogent evidence within both the Positive Youth Development and risk factor research fields that risk and protective factors exhibit a 'causal' influence or any predictive or directional influence on behaviours and outcomes (evidence is typically correlational) which can then be confidently targeted by programmes; nor is there robust evidence of substantive relationships between the risk and protective factors themselves (Case and Haines 2009). The common aetiology hypothesis is based on an imputation that the risk and protective factors measured influence behaviours and outcomes and that they are closely related to one another, for example as functional dichotomies, moderators/mediators (see Pollard, Hawkins and Arthur 1999; Kraemer, Stice, Kazdin, Offord and Kupfer 2001) or are 'causally reciprocal' (Thornberry 1987). These understandings illustrate the 'restricted evolution of the protective factor' (Case and Haines 2011) entirely in terms of risk (factors), rather than as potentially independent factors exerting influence on a range of positive behaviours and outcomes that are themselves potentially independent from negative behaviours and outcomes. In other words, we need to look beyond the illusory 'relationship' between (the absence of) risk factors and (the absence of) negative behaviours and outcomes that has characterised so-called 'positive' and 'promotional' interpretations of the RFPP, notably the early development of the Positive Youth Development model. This progression has been evidenced in subsequent research that has reconceptualised protective factors as *promotive factors* linked to positive outcomes for children (Ashcroft, Daniels and Hart 2004; McCarthy, Laing and Walker 2004; Prelow, Loukas and Jordan-Green 2007), although even this nascent promotive focus 'has been grounded in the somewhat uncritical importation of established lists of risk factors into concepts of protection and promotion limited to the psychosocial domains ... [and] has retained risk, deficit and problem behaviour as its normative touchtone' (Case and Haines 2009: 41–2). In CFOS, and indeed in other, similar international models such as the New Zealand-based '10 Characteristics of a Good Youth Justice System' model (Harding and Becroft 2013; see Chapter Two), the focus is on enhancing the extent to which children are enabled to achieve a range of positive outcomes.

Case study: extending and enabling entitlements as positive promotion

The Welsh government's Extending Entitlement youth inclusion strategy (National Assembly Policy Unit 2000) determines that practitioners and organisations working with children should provide opportunities, support, services and guidance to enable all children aged 11–25 in Wales to have unconditional access to 10 universal entitlements: education, training and employment; basic skills; volunteering and citizenship; responsive, and accessible services; careers advice and counselling services; personal life; health and housing; recreation and social life; sport, art and music; consultation and participation regarding decision making that affects them. The concept of 'entitlements' is grounded in a forward looking and proactive approach to the pursuit of *maximum outcomes* for children in terms of the (adult-facilitated) realisation of the support and service they can expect from adults, rather than the rights-based *minimum standards* for service established by the UNCRC (UNICEF 1989). As such, the concepts of children's entitlements and children's rights remain philosophically and practically distinct.

The independent evaluation of the Welsh government's Extending Entitlement strategy (conducted 2005–08) employed self-report questionnaires with over 3,000 secondary schoolchildren across Wales to identify their PLATE and their strength of agreement (on a five-point Likert scale) with a series of statements related to exposure to psychosocial risk and protective factors (Haines et al 2004; Case et al 2005). The PLATE concept was conceived as a dichotomous outcome measure, with 'lower PLATE' considered to be indicative of a negative outcome and 'higher PLATE' as an innovative, positive outcome measure symbiotic with the entitlements-based principles of CFOS. For example, the 'Education' entitlement was measured with the question 'The Welsh Assembly Government believes you are entitled to AN EDUCATION that meets your needs. How well does your education meet your needs? Not at all, very little, some, quite a lot, to the maximum?'. Children reporting 'not at all' or 'very little' were considered as having lower PLATE in relation to education, whereas 'quite a lot' and 'to the maximum' indicated higher PLATE. Risk and protective factor statements were also considered to be dichotomous, worded such that disagreement indicated the presence of a risk factor (in the case of a statistical relationship with lower PLATE) and agreement indicated the presence of a protective factor (in the case of a statistical relationship with higher PLATE). For example, the issue of 'Feeling confident in the educational environment' was assessed with the question 'Have you felt confident about yourself at school or college? Not at all, very little, some, quite a lot, a lot?'. The responses 'not at all' and 'very little' were indicative of a potential risk factor, while 'quite a lot' and 'a lot' were indicative of a potential protective factor.

Questionnaire data was analysed (using linear regression) for statistical associations between 'composite' protective factors and risk factors (identified using factor analysis) and PLATE. The protective factors linked to higher PLATE were: positive relationships and interactions in the family and school environments, commitment to school, constructive use of leisure time, positive perceptions of local neighbourhood, psychological well-being. Furthermore, children reporting higher PLATE were more likely (than those reporting lower PLATE) to have never offended, never used illegal drugs and never used alcohol underage. The risk factors linked to lower PLATE were: impulsivity, risk taking, negative thoughts and acceptance of and exposure to antisocial behaviour. Children reporting lower PLATE were statistically more likely to also report active (in the past year) offending, illegal drug use and underage alcohol use (Case et al 2005).

The evaluation findings highlighted higher PLATE as a practical, original CFOS outcome measure and suggested that the protective factors identified should be more accurately defined as *enabling factors* because they appeared to facilitate children's attainment of a positive outcome, rather than simply protecting them from a negative outcome. The Extending Entitlement evaluation, therefore, progressed the prevention focus beyond that of the RFPP by linking enabling factors (identified as independent from risk factors) to a new, principled positive outcome measure, rather than remaining restricted to identifying protective factors (as the functional dichotomy of risk factors) and the absence of negative outcomes (which does not indicate the presence of a positive outcome). When this principled, positive, future-oriented, entitlements-led approach is consolidated by responsibilising adults to ensure that children access their entitlements in reality (not just in perception), the increased likelihood of positive behaviours and outcomes (as evidenced in the evaluation of Extending Entitlement) is manifest.

Children First, Offenders Second prevention-promotion

We have explored the complex, contested and ambiguous nature of *prevention* work with children by exploring the disparate and competing approaches to its definition, measurement and implementation. Much prevention policy and practice has embodied targeted early intervention and reduction methods and objectives, grounded in retrospective, risk-focused, offender-first approaches that individualised (psychosocial) risk factors and the prevention of *negative* behaviours by, and outcomes for, children. We have characterised this as a neoconservative correctionalist approach to prevention that *individualises* the blame for offending and feeds into the neoliberal responsibilisation of children for failing to resist and negotiate their exposure to psychosocial and socio-structural risk (factors). Furthermore, we have argued that this approach is symbolic of that adopted in English policy (see Chapter Three). Within this neoliberal approach, children's perspectives and experiences are neglected and they are afforded little influence over the interpretation of their lives (as bundles of risk factors) and the (adult-centric) decision-making processes that result in relation to sentencing, choice of disposal and nature of intervention. The alternative CFOS model of prevention is anti-risk – moving beyond the traditional prevention and reduction of the negative to prioritise *promotion of the positive*: positive behaviours and positive outcomes for children within and outside the YJS. CFOS prevention is grounded in child-friendly principles of universalism, diversion and normalisation. It is progressed through inclusionary, participatory, engaging and legitimate practice and evidenced through substantive, measurable behaviours and outcomes such as *participation* in decision making, *engagement* with youth justice assessment and interventions and *access* to entitlements and rights. CFOS consolidates, animates and extrapolates the policy perspective articulated in the AWYOS ('prevention is better than cure', 'children first and offenders second' – WAG and YJB 2004: 3) to proffer a positive, participatory and entitlements-based approach to promotion (rather than prevention) with *all* children, including (but not limited to) those who come to the attention of the YJS.

The prevention of (first-time) offending by children and the reduction of identified offending (that is, the reduction of *re*offending) by children already officially recorded as having offended should both be reframed, turned on their heads, moved away from their obsession with preventing the negative and towards the *promotion* of measurable, demonstrable and achievable positive behaviours and outcomes. The absence of a negative behaviour or outcome does not constitute or imply the presence of a positive behaviour or outcome, nor does the presence of a protective factor promote positive behaviours and outcomes, simply because it represents the absence of a risk factor. However, these uncritical assumptions have formed the basis of much prevention theory, policy and practice. It is imperative that we seek to establish specific, measurable, achievable and meaningful indicators of positive behaviours (for example school achievement, prosocial behaviour, engagement, participation) and positive outcomes (for example social inclusion, employment, qualifications, access to rights and entitlements) around which to cohere CFOS prevention.

Positive behaviours and outcomes should be the targets for targeted (and universal) prevention practice under the umbrella of CFOS – not a narrow, reductionist focus on avoiding negativity, deficit, risk and harm. Participation, engagement and legitimacy are the vehicles with which to achieve these targets and are worthy principles for practice in their own right. This forward-looking, promotional focus distinguishes CFOS from ostensibly similar 'positive' models such as Positive Youth Development and Positive Futures (see earlier in this chapter), which remain wedded to reducing risk and promoting the absence of negativity through resilience- and desistance-based behaviours.

CFOS prevention (like its corresponding approach to diversion) normalises (rather than problematises) offending as only a small element of a child's broader identity. The status of 'child' is paramount in all policy and practice, which demands an acceptance of the child's inherent vulnerability by virtue of age, immaturity (biological, cognitive), their relative powerlessness, restricted socio-structural position (see also Robinson 2014) and their entitlements and rights to access support, guidance and opportunities from (responsibilised) adults and society. Prevention viewed through the lens of CFOS demands the rejection of offender-first and offence-first approaches driven by retributive and punitive practices that target the negative, in favour of a focus on promoting positive behaviour and positive outcomes for *all* children (that is, universal promotion). The prevention of offending by children is an objective best achieved through the promotion of positive behaviour via universal services that safeguard children, are normalising, and decriminalising, and located outwith the formal YJS (see also Goldson and Muncie 2006). CFOS interventions view the child as part of the solution, not part of the problem. Therefore, intervention should be provided through a non-responsibilising, inclusionary model that engages children and enables their participation in decision-making processes that affect them, such as the planning, implementation and evaluation of responsive interventions. The third-generation evolution of prevention-promotion work in Swansea, the Positive Promotion Project, provides an evidenced animation of the aspirations of CFOS as the final stage (for now) of a reflective intellectual policy and practice journey locally.

Case study: Positive Promotion Project (2007–present)

In 2007 there was a series of incidents of antisocial behaviour by children in a local Swansea community experiencing high levels of social disadvantage.[78] In response to these incidents, key youth justice and related local agencies (YOT, the local secondary school, South Wales Police, Children and Young People Strategy Unit, Anti-Social Behaviour Unit, Education Department, YIP, Careers Wales) met to discuss a partnership approach to addressing this behaviour and its associated personal and social problems through the promotion of positive behaviours and outcomes – in accordance with the evolving prevention agenda locally and the emerging social policy direction at the national level in Wales. As a result, the multi-agency Positive Promotion Project (PPP) was established to provide an holistic service delivery project which could assist children by deploying universal and targeted prevention-promotion interventions in their community context. PPP was underpinned by principles of participation, restorative practice, children's rights (UNCRC 1989; Rights of Children and Young Persons (Wales) Measure 2011), early assessment and early and *appropriate* intervention (that is, suitable, proportionate, meaningful and responsive to expressed needs and promotional objectives). PPP was constructed as an intensive, holistic, multiple-intervention,

[78] Above local and national average levels of social deprivation (for example low income, unemployment), family deprivation (for example overcrowding, single parenthood, poor quality accommodation, high uptake of free school meals), school truancy, school exclusion, children 'not in education, employment or training' (NEETs), referrals for mental health problems, along with offending, substance use and antisocial behaviour by children, with lower than average levels of educational attainment at key stages one–four (Swansea Children and Young People's Strategy Unit (CYPSU) 2007).

community-based response to meeting the needs of children aged 11–16 years (secondary school age in England and Wales), with the objectives of:

- *early intervention* to maximise children's access to opportunities, to encourage positive behaviours and outcomes and to prevent the build up of problems;
- *working in partnership* with children and families to build a safe and prosperous future for the community;
- *enabling children's positive personal development* in the home, school and community;
- *helping children to fulfil their potential* and to maximise their talents in order to enjoy a fulfilling, happy and healthy life. (Case, Charles and Haines 2012)

PPP comprised a series of coordinated programmes (for example youth nights, restorative initiatives, peer-led education, Prince's Trust activities), with the main focus being on two key programmes – the Team Around the Child (TAC) and Someone to Listen to, Something to Do (SoToDo). Both programmes are underpinned by the principles of social inclusion, consultation, multi-agency working, information sharing and early intervention with children who display need through the Common Assessment Framework.[79] However, each has a specific focus – TAC's being that of a general (primary) prevention project, whereas SoToDo consists of more targeted, responsive preventive interventions.

- **SoToDo** – a multi-agency, early intervention and prevention programme adapted from a model outlined in a Children's Commissioner for Wales report, advocating for 'effective partnership working and the establishment of an integrated holistic model of support and services' (Towler 2007: 3) to address the problem of antisocial behaviour and offending resulting from boredom and children lacking constructive

[79] A needs-based assessment framework used in the social work and child welfare fields with children likely to require support beyond universal services.

activities and facilities in their local area. SoToDo projects existed across Wales at the time of PPP's inception and a local SoToDo programme was immediately established as a foundational activity of PPP, with the partnership consisting of the police, YOT, the local authority education, social services, youth and housing departments, the local secondary school and relevant third sector organisations. A series of interventions were linked to the project from its outset, notably one-to-one support through the Swansea YIP and dedicated, needs-led prosocial activities including sports and mentoring

- **TAC** – the TAC is more social-work oriented (than SoToDo) in its use of the Common Assessment Framework (CAF) as a needs assessment tool with which to prioritise service in accordance with the Children Act 2004. The TAC situates local children and planned services on a 'continuum of needs', from *universal* (provision for all children) to *vulnerable* (targeted services for children with additional needs) to *complex* (specialist services for children with multiple needs) to *acute* (specialist services for children in immediate need of care and protection) – locating the child and family at the centre of services throughout. Once a referral is made to the TAC and a child is assessed (through CAF) as having a sufficient level of need, informed consent is elicited from the child and their parent/carer to attend a multi-agency TAC meeting to facilitate the generation of a support team of practitioners and services around the individual child and family, leading to an action plan and referral to the appropriate agency/ies. The core focus of the TAC in this context is to assess need, promote multi-agency dialogue and the engagement of children in support services and interventions that promote positive behaviours, positive outcomes, quality of life and access to their entitlements.

PPP was evaluated from 2010 to 2012 (Case, Charles and Haines 2012), with each evaluation element monitored and informed by a multi-disciplinary steering group, with representation from Swansea YOT, the local secondary school, Swansea University CCJC, South Wales Police, the local authority Education Department and Child and Family Services Department, and the project managers of SoToDo and the TAC. The main research objectives were:

1. Has PPP increased the extent and nature of *positive outcomes* such as improved school attendance (number of days per year), academic success (academic and vocational qualifications), prosocial leisure activities (for example membership of community groups, participation in local/school sports teams, volunteering), transition to college, transition to employment?
2. Has PPP reduced the extent and seriousness of officially recorded *problematic outcomes* such as substance use, offending, antisocial behaviour, teenage pregnancy, NEETs, mental-health referrals and school exclusion for children?
3. Has PPP met and reduced *children's needs* (as expressed through the CAF instrument)?
4. Has PPP improved the efficacy, quality and efficiency of *multi-agency working* with, and service provision for, children locally as perceived by key stakeholders?

The evaluation questions were drawn directly from the objectives of PPP, while the chosen method built on the empirically evidenced benefits of participatory action research with children – encouraging children's exploration, reflection and action upon their environment, developing children's capacity for self-determination, producing policy-relevant information.

A two-stage evaluation methodology was employed, consisting of quantitative secondary data analysis and qualitative interviews (one-to-one and focus group) with key stakeholders (children and practitioners working within PPP).

Quantitative secondary data analysis

Comprehensive datasets covering the period 2004–10 (three years pre- and post-PPP) relating to key measures of positive and negative behaviours and outcomes for children were accessed through existing relationships with partner agencies (for example YOT, Anti-Social Behaviour Unit, YIP, Education Department, Careers Wales – formerly Careers Business Company) who granted unconditional access to their data management systems. Local community data was analysed and compared to Swansea-wide statistics in relation to:

- education and learning – academic attainment, attendance, career pathways, school exclusion;
- crime and disorder – entry into and engagement with the YJS, involvement in the antisocial behaviour system.

Secondary data analysis (2004–10) identified that children aged 11–16 years in the local area experienced high levels of *social deprivation* compared to local (Swansea) and national (Wales) averages, as measured by living in the top 30% of deprived local wards/areas in Wales, eligibility for free school meals and being recorded as having special educational needs (Case, Charles and Haines 2012). The implication is that links between social deprivation, unmet needs and problematic behaviour in this community validate the necessity for PPP and its promotional ethos that shifts the practice focus from individualised, psychosocial risk factors and negative behaviours towards broader socio-structural and community-based needs and problems that adults are responsible for ameliorating. Since the inception of PPP in 2007, several promising positive outcomes have emerged from local community data sources.

Educationally, in terms of *academic attainment*, although remaining below the Swansea average, children in the local area have evidenced improvements (compared with 2004–06) in levels one and two attainment thresholds and 100% of pupils have gained at least one GCSE at grade A–G (both of which are positive outcome measures), which was not the case pre-PPP. Both school attendance (positive outcome) and school exclusion (negative outcome) levels have remained stable from 2007 to 2010, compared with prior trends of annual decreases in attendance and annual increases in exclusion beyond the Swansea average. From 2007 the percentage of local pupils entering further education and entering work-based training (both positive outcomes) have increased annually to levels above the Swansea average for these learning pathways. Furthermore, the percentage of children designated as NEETs (a negative outcome measure), has decreased annually since PPP began.

The crime and disorder data has illustrated some equally encouraging findings. From 2007, there have been annual decreases in the numbers of children in the local area recorded with negative outcomes, typically reflecting previous decreasing trends from 2004 to 2007 (pre-PPP), but steepening and accelerating these trends post-PPP from 2007 to 2010. There were annual decreases in the number of children receiving pre-court disposals (23% decrease pre-PPP; 50% decrease post-PPP) and those receiving court sanctions/prosecutions (27% decrease pre-PPP; 53% decrease post-PPP). Similarly, there were annual decreases in the number of offences committed by children (4% from 2004 to 2007, 64% decrease post-PPP) and the number of local children recorded as reoffending (decreased 32% pre-PPP; 29% decrease up to 2009 – the 2010 figure was unavailable). Since PPP began, no local children have been given ABCs or ASBOs through the local *antisocial behaviour system* (see Chapter Five) and the numbers of children entering stages one and two decreased annually.

Qualitative interviews and focus groups

Individual and focus group interviews were conducted with a purposive sample of key stakeholders: 64 local children in receipt of PPP provision (drawn from mainstream school and 'hard to reach' YOT and antisocial behaviour samples) and 15 key stakeholder staff from three groups: strategic directors, operational managers and ground-level practitioners. The qualitative analysis highlighted a series of critical themes emerging from key stakeholders' perceptions of PPP. Children were most concerned with how PPP had contributed to their perceptions of reducing levels of crime, antisocial behaviour and substance use in their area (including a reduced fear of these negative behaviours and their personal likelihood of participating in them), increasing respect between children and adults (for example pride and confidence in the community and in supportive child–adult relationships) and improved service effectiveness (in terms of children's views of the appropriateness and quality of the services they receive and the implications of this service delivery for their positive futures). For adult stakeholders, the most important aspects of PPP were their perceptions of reducing levels of crime, antisocial behaviour and substance use in their area (a theme shared with children, but defined by adults more in terms of how it had been achieved by integrating services and broader understandings of prevention-promotion); engagement with children (finding promotional, positive ways that children can realise their rights and be engaged within PPP process) and multi-agency working (information sharing, culture change and resource implications). A clear example of the engaging, promotional, multi-agency ethos of PPP was offered by the key operational manager from South Wales Police, who asserted that '[M]y view on prevention now is to prevent a young person from not being left on the heap, rather than prevent crime' (South Wales Police Divisional Commander, in Case, Charles and Haines 2012).

The post-PPP improvements in a series of positive educational and crime and disorder outcomes for children were consolidated by early qualitative indications that key stakeholders (children and adults) perceived these outcomes as due to improvements in the nature of (engaging, rights-based and respectful) relationships between children and adults locally, enhancements to service effectiveness (appropriateness, quality) and better multi-agency working in the community. When evaluating the central foci and practices of the programme, a key stakeholder reflected that 'these aspects present themselves as a continuum around PPP, all melding together and creating a dynamic in which it was possible to go further than we've been able to do in other locations around the issues about pupil participation' (YOT Manager, in Case, Charles and Haines 2012).

The evaluation of PPP concluded that the project offers an innovative model that combines prevention and promotion in addressing key strategic foci that intimately affect the lives of children and by seeking to resolve the issues facing local children through participative discourse, culture change and inter-agency cooperation. PPP is third-generation prevention-promotion because it moves beyond first-generation provision within schools (PPB – see Haines and Case 2003) and second generation community-based out-of-school services (*Promoting Prevention* – see Haines and Case 2003) to universal service delivery that aims to penetrate the everyday lives of all children through systemic changes to how agencies and children engage with one another to achieve positive life-changing outcomes. Since the evaluation, the local secondary school has become the first in Wales to be recognised as a 'Rights Respecting' school – placing the UNCRC at the forefront of its planning, policies and practices (UNICEF UK 2014).The school's Rights Respecting status is monitored and evolved through a 'Child Rights Committee' to inform school policy and practice and to engage children in the development and implementation of school policies (see Charles and Haines 2014). PPP animates CFOS elements that cohere around the promotion of positive behaviours and outcomes for children (alongside the promotion of positive adult perceptions of children, a much-overlooked positive outcome). As such, PPP has the potential to address the increasingly separate, 'special' and specialised treatment of children who offend across the international child welfare systems, which has resulted from managerialist concerns with policy implementation, organisational structures and financial resources and that has largely been pursued through targeted, preventive services and stand-alone projects (Haines 1997). Unfortunately, increasing numbers of specialised and targeted services and formal responses run the risk of contributing to the labelling, stigmatisation and marginalisation of children in conflict with the law and the youth justice system, rather than seeking to improve their lives through social inclusion, universalism and the normalisation of behaviour – priority outcomes for PPP.

Children First, Offenders Second prevention-promotion: protecting, promoting, progressing

In this chapter, we have demonstrated how the contemporary prevention provision delivered by youth justice services (for example, multi-agency YOTs, the Secure Estate) since the Crime and Disorder Act 1998 has pursued reductionist and interventionist goals – typically through the targeting of risk factors and negative behaviours and outcomes (stages four–six on the prevention-promotion constellation). Grounding prevention policy and practice in the RFPP has engendered a neoliberal, neo-correctionalist prevention model that 'promotes' negative views of children and negative experiences and outcomes for children (Kelly 2012). These criticisms themselves overlook the issue that prevention work is predominantly conducted with identified 'offenders' and 'at risk' children, thus is situated firmly within the formal YJS – reflecting ongoing confusion and conflation of the prevention of offending, early intervention and the reduction of reoffending. However, such confusion and conflation has only been compounded by the recent retrenchment of prevention activity due to economic austerity measures, which have prompted an increased emphasis on targeting time and resources on children assessed as at 'high risk' of reoffending (MoJ 2010; see also Haines 1997).

We have argued that the youth justice prevention agenda as currently conceived is highly problematic, not only due to its creation of negative and restricted understandings of children and their behaviour, but also on methodological grounds. The evidential basis for prevention approaches is dubious – beset by ambiguities and divergences regarding appropriate targets, objectives and evidence base. The precise nature of the *targets* for youth justice prevention activity have been heterogeneous and contested (notwithstanding the consensual focus on the negative), with interventions often targeting one or more of a range of possible negative behaviours (for example first-time offending, reoffending, serious offending, drug use, alcohol use, antisocial behaviour, violence, self-harm, risk taking) and negative outcomes (for example first-time entry into the YJS, conviction, reconviction, social exclusion, school exclusion, unemployment, disaffection). There have been further ambiguities regarding the *objectives* of prevention activity. As demonstrated by the prevention-promotion constellation, youth justice prevention approaches have vacillated between the pure *prevention* of the onset of negative behaviours and outcomes, to *early intervention* with children identified as 'at risk' of developing problem trajectories, to the *reduction* of identified, established behaviours and outcomes. Indeed, much activity defined as 'prevention' can be more accurately portrayed as 'reduction' because it seeks to reduce negative behaviours and outcomes and exposure to identified, existing risk factors in the child's life.

We have discussed how a CFOS model of prevention is no more focused on the *prevention* of emerging problems, negative behaviours and outcomes than is the risk-focused, targeted early intervention and reduction policy and practice of the UK government. Instead, CFOS prevention replaces traditional youth justice prevention with a focus on *promotion* – a positive youth justice that promotes positive circumstances, experiences, opportunities, capacities, behaviours and outcomes for children through their inclusion, participation and engagement in the evidence-based partnerships that develop and implement interventions to respond to children's expressed needs and problems (see also Pittman et al 2003). These interventions are coordinated through systems management that maintains their child-friendly and child-appropriate nature, and are underpinned by universalism and facilitated access to rights and entitlements.

A principled, embedded and consistent CFOS approach to working with children, animated by targeted and universal promotion, replacing the punitive, interventionist, net-widening and criminalising excesses of previous and current youth justice prevention, remains aspirational to a large degree in England and Wales. Social policy in Wales has espoused broad commitments to universalism and the CFOS principles of multi-agency (evidence-based) partnership working, consultation with children and ensuring access to children's rights as standard, yet much of this policy and associated practice remains wedded to the negative-facing, deleterious RFPP, which is anathema to CFOS. Similarly, the Positive Youth Development movement emanating from the US has made encouraging steps towards the promotion of positive behaviour, but the movement seems intent on restricting its own potential by privileging risk, protection from risk and the child's resilience to risk, at the expense of its more progressive pursuit of positive characteristics, behaviours and outcomes (see also Case and Haines 2009). A promising approach to animating and evidencing CFOS prevention has been the experience of the three generations of prevention-promotion work in Swansea, developed through evidence-based partnership with children and with academic researchers through Reflective Friend Research. Although the evolving programmes have reflected an undercurrent of faith in the RFPP (at least to some degree), they have consistently moved the local agenda towards the promotion of positive behaviours and outcomes, such that the third-generation PPP initiative has significantly marginalised the risk focus in favour of positive objectives and addressing expressed needs, rather than risks. These local developments, consolidated by interview testimony from practitioners, policy makers and children, offer tentative indications of an evidence-based approach to 'prevention' that has been able to animate the promotional ethos of CFOS.

SEVEN

Conclusion

Society treats children in conflict with the law and the youth justice system in 'special' ways, but often with a negative focus, in relation to the perceived threat they present and the problems they may cause others, rather than offering children support and protection due to their vulnerability, lack of maturity and relative lack of power in society. In response to this situation, we have asserted a principled, progressive and positive model of youth justice that can shape the 'special treatment' of children in conflict with the law and the youth justice system by adhering to the tenets/touchstones of diversion, inclusion, evidence-based partnership, legitimacy, systems management, partnership with the state and responsibilising adults. Accordingly, this book has laid out the Children First, Offenders Second (CFOS) approach to positive youth justice.

In the opening two chapters we outlined the thinking that underpins the approach and the fundamental elements of CFOS. We argued that CFOS positive youth justice is a modern, economic-normative paradigm driven by a series of principles that sustain and promote child-friendly and child-appropriate policy and practice. As such, CFOS is both reactionary against the negative, correctionalist, reductionist, interventionist and stigmatising approaches that have dominated youth justice and progressive in offering a distinctive, positive youth justice that prioritises the normalisation of childhood behaviour, children's access to their universal entitlements and children's achievement of positive behaviours and outcomes.

In Chapter Three we explored the complex and contentious differences and divergences between Wales and England in terms of their social *policy* for children generally and in the youth justice arena in particular. We argued that from the end of the 1990s, youth justice policy in England took a neoliberalist, offender-first, punitive turn, predicated on notions of risk and responsibilisation. In contrast, the Welsh government has sought to enshrine a rights- and entitlements-based social policy for children and has placed those children in conflict with the law and the youth justice system at the heart of this approach. While noting that youth justice is not a matter of devolved responsibility – remaining the province of the Westminster government and the Youth Justice Board for England and Wales – we pointed out that many of those employed to provide youth justice services in Wales are employed within organisations for whom the Welsh government does have devolved responsibility. As a consequence of these complexities in constitutional arrangements, bespoke structures have been established – notably YJB Cymru and the Wales Youth Justice Advisory Panel – to manage the differences between jurisdictions and to pursue the distinctive Welsh social policy-making identity in work with children in conflict with the law and the youth justice system.

In Chapters Four, Five and Six, we explored the potentialities for adopting a CFOS approach to working with children within the formal youth justice system (YJS) and in less formal diversionary and prevention-promotion contexts, using a body of evidence generated through local research partnership working guided by Welsh social policy for children and young people. However, while it is important to reflect on the specific (potential) impact of CFOS locally and within Wales, it is equally vital to address the *transferability* and *applicability* of the model to other places and settings where work with children is conducted. The established extent of local variations in practice (between and within countries) establishes the space for professionals working with children in conflict with the law and the youth justice system to adopt and adapt their practice. Indeed, other countries and areas outside Wales are already moving to a set of practices that are consistent with CFOS principles, for example, diversionary models (compare Durham Pre-Remand Disposal, Hull Triage – Smith 2014) and innovative 'post-YOT' participation and engagement strategies in England (compare Surrey Youth Support Service – Byrne and Brooks 2015), the emerging diversionary focus in Australia (compare Richards 2014), the emphasis on a fusion of diversion and engagement in

New Zealand (compare Henry, Henaghan, Sanders and Munford 2015) and the positive youth justice model in the US (Butts et al 2010). Therefore, there is a nascent but growing Welsh, English and international consensus that CFOS principles offer a coherent, evidence-based and philosophically robust basis for the future of youth justice.

Alongside policy and practice divergences between (also within) different *countries*, there are also well-known and well-established divergences between policy and practice *within* countries (the 'policy–practice divide'), despite over two decades of ever more intrusive managerialism. The relationship between policy and practice is a complex one, and this is certainly true in youth justice. Indeed, we are mindful throughout of the local mediation of centralised policy in practice, notably across England and Wales. There is no suggestion, therefore, that a straight-line relationship exists between policy and practice. There are, indeed, what we would characterise as good and bad examples of practice in both countries (see for example, Sutherland 2009; Haines and Case 2012) – illustrating that the relationship between policy and practice can be highly attenuated by extraneous and exogenous factors such as local mediation, organisational culture, within- and between-agency differences and socio-economic and socio-political pressures. What we see as one of the key determinants of the extent of divergence between policy and practice is the existence and penetration of a coherent *philosophy* of approach. Indeed, for practice itself to be coherent (recognising that different practitioners within a single team may diverge in their approach), practitioners need to know why they come into work every day, they must possess (and share) a clear idea about the purpose of their work and there must be clarity about whose interests they serve, what they are in work to achieve and what outcomes they seek to promote and for whom. Only when there is clarity of philosophy can the mechanics of achieving the overall aim of the system be determined and measured.[80]

[80] See Bottoms et al (1990) for an interesting example of a typology of philosophies as they existed during the era of Intermediate Treatment and Haines and Drakeford (1998) for an account of the development, implementation and impact of *new orthodoxy* thinking.

Realising Children First, Offenders Second positive youth justice: the Children and Young People First strategy

At this point, to bring this book to a conclusion, it seems appropriate to turn to the revised All Wales Youth Offending Strategy (WAG and YJB 2004) – not least because the revised strategy has been published as we write this final chapter.

Firstly and significantly, a strong indication of the trajectory of the new strategy and its difference from the All Wales Youth Offending Strategy (AWYOS) is to be found in the title: *Children and Young People First*, which foregrounds the more descriptive sub-title *Welsh Government/Youth Justice Board Joint Strategy to Improve Services for Young People from Wales at Risk of Becoming Involved in, or in, the Youth Justice System* (Welsh Government and YJB 2014). The evident commitment to taking a CFOS approach in Wales is clearly stated in the vision statement (Welsh Government and YJB 2014: 3):

> We want a country in which we all work to prevent children and young people from entering the youth justice system. But if young people do offend, we want to ensure the system and associated services do all they can to help and support them to have the best chance of not having further convictions. Children and young people at risk of entering, or who are in, the youth justice system must be treated as children first and offenders second in all interactions with services.

It is clear from this vision statement that taking a CFOS approach is designed to enable children to lead positive lives and that this is intended to have a positive effect on reducing youth offending. It is also clear that the strategy makes adults responsible for achieving this vision. Children and Young People First sets out five *priorities* for youth justice practice:

1. a well-designed partnership approach;
2. early intervention, prevention and diversion;
3. reducing reoffending;

4. effective use of custody;
5. resettlement and reintegration at the end of a sentence.

These priorities are linked to eight specific objectives for the CFOS treatment of children in the YJS: engaging children in mainstream services; multi-agency partnerships for meeting children's needs; diversion out of the YJS and into needs-based services; challenging offending behaviour and responding proportionately; recognising vulnerability and safeguarding children; enhancing the values, attitudes, knowledge and skills of practitioners to enable children's desistance and crime-free lives; custody as a last resort; enabling transitions from the YJS into an independent, crime-free life. Each of these objectives is to be pursued through eight key principles of practice:

1. Children First, Offenders Second;
2. children in the YJS have the same access to their rights and entitlements as any other child;
3. the voice of the child is actively sought and listened to;
4. early intervention and holistic multi-agency support;
5. effective practice as fundamental to improving outcomes for children;
6. accountable services that address children's needs;
7. supporting the YJS to develop the knowledge and skills to understand and address children's needs;
8. victim consultation and meaningful participation.

Crucially, the priorities, objectives and principles of Children and Young People First reflect, map onto and animate the guiding features of CFOS positive youth justice. The bedrock and driving force of the strategy is multi-agency *partnership* working. Having outlined 'a well-designed partnership approach' as its first priority, Children and Young People First (Welsh Government and YJB 2014: 7) goes on to assert an expectation that services

> work together to provide coordinated, multi-agency, wrap-around support which is consistent across Wales so young people do not fall into 'service gaps'; or move back and forth between services where

> there are disputes with regard to who is responsible for providing the relevant support. ... Partnership working is fundamental to ensuring young people have access to services when they need them.

These partnerships are not just those between the agencies that comprise the YJS – as important as these partnerships are – they extend to include and direct children towards those agencies that provide 'mainstream' and other targeted services to children.[81] Furthermore, the partnership approach applies to the delivery of services from diversion and prevention (strategy priority two), through to those children embroiled in the YJS (priorities three and four), to those children transitioning out of the system (priority five) – at all stages and ages. The strategy clearly states that 'prevention in all its forms is the key to stopping young people coming into the justice system' (Welsh Government and YJB 2014: 12). This is to be achieved through a tiered approach that moves from early intervention and prevention services (tier one) to targeted YOT prevention (tier two) to alternatives to charging and diversion (tier three). While the strategy uses the terms 'early intervention and prevention' (compare our criticisms in Chapter Six of these terms, their usage and application), the intention here is clear and avowedly children first and entitlements/rights focused. Intervention in the lives of children in Wales is presented as a good thing and predicated on improving children's access to their entitlements (under Extending Entitlement – see Chapter Three) in a proactive, forward-looking manner in which the outcomes for children are improved. The strategy sees a proper and full role for YOTs in both tier one and two prevention (Welsh Government and YJB 2014: 14), in a manner consistent with the CFOS principle of partnership:

> There will be young people who risk falling into a 'service gap' because their needs are too complex for easy integration into universal services yet who

[81] See our thoroughgoing criticism of managerialism, neoliberalism and the cuts to children's services wrought in the name of austerity.

> have not met the threshold for statutory intervention … It is in instances like these we believe targeted multi-agency prevention is appropriate. YOTs are the primary providers of services to identify and prevent children and young people from offending, however this work is often delivered in partnership with others from the voluntary and public sectors.

In line with CFOS principles, the strategy prioritises *diversion* from prosecution and formal system contact for children in conflict with the law and the youth justice system. Diversion is framed within an overarching early intervention and *prevention* focus (which also incorporates the prevention of/diversion from future (re)offending), with a commitment to 'prevent young people entering the youth justice system' (Welsh Government and YJB 2014: 14) – a principle we explored in Chapter Five as 'diversion from the formal YJS'. Children and Young People First asserts that 'Police-led alternatives to charging exist as a mechanism for diverting children and young people away from the youth justice system and into mainstream services' (Welsh Government and YJB 2014: 14). Notably, the Bureau model is highlighted as the key (police-led, alternative to charging) vehicle to achieve the strategy's diversion-prevention objectives, as evidenced by our own research into the reduction of first-time entrants into the YJS and the reduction of reoffending (Haines, Case, Charles and Davies 2013; see Chapter Five).

The problems faced by those children now entering the YJS and the challenges this poses to YOTs and others are growing more complex and this is acknowledged in the strategy's focus on children demonstrating multiple, complex needs (for example emotional and mental health issues, substance use, victimisation) as the group at highest risk of reoffending. In the face of this challenge, the strategy offers support for the CFOS principle of systems management as a tool to unblock children's restricted societal opportunities (Welsh Government and YJB 2014: 16; see also France and Homel 2007) and tackling their inherent vulnerability and disadvantage: 'We will work to overcome any systemic obstacles, so service provision is based around the needs of the young person rather than how services are organised and delivered.'

In terms of working with children in the YJS, Children and Young People First heralds the new AssetPlus assessment and intervention framework for its privileging of children's 'views and experiences' and practitioners' discretion, both of which are central features of the participatory and engagement-led practice promoted by CFOS positive youth justice (see Chapter Four). However, the implementation of AssetPlus (at the time of writing) remains to be tested. We believe that AssetPlus has the potential to lead to improvements in the delivery of youth justice services to children in Wales and England (Haines and Case 2012; Case 2014; Case and Haines, in Goldson and Muncie 2015c). We have argued that this potential can be increased (see Chapter Four) if AssetPlus is augmented in the service of a coherent philosophy – something that it currently lacks – and we have argued throughout our book that CFOS provides such a philosophy through its underpinning principles for practice: engagement with children, families and practitioners (for example enhancing participation and discretion), advocacy of a thoroughgoing entitlements-led (anti-risk) focus for all work with children and cohering policy and practice around the promotion of positive behaviours and outcomes, rather than the prevention of the negative.

Children and Young People First represents a bold statement from Welsh government and the Youth Justice Board of a distinctively Welsh approach to youth justice. In contrast with the AWYOS, which presented an uneasy compromise between English and Welsh principles (Haines 2009b), Children and Young People First offers a much stronger statement of Welsh philosophy, policy and practice. Gone are notions of punishment, risk factors and responsibilising children. In their place is a positive view of children, a positive view of and (legitimate) role for the state (at national and local levels), a positive view of intervention and the utilisation of systems management focused on achieving positive outcomes for children and a positive commitment to responsibilising adults – all in the service of a CFOS philosophy and achieving maximum positive outcomes for all children. However, the clear and robust *policy* standpoint of Children and Young People First remains a significant challenge in terms of its implementation in *practice* across Welsh youth offending teams (YOTs). Youth justice practice in Wales is characterised by local variation in the mediation and animation of policy (as in England), with YOTs occupying a dynamic, yet ambiguous 'constitutional' position somewhere in between mainstream local management structures (for example local authority social services departments) and national governing bodies (for example YJB Cymru). The influence on policy and practice of the emerging contexts of both 'localism' and economic austerity have both constrained practice and (ironically) precipitated conditions ripe for local variations and innovations in practice. While a degree of local discretion is both desirable and necessary to enable flexible and appropriate responses to specific localised contexts, the challenge remains, across Wales and England, to cohere local variation around a consistent philosophy and approach (Haines and Case 2015). Children and Young People First offers the first step in this process.

The ultimate aim of this book is to establish CFOS as the dominant philosophy of youth justice – not just as it exists in Welsh policy, but to extend it much more assiduously to Welsh practice and to policy and practice in other countries around the world. Our experience of developing and implementing CFOS across Wales has, however, been mixed. Most (if not all) YOTs, YOT managers and YOT practitioners in Wales would say that their practice adheres to a CFOS philosophy even where it is fairly clear, to us, that it does not. This incongruence is partly a product of the aforementioned policy–practice divide and partly due to ongoing ambiguity, debate and uncertainty over the precise nature of CFOS positive youth justice – hopefully an issue that can be resolved upon reading of the arguments in this book. There is much still to learn about what exactly constitutes CFOS practice, much still to learn about practice that is CFOS compliant and much still to learn about how to implement CFOS in practice. For this reason, we used Chapters Four, Five and Six to discuss and evidence our experience of developing and implementing CFOS in a local youth justice context. We also use the evidence-based chapters in particular to illustrate the principles and practices of CFOS in a practical manner –

to bring to life positive youth justice practice that is consistent with a CFOS philosophy. In this vein, we have argued that the CFOS model shapes and puts boundaries around youth justice practice, but that there is much scope and need for practitioner discretion and the development of professional practice, much to be gained from using a reflective research-practice partnership to develop CFOS practice and great potential in facilitating children's participation and engagement to contribute to child-friendly and child-appropriate youth justice (see Case and Haines, 2015b). We highly commend the Reflective Friend Research model of engagement-focused partnership working between children, practitioners, policy makers and researchers as a conduit to CFOS positive youth justice. For us, effective Reflective Friend Research coheres around *situated learning* through researcher immersion in the everyday practice contexts and lived realities of partners, which facilitates *enhanced access* to a broader range of (more valid) data and evidence than would be possible through the traditional researcher–subject relationship. Situated learning and enhanced access, in turn, facilitate *reflective engagement* with data, evidence and practice through relationships founded on trust, respect, confidence and reciprocity, which itself enables a *critical friendship* role for researchers, to utilise for constructive evaluation and critique of policy and practice and the recommendation of development/enhancement opportunities (Case and Haines 2014a).

In conclusion, it is crucial to emphasise that:

- CFOS is, and always will be, a work in progress;
- it takes time and concerted effort to implement CFOS and to realise its benefits;
- local factors are important in shaping CFOS delivery; our local experiences are not a model or a blueprint, but are illustrative of the type of issues that may be faced and methods that can be transferred and applied in other geographical areas and to other practice contexts that involve work with children.

What we have sought to outline is a practical, progressive, participatory and promotional model of evidence-based partnership working with children that can be adapted and adopted elsewhere for the benefit of children, families, communities, practitioners and policy makers – a positive youth justice that puts *children first*.

References

Agnew, R. (2005) *Why do criminals offend? A general theory of crime and delinquency*, Oxford: Oxford University Press

Alderson, P. (2008) *Young children's rights: Exploring beliefs, principles and practice*, London: Jessica Kingsley, 105–14

Allen, R. (1991) Out of jail: The reduction in the sue of penal custody for male juveniles 1981-88, *Howard Journal* 30, 1, 30–52

Allen, R. (2009) International Centre for Prison Studies (ICPS) Press release 16/09, 26 January

ARCS Ltd (2008) *Reviewing the effectiveness of community safety policy and Practice – An overview of current debates and their background*. Montreal: International Centre for the Prevention of Crime

Armstrong, D. (2004) A risky business? Research, policy, governmentality and youth offending, *Youth Justice* 4, 2, 100–16

Ashcroft, J., Daniels, D. and Hart, S. (2004) *Evaluating GREAT: A school-based gang prevention program*, Washington, DC: National Institute of Justice, US Department of Justice

Ashford, B. (2007) *Towards a crime prevention strategy*, London: YJB

Asquith, S. (1998) The Scottish Children's Hearings in an international context, in A. Lockyer and F. Stone (eds) *The Scottish Children's Hearings*, Edinburgh: T & T Clarke

Atkinson, W., Roberts, S. and Savage, M. (2012) *Class inequality in austerity Britain: Power, difference and suffering*, London: Sage

Audit Commission (1996) *Misspent youth: Young people and crime*, London: Audit Commission

Audit Commission (2004) *Youth justice*, London: Audit Commission

Bailey, R. and Williams, B. (2000) *Inter-agency partnerships in youth justice: Implementing the Crime and Disorder Act 1998*, Sheffield: University of Sheffield,

Baker, K. (2005) Assessment in youth justice: Professional discretion and the use of Asset, *Youth Justice*, 5, 106–22

Baker, K. (2012) AssetPlus *Rationale*, London: YJB

Bandalli, S. (2000) Children, Responsibility and the New Youth Justice, in B. Goldson, (ed) *The New Youth Justice*, Lyme Regis: Russell House, 81–95

Banks, R. and Laurie, H. (2000) From PAPI to CAPI: The case of the British Household Panel Survey, *Social Science Computer Review*, 18, 4, 397–406

Barry, M. and McNeill, F. (eds) (2009) *Youth Offending and youth justice*, London: Jessica Kingsley Publishers

Baskerville, D. and Goldblatt, H. (2009) Learning to be a critical friend: From professional indifference through challenge to unguarded conversations. *Cambridge Journal of Education*, 39, 2, 205–21,, ,–

Bateman, T. (2011) Punishing poverty: the 'scaled approach' and youth justice practice, *Howard Journal of Penal Reform*, 50, 2, 171–83

Bateman, T. (2012) *Children in conflict with the law: An overview of trends and developments – 2010/2011*, London: NAYJ

Beck, U. (1992) *Risk society: Towards a new modernity*, London: Sage

Becker, H. (1963) *Outsiders: Studies in the sociology of deviance*, New York: The Free Press

Behlmer, G. (1998) *Friends of the family: The English home and its guardians, 1850-1940*, Stanford: Stanford University Press

Beinert, S., Anderson, B., Lee, S. and Utting, D. (2002) *Youth at risk? A national survey of risk factors, protective factors and problem behaviour among young people in England, Scotland and Wales*, York: JRF

Bell, C. and Haines, K. (1991) Managing the transition: Implications of the introduction of a Youth Court in England and Wales – A moving frontier, in T. Booth (ed) *Juvenile justice in the new Europe*, Social Services Monographs: Research in Practice

Bessant, J., Hill, R. and Watts, R. (2003) *Discovering risk: Social research and policy making*, New York: Peter Lang

Birdwell, J. and Bani, M. (2014) Today's teenagers are more engaged with social issues than ever ..., *Introducing generation citizen*, London: Demos

Blyth, M. and Solomon, E. (2009) *Prevention and youth crime: Is early intervention working*? Bristol: Policy Press

Bobo, L.D. and Thompson, V. (2006) Unfair by Design: The War on Drugs, Race, and the Legitimacy of the Criminal Justice System, *Social Research*, 73, 2, 445–72

Bottoms, A., Brown, P., McWilliams, B., McWilliams, W., Nellis, M. with Pratt, J. (1990) *Intermediate treatment and juvenile justice*, London: HMSO

Braithwaite, J. (1989) *Crime, shame and reintegration*, Cambridge: Cambridge University Press

Braithwaite, J. (2002). *Restorative justice and responsive regulation*, New York: Oxford University Press

Braithwaite, J. and Mugford, S. (1994) Conditions of successful reintegration ceremonies, *British Journal of Criminology*, 34, 2, 139–71

Bredo, E. (2005) Reconstructing educational psychology, in P. Murphy (ed) *Learners, learning and assessment*, London: Paul Chapman Publishing

Briggs, D. (2013) Conceptualising risk and need: The rise of actuarialism and the death of welfare? Practitioner assessment and intervention in the youth offending service, *Youth Justice*, 13, 1, 17–30

Brittan, L. (1984) Foreword. *Criminal justice: A working paper.* London: Home Office

Brown, S. (2005) *Understanding youth and crime. Listening to youth?*, Maidenhead: Open University Press

Burnett, R. (2007) Never too early? Reflections on research and interventions for early developmental prevention of serious harm, in M. Blyth, E. Solomon and K. Baker (eds) *Young people and risk*, Bristol: Policy Press

Burnett, R. and Appleton, K. (2004) Joined-up services to tackle youth crime. A case-study in England, *British Journal of Criminology*, 44, 1, 34–54

Burney, E. (2009) *Making people behave*, Cullompton: Willan

Butts, J.A., Bazemore, G. and Meroe, A.S. (2010) *Positive youth justice: Framing justice interventions using the concepts of positive youth development*, Washington, DC: Coalition for Juvenile Justice

Carlile, A. (2014) Written Evidence to the Inquiry by Parliamentarians into the operation and effectiveness of the Youth Court, London: NCB and Michael Sieff Foundation

Carrabine, E. (2008) Youth Justice in the UK, paper presented at the UKIERI Child Rights Conference, University of Essex, April 2008

Casanovas, P. (2008) Concepts and fields of relational justice, in J.G. Carbonell and J. Siekmann, *Lecture notes in artificial intelligence 4884*, Berlin, Heidelberg: Springer, 323–340

Case, S.P. (2004) *Promoting prevention: Evaluating a multi-agency initiative to prevent youth offending in Swansea*, unpublished PhD Thesis, Swansea: Swansea University

Case, S.P. (2006) Young people 'at risk' of what? Challenging risk-focused early intervention as crime prevention, *Youth Justice*, 6, 3, 171–9

Case, S.P. (2007) Questioning the 'evidence' of risk that underpins evidence-led youth justice interventions, *Youth Justice*, 7, 2, 91–106

Case, S.P. (2008) Intermediate Treatment, in B. Goldson (ed) *Dictionary of Youth Justice*, Cullompton: Willan

Case, S.P. (2009) Preventing and reducing risk, in W. Taylor, R. Earle and R. Hester (eds) *Youth Justice Handbook*, Cullompton: Willan

Case, S.P. (2011) A New Response to Youth Crime (D J Smith), *Youth Justice*, 11, 1, 106–8

Case, S.P. (2014) Strategic complexities and opportunities in Welsh youth justice: Exploring YJB Cymru, *Safer Communities* 13, 3, 109–19

Case, S.P. and Haines, K.R. (2004) Promoting prevention: Evaluating a multi-agency initiative of youth consultation and crime prevention in Swansea, *Children and Society* 18, 5, 355–70

Case, S.P. and Haines, K.R. (2009) *Understanding youth offending: Risk factor research, policy and practice*, Cullompton: Willan.

Case, S.P. and Haines, K.R. (2011) Protection, prevention and promotion: The restricted evolution of the protective factor in criminological research, *Social Work Review*, 2, 109–22

Case, S.P. and Haines, K.R. (2012) Supporting an evolving and devolving Youth Justice Board, *Criminal Justice Matters*, 88, 1, 38–40

Case, S.P. and Haines, K.R. (2014a) Reflective friend research: the relational aspects of social scientific research, in K. Lumsden (ed) *Reflexivity in criminological research*, London: Palgrave

Case, S.P. and Haines, K.R. (2014b) Youth justice: From linear risk paradigm to complexity, in A. Pycroft and C. Bartollas (eds) *Applying complexity theory: Whole systems approaches in criminal justice and social work*, Bristol: Policy Press

Case, S.P. and Haines, K.R. (2015a) Children first, offenders second positive promotion: Reframing the prevention debate, *Youth Justice Journal*, http://yjj.sagepub.com/content/early/2014/12/12/1473225414563154.full.pdf+html

Case, S.P. and Haines, K.R. (2015b) Children first, offenders second: The centrality of engagement in positive youth justice, *The Howard Journal of Criminal Justice*, 54, 2, 157–75.

Case, S.P. and Haines, K.R. (2015c) Risk management and early intervention, in B. Goldson and J. Muncie (eds) *Youth, Crime and Justice*, London: Sage

Case, S.P. and Hester, R. (2010) Professional education in youth justice. Mirror or motor? *British Journal of Community Justice*, 8, 2, 45–56

Case, S.P., Charles, A.D. and Haines, K.R. (2012) *Positive Promotion Project. Report for the National Institute for Social Care and Health Research*, Swansea: NISCH

Case, S.P., Clutton, S. and Haines, K.R. (2005) Extending Entitlement: A Welsh policy for children, *Wales Journal of Law and Policy* 4, 2, 187–202

Catalano, R.F. and Hawkins, J.D. (1996) The social development model: a theory of anti-social behaviour, in J. Hawkins (ed) *Delinquency and crime: Current theories*, Cambridge: Cambridge University Press

Catalano, R.F., Berglund, L.M., Ryan, J.A.M., Lonczak, H.S. and Hawkins, D.J. (2004) Positive Youth Development in the United Sates: Research Findings on Evaluations of Positive Youth Development Programs, *Prevention and Treatment* 5, Article 15, American Psychological Association

Catch 22 (2014) www.catch-22.org.uk/expertise/social-action/positive-futures/

Cavadino, M. and Dignan, J. (2002) *The penal system: An introduction*, London: SageCavadino, M. and Dignan, J. (2006) *Penal policy and political economy*, London: Sage

Centre for Mental Health (2009) *Diversion: A better way for criminal justice and mental health*, London: Centre for Mental Health

Centre for Social Justice (2007) *Being tough on the causes of crime: Tackling family breakdown to prevent youth crime*, London: CSJ

Centre for Social Justice (2011) *Making sense of early intervention*, London: CSJCentre for Social Justice (2012) *Rules of engagement: Changing the heart of youth justice*, London: CSJ

Charles, A.D. (2011) *Young people's participation in everyday decision-making*, unpublished PhD thesis, Swansea: Swansea University

Charles, A. and Haines, K. (2014) Measuring young people's participation in decision making, *International Journal of Children's Rights*, 22, 3, 641-59

Children and Young People Now (2011) Intervene in the early years to bring down youth offending, urges justice minister, 7 February 2011, www.cypnow.co.uk/cyp/news/1044941/intervene-bring-youth-offending-urges-justice-minister

Children and Young People Now (2012) Ex-Chair Rod Morgan rejects YJB custody claim, 12 April, www.cypnow.co.uk/cyp/news/1043084/ex-chair-rod-morgan-rejects-yjb-custody-claim

City and County of Swansea Cabinet (2013) *Cabinet minutes January 31st, 2013*, Swansea: CCS

Cloward, R. and Ohlin, L. (1960) *Delinquency and opportunity* New York: Free Press

Cohen, A.K. (1955) *Delinquent boys: The culture of the gang*, New York: The Free Press

Cohen, S. (1985) *Visions of social control: Crime, punishment and classification*, London: Polity Press

Cole, D. (1999) *No equal justice: Race and class in the American criminal justice*, New York: New Press

Commission on Devolution in Wales (2014) *Empowerment and responsibility: Legislative power to strengthen Wales*, Cardiff: Welsh Government

Cousin, G. and Deepwell, F. (2005) Designs for network learning: A communities of practice perspective, *Studies in Higher Education*, 30, 1, 57–66

Crawford, A. (2002) Joined up but fragmented: Contradiction, ambiguity and ambivalence at the heart of New Labour's 'third way', in R. Matthews and J. Pitts (eds) *Crime, Disorder and Community Safety*, London: Routledge, 54–80

Crawford, A., (2009) Governing through anti-social behaviour: Regulatory challenges to criminal justice, *British Journal of Crimino*logy, 49, 6, 810–31

Crawford, A. and Newburn, T. (2003) *Youth offending and restorative justice*, Cullompton: Willan

Creaney, S. (2012) Targeting, labelling and stigma: Challenging the criminalisation of children and young people, *Criminal Justice Matters*, 89, 1, 16–17

Creaney, S. (2014) The benefits of participation for young offenders, *Safer Communities*, 13, 3, 126–32

Creaney, S. and Smith, R. (2014) Youth justice back at the crossroads, *Safer Communities*, 13, 2, 83–7

Cromby, J. and Willis, M. (2014) Nudging into subjectification: governmentality and psychometrics, *Critical Social Policy*, 34, 2, 241–59

Daly, K. (2003) Mind the gap: Restorative justice in theory and practice, in Andrew von Hirsch, et al (eds) *Restorative justice and criminal justice: Competing or reconcilable paradigms?* Oxford and Portland, Oregon: Hart Publishing, 219–36

Davis, G., Boucherat, J. and Watson, D. (1989) Pre-court decision making in juvenile justice, *British Journal of Criminology*, 29, 3, 219–35 (1995) *Diversion and informal social control*, Berlin, New York: De Gruyter

Delgrado, R. (2000) Prosecuting violence: A colloquy on race, community and justice. Goodbye to Hammurabi: Analysing the atavistic appeal of restorative justice, *Stanford Law Review*, 52, 4, 751–75

Department for Children, Schools and Families (2008) *Youth Task Force action plan: Give respect, get respect*, London: DfCSF

Department for Education (2004) *Every child matters*. London: DoE

Department for Education and Skills (2004) *Every child matters*, London: DfES

Department for Education and Skills (2005) *Youth matters*, London: DfES

Department for Education and Skills (2007) *Children's plan*. London: DfES

Department of Health (1994) *Responding to youth crime: Findings from inspections of youth justice sections in five local authority social services departments*, London: HMSO

Department of Justice Northern Ireland (2011) *Report of the Youth Justice System in Northern Ireland*, Belfast: Department of Justice

Dorling, D. (2014) *Inequality and the 1%*, New York: Verso

Dottridge, M. (2004) *Kids as commodities? Child trafficking and what to do about it*, Geneva: Fédération Internationale Terre des hommes

Drake, D.H., Fergusson, R. and Briggs, D.B. (2014) Hearing new voices: Re-viewing youth justice policy through practitioners? Relationships with young people, *Youth Justice* 14 22–39

Drakeford, M. (2009) Children first, offenders second: youth justice in a devolved Wales, *Criminal Justice Matters* 78, 1, 8–9,,

Durnescu., I. (2012) What matters most in probation supervision: Staff characteristics, staff skills or programme? *Criminology and Criminal Justice*, 12, 2, 193–216

Dutton, J.E. and Dukerich, J.M. (2006) The relational foundation of research: An underappreciated dimension of interesting research, *Academy of Management Journal*, 49, 1, 21–6

Early Intervention Foundation (2014) Right for children, better for the economy, www.eif.org.uk/

Edwards, A. and Hughes, G. (2008) Inventing community safety, in P. Carlen (ed) *Imaginary Penalities*, Cullompton, Willan

Edwards, A. and Hughes, G. (2009) The preventive turn and the promotion of safer communities in England and Wales, in A. Crawford (ed) *Crime prevention policies in comparative perspective*, Cullompton: Willan

Evans, R., Pinnock, K., Beirens, H. and Edwards, A. (2006) Developing preventative practices: The experiences of children, young people and their families in the Children's Fund, *The National Evaluation of the Children's Fund*. London: DfES

Fagan, J. and Zimring, F. (2000) *The changing borders of juvenile justice*, Chicago: University of Chicago Press

Farrington, D.P. (1996) *Understanding and preventing youth crime*, York: Joseph Rowntree Foundation

Farrington, D. (2000) Developmental criminology and risk-focussed prevention, in M. Maguire, R. Morgan and R. Reiner (eds) *The Oxford handbook of criminology* (3rd edn) Oxford: Oxford University Press

Farrington, D. (2007) Childhood risk factors and risk-focused prevention, in M. Maguire, R. Morgan and R. Reiner (eds) *The Oxford handbook of criminology* (4th edn) Oxford: Oxford University Press

Farrow, K., Kelly, G. and Wilkinson, B. (2007) *Offenders in focus*, Bristol: Policy Press

Fionda, J. (1998) The age of innocence? – the concept of childhood in the punishment of young offenders, *Child and Family Law Quarterly*, 10: 77–88

France, A. (2008) Risk factor analysis and the youth question, *Journal of Youth Studies*, 11, 1, 1-15

France, A. and Crow, I. (2005) Using the 'risk factor paradigm' in prevention: lessons from the evaluation of Communities that Care, *Children and Society*, 19, 2, 172–84

France, A. and Homel, R. (2006) Societal access routes and developmental pathways: Putting social structure and young people's voices into the analysis of pathways into and out of crime, *Australian New Zealand Journal of Criminology*, 39, 3, 295-309

France, A. and Homel, R. (2007) *Pathways and crime prevention*, Cullompton: Willan

France, A. and Utting, D. (2005) The paradigm of 'risk and protection-focused prevention' and its impact on services for children and families, *Children and Society*, 19, 2, 77–90

Freeman, M. (2007) *Article 3: The best interests of the child*, Leiden: Martinus Nijhoff Publishers

Fuller, D. (2004) Going Native, in M.S. Lewis-Beck, A. Bryman and T. Futing Liao (eds) *The Sage encyclopedia of social science research methods*, London: Sage

Funky Dragon (2007) *Our rights, our story*, Cardiff: Funky Dragon

Garland, D. (1996) The limits of the sovereign state: Strategies of crime control in contemporary society *British Journal of Criminology*, 36, 4) 445–71

Garland, D. (2002) *The culture of control*, Oxford: Oxford University Press

Gelsthorpe, L. and Morris, A. (1994) Juvenile justice 1945–1992, in M. Maguire, R. Morgan and R. Reiner (eds) *The Oxford handbook of criminology* Oxford: Oxford University Press

Gelsthorpe, L. and Morris, A. (2002) Restorative youth justice: the last vestiges of welfare? in J. Muncie, G. Hughes and E. McLaughlin (eds) *Youth justice: Critical readings*, London: Sage

Ghate, D. and Ramella, M. (2002) Positive parenting: The national evaluation of the Youth Justice Board's Parenting Programme, London: YJB

Giddens, A. (1990) *The consequences of modernity,* Cambridge: Polity

Giddens, A. (1998) *The third way. The renewal of social democracy*, Cambridge: Polity

Gillis, J.R. (1975) The evolution of juvenile delinquency in England 1890–1914, *Past and Present*, 67, 96–126

Gittell, J.H. (2003) A theory of relational coordination, in K.S. Cameron, J.E. Dutton and R.E. Quinn (eds) *Positive organizational scholarship: Foundations of a new discipline*, San Francisco, CA: Berrett-Koehler Publishing

Glueck, S. and Glueck, E. (1930) *500 criminal careers*, New York: Alfred Knopf

Goldson, B. (2000) *The new youth justice*, Lyme Regis: Russell House

Goldson, B. (2003) 'Tough on children: Tough on justice', paper presented at the Centre for Studies in Crime and Social Justice (Edge Hill) in collaboration with the European Group for the Study of Deviance and Social Control, Chester, UK

Goldson, B. (2005) Taking liberties: Policy and the punitive turn, in H. Hendrick (ed) *Child welfare and social policy*, Bristol: Policy Press

Goldson, B. (2010) The sleep of (criminological) reason: Knowledge-policy rupture and New Labour's youth justice legacy, *Criminology and Criminal Justice*, 10, 2, 155–78

Goldson, B. (2011) The Independent Commission on Youth Crime and Antisocial Behaviour: Fresh start or false dawn? *Journal of Children's Services*, 6, 2, 77–85

Goldson, B. and Hughes, G. (2010) Sociological criminology and youth justice: Comparative policy analysis and academic intervention, *Criminology and Criminal Justice*, 10, 2, 211–30

Goldson, B. and Muncie, J. (2006) Rethinking youth justice: Comparative analysis, international human rights and research evidence, *Youth Justice*, 6, 2, 91–106

Goldson, B. and Muncie, J. (2006) *Youth, crime and justice*, London: Sage

Görgen, T., Evenepoel, A., Kraus, B. and Taef, A. (2013) Prevention of juvenile crime and deviance: Adolescents' and experts' views in an international perspective, *Journal of Criminal Justice and Security*, 15, 4, 531–50

Graham, J. and Bowling, B. (1995) *Young people and crime*, London: Home Office

Gray, P. (2013) Assemblages of penal governance, social justice and youth justice partnerships, *Theoretical Criminology: An International Journal*, 17, 4, 516–33

Haines, A., Goldson, B., Haycox, A., Houten, R., Lane, S., McGuire, J., Nathan, T., Perkins, E., Richards, S. and Whittington, R. (2012) *Evaluation of the Youth Justice Liaison and Diversion (YJLD) pilot scheme. Final report*, Liverpool: University of Liverpool

Haines, K.R. (1996) *Understanding modern juvenile justice: the organisational context of service provision*, Aldershot: Avebury

Haines, K.R. (1997) Young offenders and family support services: A European perspective, *International Journal of Child and Family Welfare*, 97, 1, 61–73

Haines, K.R. (2008) Systems management, in B. Goldson (ed) *The dictionary of youth justice*, Cullompton: Willan

Haines. K.R. (2009a) Systems management, in B. Goldson (ed) *Dictionary of youth justice*, Cullompton: Willan

Haines, K.R. (2009b) The dragonisation of youth justice, in W. Taylor, R. Hester and R. Earle (eds) *Youth justice handbook*, Cullompton: Willan

Haines, K.R. and Case, S.P. (2003) Promoting positive behaviour in schools: The youth social audit, *Youth Justice*, 3, 2, 86–103

Haines, K.R. and Case, S.P. (2005) Promoting Prevention: targeting family-based risk and protective factors for drug use and youth offending in Swansea, *British Journal of Social Work*, 35, 2, 1–18

Haines, K.R. and Case. S.P. (2007) Individual differences in public opinion about youth crime and justice in Swansea, *Howard Journal*, 46, 4, 338–55

Haines, K. R. and Case, S.P. (2008) The rhetoric and reality of the 'Risk factor prevention paradigm' approach to preventing and reducing youth offending, *Youth Justice Journal*, 8, 1, 5–20

Haines, K.R. and Case, S.P. (2009) Putting children first in Wales: The evaluation of Extending Entitlement, *Social Work Review*, 3–4, 22–30, www.revistadeasistentasociala.ro/index.pl/numar_3_4_2009

Haines, K.R. and Case, S.P. (2011) Risks, rights or both? Evaluating the common aetiology of negative and positive outcomes for young people to inform youth justice practice, *Social Work Review*, 2, 109–22

Haines, K.R. and Case, S.P. (2012) Is the Scaled Approach a failed approach? *Youth Justice*, 12, 3, 212–28

Haines, K.R. and Case, S.P. (2015) Youth justice policy in Wales. Children First, Offenders Second. *Howard League ECAN Bulletin*, 5–10, https://d19ylpo4aovc7m.cloudfront.net/fileadmin/howard_league/user/pdf/Research/ECAN/ECAN_bulletin_26.pdf

Haines, K.R. and Drakeford, M. (1998) *Young people and youth justice*, London: Macmillan

Haines, K.R. and O'Mahony (2006) Restorative approaches, young people and youth justice, in B. Goldson and J. Muncie (eds) *Youth crime and justice*, London: Sage

Haines,K.R., Case, S. and Portwood, J. (2004) *Extending entitlement – creating visions of effective practice for young people in Wales*, Cardiff: Welsh Assembly Government

Haines, K.R., Jones, R. and Isles, E. (2001) The causes and correlates of school exclusion: Can targeted social provision prevent school breakdown? Promoting positive behaviour in schools, *Spotlight 58*, Cardiff, Wales Office for Research and Development

Haines, K.R., Case, S., Isles, E. Rees, I. and Hancock, A. (2004) *Extending entitlement: Making it real*, Cardiff: Welsh Assembly Government, www.learning.wales.gov.uk/pdfs/extending-entitlement-making-real-e.pdf,

Haines, K.R., Case, S.P., Charles, A.D. and Davies, K. (2013) The Swansea Bureau: A model of diversion from the youth justice system, *International Journal of Law, Crime and Justice*, 41, 2, 167–87

Hall, G.S. (1905) *Adolescence: Its psychology and its relations to physiology, anthropology, sociology, sex, crime, religion and education*, volume 2. New York: D. Appleton.

Hallett, C. and Prout, A. (eds) (2003) *Hearing the voices of children*, Basingstoke: Taylor and Francis

Hammarberg, T (2008) A juvenile justice approach built on human rights principles, *Youth Justice*, 8, 3, 193–6

Harding, C.J. and Becroft, A.J. (2013) *10 Characteristics of a good youth justice system*. A paper for The Pacific Judicial Development Programme Family Violence and Youth Justice Workshop, Port Vila, Vanuatu

Harris, R. and Webb, D. (1987) *Welfare, power and juvenile justice: The social control of delinquent youth*, London: TavistockHart, D. (2012) *Pre-court arrangements for children who offend*, NAYJ Briefing, NAYJ

Hart, D. and Thompson, C. (2009) *Young people's participation in the youth justice system*, London: NCB

Hart, R. (1992) *Children's participation: From tokenism to citizenship*, Florence: UNICEF

Hawes, M. (2013) Legitimacy and social order: A young people's perspective, unpublished PhD thesis, Swansea: Swansea University

Hawkins, J.D. and Catalano, R.F. (1992) *Communities that care*, San Francisco: Jossey-Bass

Hawkins, J.D. and Weis, J.G. (1985) The social development model: An integrated approach to delinquency prevention, *Journal of Primary Prevention*, 6, 73–97

Hawkins, J.D., Smith, B.H., Hill, K.G., Kosterman, R., Catalano, R.F. and Abbott. R.D. (2003) Understanding and preventing crime and violence. Findings from the Seattle Social Development Project, in T.P. Thornberry and M.D. Krohn (eds) *Taking Stock of Delinquency: An overview of findings from contemporary longitudinal studies*, New York: Kluwer, 255–312

Hayden, C. (2007) *Children in trouble*, Basingstoke: Palgrave/MacMillan

Hazel N. (2008) *Cross-national comparison of youth justice*, London: Youth Justice Board

Hendrick, H. (2003) *Child welfare: Historical dimensions, contemporary debate*, Bristol: Policy Press

Hendrick, H. (2006) Histories of youth crime and justice, in B. Goldson and J. Muncie (eds) *Youth crime and justice*, London: Sage

Henry, S., Henaghan M., Sanders, J. and Munford, R. (2015) Engaging youth in youth justice interventions: Well-being and accountability *Youth Justice* (Online First), http://yjj.sagepub.com/content/early/recent

Hill, M., Lockyer, A. and Stone, F. (2007) *Youth justice and child protection* London: Jessica Kingsley

Hine, J. (2006) Young people, pathways and crime: context and complexity. *Pathways into and out of crime: Taking stock and moving forward: international symposium*. Leicester, April

Hinks, N. and Smith, R. (1985) Diversion in practice: Northants Juvenile Liaison Bureaux, *Probation Journal*, 32: 48–50

Hirschi, T. (1969) *Causes of delinquency* Berkeley: University of California

HM Government (2003) *Respect and responsibility: Taking a stand against antisocial behaviour*, London: HMSO

HM Government (2008) *Youth Crime Action Plan 2008*, London: HMSO

HMI Probation (2009) *Joint inspection findings of youth offending teams in Wales 2003–2008*, London: HMI Probation

Hoffman, S. and Macdonald, S. (2011) Tackling youth anti-social behaviour in devolving Wales: A study of the tiered approach in Swansea', *Youth Justice*, 11, 2, 150–67

Holman, B. and Ziedenberg, J. (2006) *Juvenile offenders and victims 2006 national report*, Washington, DC: US Department of Justice

Home Office (1994) *The cautioning of offenders. Circular 18/1994*, London: Home Office

Home Office (1997) *No more excuses: a new approach to tackling youth crime in England and Wales*, London: HMSO
Home Office (2002) *Offences brought to justice*, London: Home Office
Home Office (2005) *Guidance on publicising anti-social behaviour orders*, London: HMSO
Home Office (2008) *A guide to anti-social behaviour tools and powers*, London: Home Office
Home Office (2011) *More effective responses to antisocial behaviour*, London: Home Office
Home Office and Ministry of Justice (2009) *Prolific and other priority offender programme five years on: Maximising the impact*, London: Home Office/MoJ
Hope, T. (2005) Pretend it doesn't work: The 'anti-social' bias in the Maryland Scientific Methods Scale, *European Journal on Criminal Policy and Research*, 11, 3, 275–96
Hope, T. and Walters, R. (2008) *Critical thinking about the uses of research*, London: Centre for Crime and Justice Studies
Houghton, J. (2011) The partnership approach as a process in dealing with crime and disorder reduction, *Safer Communities*, 10, 4, 14–18
House of Commons Justice Committee (2013) *Youth Justice – Justice Committee*, www.publications.parliament.uk/pa/cm201213/cmselect/cmjust/339/339we07.htm
Howard League for Penal Reform (2007) *The ASBO: Wrong turning, dead end*, London: Howard League
Howe, N. and Strauss, W. (1992) *Generations*, New York: Harper-Collins
Howell, J.C., Krisberg, B., Hawkins, J.D. and Wilson, J.J. (1995) *Guide for implementing the Comprehensive Strategy for Serious, Violent, and Chronic Juvenile Offenders*, Washington, DC: Office of Juvenile Justice and Delinquency Prevention, US Department of Justice
Hoyle, D. (2008) Problematizing Every Child Matters, www.infed.org/socialwork/every_child_matters_a_critique.htm
Hudson, B. (2003) *Justice in the risk society*, London: Sage
Hughes, G. (2004) The community governance of crime, justice and safety: challenges and lesson-drawing, *British Journal of Community Justice*, 2, 3, www.cjp.org.uk/bjcj/volume-2-issue-3/
Hughes, G. (2007) *The politics of crime and community*, Basingstoke, Palgrave Macmillan

Hughes, G., Wright, S., Adams, A., Case, S., Liddle, M. and Haines, K. (2009) *Evaluation of the effectiveness of the Safer Communities Fund 2006–2009*, Final report submitted to the Welsh Assembly Government by Cardiff University, Swansea University and ARCS (UK) Ltd

Iedema, R., Degeling, P. White, L. and Braithwaite, J. (2004) Analysing discourse practices in organisations, *Qualitative Research Journal*, 4, 1, 5–25

Ignatieff, M. (2000) *The rights revolution*, Toronto: House of Anansi Press

ICYCAB (2011) *Time for a fresh start*, London: ICYCAB www.youthcrimecommission.org.uk/

Institute for Criminal Policy Research (2012) *Assessing young people in police custody: An examination of the operation of Triage schemes*, London: Home Office

Ipsos MORI (2010) *A review of techniques for effective engagement and participation*, London: YJB

James, A. and Prout, A. (1997) *Constructing and reconstructing childhood: Contemporary issues in the sociological study of childhood*, London: Routledge

Jamieson, J. (2005) New Labour, youth justice and the question of 'Respect', *Youth Justice Journal*, 5, 180–93

Jepsen, J. (2006) Juvenile justice in Denmark: from social welfare to repression, in E. Jensen and J. Jepsen (eds) *Juvenile law violators, human rights and the development of new juvenile justice*, Oxford: Hart Publishing

Johnstone, G. (2002) *Restorative justice: Ideas, values and debates*, Cullompton: Willan

Jordan, L. and Farrell, J. (2013) Juvenile justice diversion in Victoria: A blank canvas?, *Current Issues in Criminal Justice*, 24, 3, 419–37

Kellett, M. (2011) *Children's perspectives on integrated services: Every child matters in policy and practice*, London: Palgrave Macmillan

Kelly, L. (2012) Representing and preventing youth crime and disorder: Intended and unintended consequences of targeted youth programmes in England', *Youth Justice: An International Journal*, 12, 2, 101–17

Kemshall, H. (2008) Risks, rights and justice: Understanding and responding to youth risk, *Youth Justice* 8, 1, 21–37

Kelly, L., Armitage, V. and Phoenix, J. (2014) Diverse diversions: Youth justice reform, localised practices, and a 'new interventionist diversion'?, paper presented to the British Society of Criminology annual conference, University of Liverpool, UK

Kemshall, H. (2008) Risk, rights and justice: Understanding and responding to youth risk, *Youth Justice*, 8, 1, 21–38

Kilkelly, U. (2008) Youth justice and children's rights: Measuring compliance with international standards, *Youth Justice: An International Journal*, 8, 3, 187–92

King, M. and Szymanski, L. (2006) National Overviews, *State Juvenile Justice Profiles*, Pittsburgh, PA: National Center for Juvenile Justice

Kirby, P. and Bryson, S. (2002) *Measuring the magic: Evaluating and researching young people's participation in public decision-making*, London: Carnegie Young People Initiative

Koocher, G.P. and Keith-Spiegel, P. (1990) *Children, ethics, and the law: Professional issues and cases*, University of Nebraska Press

Kraemer, H.C., Stice, E., Kazdin, A., Offord, D. and Kupfer, D. (2001) How do risk factors work together? Mediators, moderators, and independent, overlapping, and proxy risk factors, *American Journal of Psychiatry*, 158, 848–56

Labour Party (1997) *New Labour because Britain deserves better*, London: Labour Party

Lancaster, Y.P. and Broadbent, V. (2003) *Listening to young children* Maidenhead: Open University Press

Lash, S. and Urry, J. (1988) *The end of organized capitalism*, Wisconsin: The University of Wisconsin Press

Lave, J. and Wenger, E. (2002) Legitimate peripheral participation in community of practice, in R. Harrison, F. Reeve, A. Hanson and J. Clarke (eds) *Supporting lifelong learning: Perspectives on learning*, London and New York: Routledge Falmer

Lelliott, K. (2013) To what extent is Swansea Youth Offending Service review system promoting participatory practice for young people?, unpublished dissertation, Swansea: Swansea University

Lemert, E. (1951) *Social pathology*, New York: McGraw-Hill

Lemert, E. (1967) *Human deviance, social problems and social control*, Englewood Cliffs, NJ: Prentice-Hall

Lemert, E. (1972) *Human deviance, social problems, and social control*, New York: Prentice-Hall

Liddle, M. and Gelsthorpe, L. (1994) *Crime prevention and inter-agency co-operation*, Police Research Series Paper 53, London: Home Office

Lipsey, M.W. and Howell, J.C. (2012) A broader view of evidence-based programs reveals more options for state juvenile justice systems, *Criminology and Public Policy*, 11, 515–23

Lister, R. (1998) From equality to social inclusion: New Labour and the welfare state, *Critical Social Policy*, 18, 55, 215–25

Loader, I. and Sparks, R. (2010) *Public criminology?* London: Routledge

Loeber, R. and Farrington, D.P. (1998) *Serious and violent juvenile offenders: Risk factors and successful interventions*, Thousand Oaks, CA: Sage

London, J. (2007) Power and pitfalls of youth participation in community-based action research, *Children, Youth and Environments*, 17, 2, 406–32

Losada, M. and Heaphy, E. (2004) The role of positivity and connectivity in the performance of business teams: A nonlinear dynamics model, *American Behavioral Scientist*, 47, 6, 740–65

Loveday, B. (2006) Learning from the 2004 crime audit: Crime prevention and community safety, *Crime Prevention and Community Safety*, 8, 3, 188–201

Macdonald, R. and Marsh, J. (2005) *Disconnected youth? Growing up in Britain's poor neighbourhoods*, Basingstoke: Palgrave

Mackenzie, S. (2008) Second-chance punitivism and the contractual governance of crime and incivility: New Labour, old Hobbes, *Journal of Law and Society*, 35, 2, 214–39

Marchant, R. and Kirby, P. (2005) The participation of young children: communication, consultation and involvement, in C. Willow, R. Marchant, P. Kirby, and B. Neale, *Young Children's Citizenship*, York: Joseph Rowntree Foundation

Marková, I. and Gillespie, A. (eds) (2007) *Trust and distrust: Socio-cultural perspectives*, Greenwich, CT: Information Age Publishing, Inc

Marshall, T.F. (1996) The evolution of restorative justice in Britain, *European Journal on Criminal Policy and Research*, 4, 4, 21–43

Mason, P. and Prior, D. (2008) *Engaging young people who offend*, London: YJB

McAra, L. and McVie, S. (2005) The usual suspects? Street-life, young offenders and the police, *Criminal Justice*, 5, 1, 5–36

McAra, L. and McVie, S. (2007) Youth Justice? The impact of system contact on patterns of desistance from offending, *European Journal of Criminology*, 4, 3, 315–45

McAra, L. and McVie, S. (2010) Youth crime and justice: Key messages from the Edinburgh Study of Youth Transitions and Crime, *Criminology and Criminal Justice*, 10, 211–30

McCarthy, P., Laing, K. and Walker, J. (2004) *Offenders of the future: Assessing the risk of children and young people becoming involved in criminal or antisocial behaviour*, London: Department for Education and Skills

McGuire, J. (1995) *What works: Reducing re-offending: Guidelines from research and practice*, Chichester: J Wiley and Sons

McGuire, J. (2001) What works in correctional intervention? Evidence and practical implications, in G. Bernfeld, D.P. Farrington and A. Lescheid (eds) *Offender rehabilitation in practice: Implementing and evaluating effective programs*, Chichester: John Wiley and Sons

McNeill, F. (2009) What works and what's just?, *European Journal of Probation*, 1, 1, 21–40

McNeill, F. and Maruna, S. (2008) Giving up and giving back: desistance, generativity and social work with offenders, in G. McIvor and P. Raynor (eds) *Developments in social work with offenders*. Series: Research Highlights in Social Work (48), London: Jessica Kingsley, 224–339

McNeish, D. and Newman, T. (2002) Involving children and young people in decision-making, in D. McNeish, T. Newman and H. Roberts (eds) *What works for children*, Buckingham: Open University Press, –

Merton, B., Payne, M. and Smith, D. (2004) *An evaluation of the impact of youth work in England. Research Report 606*, http://publications.dcsf.gov.uk/eOrderingDownload/RR606.pdf

Merton, R.K. (1938) Social structure and anomie, *American Sociological Review*, 3, 672–82

Middleton, E. (2006) Youth participation in the UK: Bureaucratic disaster or triumph of child rights? *Children, Youth and Environments* 16, 2, 180–90

Milbourne, L. (2009) Remodelling the third sector: Advancing collaboration or competition in community-based initiatives? *Journal of Social Policy*, 28, 2, 277–97

Miles, H. and Raynor, P. (2014) *Reintegrative justice in practice: The informal management of crime in an island community*, Farnham, Surrey: Ashgate

Millie, A. (2009) *Anti-social Behaviour*, Maidenhead: Open University Press

Millie, A., Jacobson, J., McDonald, E. and Hough, M. (2005) *Anti-social behaviour strategies*, Bristol: Policy Press

Ministry of Justice (2010) *Breaking the cycle: Effective punishment, rehabilitation and sentencing of offenders* London: MOJ

Ministry of Justice (2011) *Breaking the cycle: Government response*, London: MOJ

Ministry of Justice (2012) *Youth Justice Board for England and Wales (triennial review)* London: MOJ

Ministry of Justice (2013) *Anti-social behaviour order statistics 2012*, London: MOJ

Ministry of Justice (2014) *Effective practice library*, www.justice.gov.uk/youth-justice/effective-practice-library

Ministry of Justice, Home Office and YJB (2013) *Youth justice annual statistics 2012-13*, London: MoJ, Home Office and YJB

Ministry of Justice and Youth Justice Board (2013) *Youth out-of-court disposals guide for police and youth offending services*, London: MoJ

Moffitt, T. (1993) Adolescence-limited and life-course-persistent antisocial behavior: a developmental taxonomy, *Psychological Review*, 100, 4, 674–701

Morgan Harris Burrows (2003) *Evaluation of the youth inclusion programme* London: MHB

Morgan Report (1991) *Safer communities: The local delivery of crime prevention through the partnership approach*, London: Home Office

Morgan, R. (2002) *Annual lecture of the National Centre for Public Policy*, Swansea: Swansea University

Morgan, R. (2007) A temporary respite: Jailing young people in ever larger numbers is not the answer to tackling youth crime, Letter to the Guardian newspaper, Feb 19, 2007

Morgan, R. (2009) Report to the Welsh Assembly Government on the question of devolution of youth justice responsibilities, Cardiff: WAG

MORI (2003) *Youth survey 2003. Research Conducted for the Youth Justice Board*, London: MORI/YJB

Morris, A. and Giller, H. (1983) *Providing criminal justice for children*, London: Hodder Arnold

Muncie, J. (1999) *Youth and crime: A critical introduction*, London: Sage

Muncie, J. (2006) Governing young people: Coherence and contradiction in contemporary youth justice, *Critical Social Policy*, 26, 4, 770–93

Muncie, J. (2008a) Managerialism, in B. Goldson (ed) *The dictionary of youth justice*, Cullompton: Willan

Muncie, J. (2008b) The 'punitive' turn in juvenile justice: Cultures of control and rights compliance in Western Europe and the USA, *Youth Justice*, 8, 2, 107–21

Muncie, J. (2009) The United Nations, children's rights and juvenile justice, in: W. Taylor, R. Earle and R. Hester (eds) *Youth justice handbook: Theory, policy and practice*, Cullompton: Willan, 200–10

Muncie, J. (2010) The United Nations, children's rights and juvenile justice, in: W. Taylor, R. Hester and R. Earle (eds) *Youth justice handbook*, London: Routledge, 200–10

Muncie, J. (2011) Illusions of difference: comparative youth justice in the devolved United Kingdom, *British Journal of Criminology*, 51, 1, 40–57

Muncie, J., Hughes. G. and McLaughlin, E. (2002) *Youth justice: Critical issues*, London: Sage

Munro, E. (2007) Confidentiality in a preventive child welfare system, *Ethics and Social Welfare*, 1, 1, 41–55

Mycock, A., Tonge, J. and Jeffery, B. (2012) Does citizenship education make young people better-engaged citizens? *Political Studies*, 60, 3, 578–602

Nacro (2001) *The Nacro guide to crime audits*, London: Nacro

Nacro (2011) *Reducing the number of children and young people in custody*, London: Nacro

Nacro Cymru (2009) *Youth justice and participation in Wales*, Cardiff: Nacro Cymru

National Assembly Policy Unit (2000) *Extending entitlement: Supporting young people in Wales*, Cardiff: National Assembly for Wales

National Assembly Policy Unit (2002) Extending entitlement: support for 11 to 25 year olds in Wales. Direction and guidance, Cardiff: National Assembly for Wales

National Audit Office (2008) *The Home Office: Reducing the risk of violent crime*, London: NAO

National Audit Office (2013) *Early action: Landscape review*, London: NAO

NAYJ (National Association for Youth Justice) (2013) *Children in trouble with the law: An overview of trends and developments 2013*, London: NAYJ

Newburn, T. and Morgan, R. (2007) Youth justice, in M. Maguire, R. Morgan and R. Reiner (eds) *The Oxford handbook of criminology*, fourth edn, Oxford: Oxford University Press 1024–60

Newburn, T. and Souhami, A. (2005) Youth diversion, in N. Tilley (ed) *Handbook of crime prevention and community safety*, Cullompton: Willan

Nolas, S. (2011) Reflections on the enactment of children's participation rights through research: Between transactional and relational spaces, *Children and Youth Services Review*, 33, 7, 1196–202

O'Hara, M. (2014) *Austerity bites: A journey to the sharp end of cuts in the UK*. Bristol: Policy Press

O'Mahony, P. (2009) The risk factors paradigm and the causes of youth crime: A deceptively useful analysis? *Youth Justice*, 9, 2, 99–115

O'Malley, P. (2010) *Crime and risk*, London: Sage

Oerton, S. and Pilgrim, A.N. (2013) Devolution and difference: The politics of sex and relationships education in Wales, *Critical Social Policy*, 34, 1, 3–22

Office for National Statistics (2011) *2011 mid-year estimates*, London: ONS

Pawson, R. and Tilley, N. (1998) *Realistic evaluation*, London: Sage

Paylor, I. (2010) The scaled approach to youth justice: a risky business, *Criminal Justice Matters*, 81, 30–1

Paylor, I. (2011) Youth justice in England and Wales: A risky business, *Journal of Offender Rehabilitation*, 50, 4, 221–33

Paylor, I., Measham, F. and Asher, H. (2012) *Social work and drug use*, Maidenhead: Open University Press

Peay, J. (2012) Insanity and automatism: questions from and about the Law Commission's scoping paper, *Criminal Law Review*, 12, 927–45

Penal Reform International and Interagency Panel on Juvenile Justice (2012) *Ten-point plan for fair and effective criminal justice for children*, London: Penal Reform International

Penman, R. (2010) *Evaluating Our Rights Our Story*, unpublished MPhil thesis, Swansea: Swansea University

Peters, A. (1986) Main currents in criminal law theory, in J. van Dijk, et al (eds) *Criminal law in action*, Arnheim: Gouda Quint BV

Phoenix. J. (2009) Whose account counts? Politics and research in youth justice, in W. Taylor, R. Hester and R. Earle (eds) *Youth Justice Handbook*, Cullompton: Willan/Open University, 73–82

Phoenix, J. and Kelly, L. (2013) 'You have to do it for yourself': Responsibilisation in youth justice and young people's situated knowledge of youth justice practice, *British Journal of Criminology*, 53, 3, 419–37

Pittman, K.J. and Fleming, W.E. (1991) *A new vision: Promoting youth development. Written transcript of a live testimony by Karen J. Pittman given before The House Select Committee on Children, Youth and Families*, Washington, DC: Center for Youth Development and Policy Research

Pittman, K.J., Irby, M., Tolman, J., Yohalem, N. and Ferber, T. (2003) *Preventing problems, promoting development, encouraging engagement competing priorities or inseparable goals?* Washington, DC: The Forum for Youth Investment

Pitts, J. (1988) *The politics of juvenile crime*, London: Sage

Pitts, J. (2001) Korrectional karaoke: New Labour and the zombification of youth justice, *Youth Justice*, 1, 2, 3–16

Pitts, J. (2003) *The new politics of youth crime: Discipline or solidarity?* Lyme Regis: Russell House

Piven, F.F. and Cloward, R. (1982) *The new class war: Reagan's attack on the welfare state*, New York: Pantheon

Pollard, J.A., Hawkins, J.D. and Arthur, M.W. (1999) Risk and protection: Are both necessary to understand diverse behavioral outcomes in adolescence? *Social Work Research*, 23, 3, 145–58

Pratt, J. (1989) Corporatism: The third model of juvenile justice, *British Journal of Criminology*, 29, 3, 236–54

Prelow, H., Loukas, A. and Jordan-Green, L. (2007) Socioenvironmental risk and adjustment in Latino youth: The mediating effects of family processes and social competence, *Journal of Youth and Adolescence*, 36, 465–76

Prince's Trust (2007) *The cost of exclusion. Counting the cost of youth disadvantage in the UK*, London: Prince's Trust

Prior, D. and Mason, P. (2010) A different kind of evidence. Looking for 'what works' in engaging young offenders, *Youth Justice*, 10, 3, 211–26

Puffett, N. (2012) Government warned against using payment-by-results in youth justice, *Children and Young People Now*, 23 October, www.cypnow.co.uk/cyp/news/1075071/government-warned-payment-results-youth-justice#sthash.SgmL0iTl.dpuf

Pupil Voice Wales (2014) www.pupilvoicewales.org.uk/primary/get-involved/having-a-voice/

Quinney, R. (1980) *Providence: The reconstruction of social and moral order*, New York: Longman Inc

RDS (2004) *Defining and measuring antisocial behaviour*, London: HMSO

Richards, K. (2014) Blurred lines: Reconsidering the concept of 'diversion' in youth justice systems in Australia, *Youth Justice*, 14, 2, 122–39

Robinson, A. (2014) *Foundations for youth justice*, Bristol: Policy Press

Rose, N. (1996) The death of the social? Refiguring the territory of government, *Economy and Society*, 25, 3, 327–56

Rutherford, A. (2002) *Growing out of crime: The new era*, Hook: Waterside Press

Safer Swansea Partnership (2008) *Safer Swansea crime and disorder reduction plan 2008–11*, Swansea: SSP

Safer Swansea Partnership (2011) *Safer Swansea crime and disorder reduction plan 2011–14*, Swansea: SSP

Sanders, A., Young, R. and Burton, M. (2010) *Criminal Justice*, Oxford: Oxford University Press

Save the Children (2007) *Stop, look, listen: The road to realising children's rights in Wales*, Cardiff: Save the Children

Schur, E. (1973) *Radical non-intervention: Rethinking the delinquency problem*, Englewood Cliffs, N.J.: Prentice-Hall, Inc

Scraton, P. (2008) Administrative Criminology, in B. Goldson (ed) *Dictionary of youth justice*, Cullompton: Willan

Scraton, P. and Haydon, D. (2002) Challenging the criminalisation of children and young people: Securing a rights-based agenda, in J. Muncie, G. Hughes and E. McLaughlin (eds) *Youth justice: Critical issues*, London: Sage

Scraton, P. and Haydon, D. (2002) Challenging the criminalization of children and young people, in J. Muncie, G. Hughes and E. McLaughlin (eds) *Youth justice: Critical readings*, London: Sage

Sharpe, G. (2011) *Offending girls. Young women and youth justice*, Cullompton: Willan

Sharpe, G. and Gelsthorpe, L. (2009) Engendering the agenda: Girls, young women and youth justice, *Youth Justice*, 9, 3, 195–208

Sherman, L., Gottfredson D., MacKenzie, D., Eck, J., Reuter, P. and Bushway, S. (1998) *Preventing crime: What works, what doesn't, what's promising*, Baltimore: University of Maryland, Department of Criminology and Criminal Justice

Sherman, L.W. and Strang, H. (2004) Verdicts or inventions? Interpreting results from randomized controlled experiments in criminology, *American Behavioral Scientist*, 47, 5, 575–607

Sherman, Lawrence W. and Strang, H. (2007), *Restorative justice: The evidence*, London: The Smith Institute

Smart, B. (1999) *Facing modernity: Ambivalence, reflexivity and morality*, London:

Smith, R. (2005) Welfare versus justice – again! *Youth Justice*, 5, 1, 3–16

Smith, D.J. (2010) *A new response to youth crime*, Cullompton: Willan

Smith, R. (2006) *Youth justice: Ideas, policy and practice*, Cullompton: Willan

Smith, R. (2011) *Doing justice to young people: Youth crime and social justice*, New York: Willan/Routledge

Smith, R. (2014) Reinventing diversion, *Youth justice* 14, 2, 109–21

Social Exclusion Unit (1999) *Bridging the gap*, London: SEU

Social Exclusion Unit (2000) *Report of policy action team 12: Young people*, London: SEU

Souhami, A. (2007) *Transforming youth justice. Occupational identity and cultural change*, Cullompton: Willan

Souhami, A. (2011) Inside the Youth Justice Board: ambiguity and influence in New Labour's youth justice, *Critical Social Policy*, 10, 3, 7–16

Squires, P. and Stephen, D. (2005) *Rougher justice: Antisocial behaviour and young people*, Cullompton: Willan

Stephenson, M., Giller, H. and Brown, S. (2007) *Effective practice in youth justice*, Cullompton: Willan

Such, E. and Walker, R. (2004), Being responsible and responsible beings: Children's understanding of responsibility, *Children and Society*, 18, 231–42

Sutherland, A. (2009) The 'Scaled Approach' in youth justice. Fools rush in …, *Youth Justice*, 9, 1, 44–60

Swansea Children and Young People's Strategy Unit (2007) *Swansea secondary school education statistics*, Swansea: CYPSU

Swansea YOT ASB Department (2014) *Annual ASB statistics for young people 2013–14*, Swansea: Swansea YOT

Swansea Youth Action Network (2010) www.saferswansea.org.uk/index.cfm?articleid=37099

Tankebe, J. (2008) Colonialism, legitimation, and policing in Ghana, *International Journal of Law, Crime and Justice*, 6, 68–70

Thornberry, T.P. (1987) Toward an interactional theory of delinquency, *Criminology*, 25, 4, 863–92

Thorpe, D., Smith, D., Green, C. and Paley, J. (1980) *Out of care – the community support of juvenile offenders*, London: George Allen and Unwin

Tonry, M. and Farrington, D.P. (1995) *Building a safer society: Strategic approaches to crime prevention*, Berkeley: The University of Chicago Press,

Towler, K. (2009) Treating our children as children first, *Criminal Justice Matters*, 76, 1, 42–3

Treseder, P. (1997) *Empowering children and young people, training manual*, London: Save the Children

Tuckermann, H. and Rüegg-Stürm, J. (2010) Researching practice and practicing research reflexively. Conceptualizing the relationship between research partners and researchers in longitudinal studies, *Qualitative Social Research*, 11, 3

Turnbull, G. and Spence, J. (2011) 'What's at risk? The proliferation of risk across child and youth policy in England', *Journal of Youth Studies*, 14, 8, 939–59

Tutt, N. and Giller, H. (1987) Manifesto for management – the elimination of custody, *Justice of the Peace*, 151, 200–2

Tyler, T. (2004) Enhancing police legitimacy, *Annals of the American Academy of 27 Political and Social Science* (W. G. Skogan, ed), 593, 84–99

Tyler, T. (2006) [1990] *Why people obey the law*, Princeton, NJ: Princeton University Press

Tyler, T. (2007) *Legitimacy and criminal justice: International perspectives*, New York: Russell Sage Foundation

Tyler, T.R. and Huo, Y.J. (2002) *Trust in the law: Encouraging public cooperation with the police and courts*, New York: Russell-Sage Foundation

Uggen, C. and Inderbitzen, M. (2010) Public criminologies, *Criminology and Public Policy*, 9, 4, 725–49

UK Children's Commissioners (2008) *UK Children's Commissioners' Report to UN Committee on the Rights of the Child*, www.niccy.org/uploaded_docs/uncrc_report_final.pdf

UN Committee on the Rights of the Child (2008) *Concluding observations of the UN Committee on the Rights of the Child*, Geneva: UNICEF

UNHCHR (2013) *Access to justice for children: Report of the United Nations High Commissioner for Human Rights*, Geneva: United Nations

UNICEF (1989) *United Nations Convention on the Rights of the Child 1989*, Geneva: United Nations

UNICEF (2003) *Freechild project measure for social change*, Florence: UNICEF

United Nations (1985) *United Nations standard minimum rules for the administration of juvenile justice (The Beijing Rules)*, Beijing: UN

United Nations (1990) *United Nations guidelines for the prevention of juvenile delinquency (The Riyadh Guidelines)*, 14 December, A/RES/45/112

United Nations Research Institute for Social Development (2010) *Combating poverty and inequality. Structural change, social policy and politics*, Geneva: United Nations

User Voice (2011) *What's your story? Young offenders' insights into tackling youth crime and its causes*, London: User Voice

Utting, D. (1999) *A guide to promising approaches*, London/York: Communities that Care/JRF

Walker, J., Thompson, C., Laing, K., Raybould, S., Coombes, S., Proctor, S. and Wren, C. (2007) *Youth inclusion and support panels: Preventing crime and antisocial behaviour?* London: DfES

Wallace, N. and Jacobsen, G. (2012) Children reoffend as system goes soft, Sydney, *Morning Herald*, 28 April, 1

Ward, T. and Maruna, S. (2007) *Rehabilitation*, London: Routledge

Ward, T., Yates, P.M. and Willis, G.M. (2011) The Good Lives model and the Risk Need Responsivity model: A critical response to Andrews, Bonta, and Wormith, *Criminal Justice and Behaviour*, 39, 1, 94–110

Waterhouse, L. and McGhee, J. (2002) Children's hearings in Scotland: Compulsion and disadvantage, *Journal of Social Welfare and Family Law*, 24, 3, 279–96

Weatherburn, D., McGrath, A. and Bartels, L. (2012) Three dogmas of juvenile justice, *University of New South Wales Law Journal*, 35, 779–809

Weber, M. (1978) *Economy and society: An outline of interpretive sociology*, Berkeley: University of California Press

Webster, C., MacDonald, R. and Simpson, M. (2006) Predicting criminality: Risk/protective factors, neighbourhood influence and desistance, *Youth Justice*, 6, 1, 7–22

Webster, C., Simpson, D., MacDonald, R., Abbas, A., Cieslik, M., Shildrick, T. and Simpson, M. (2004) *Poor transitions: Social exclusion and young adults*, Bristol: Policy Press

Welsh Assembly Government (2004) *Children and young people: Rights to action*, Cardiff: Welsh Government
Welsh Assembly Government (2007) *One Wales: A progressive agenda for the government of Wales*, Cardiff: Welsh Government
Welsh Assembly Government (2009) *Getting it right*, Cardiff: Welsh Government
Welsh Assembly Government and Youth Justice Board (2008) *Youth crime prevention in Wales: Strategic guidance*, Cardiff: WAG
Welsh Assembly Government and Youth Justice Board (2009) *All Wales youth offending strategy: Delivery plan 2009–11*, Cardiff: WAG
Welsh Government (2011) *Devolution of youth justice: Cabinet briefing*, Cardiff: Welsh Government
Welsh Government (2012) *Proposals to improve services in Wales to better meet the needs of children and young people who are at risk of entering, or are already in, the Youth Justice System*, Cardiff: Welsh Government.
Welsh Government and YJB (Youth Justice Board) (2014) *Children and young people first*, Cardiff: Welsh Government/YJB
Wenger, E. (1998) *Communities of practice: Learning, meaning and identity*, Cambridge: Cambridge University Press
Whyte, B. (2009) Values in youth justice: Practice approaches to welfare and justice for young people in UK jurisdictions, in W. Taylor, R. Hester and R. Earle (eds) *Youth justice handbook*, Cullompton: Willan/Open University, 221–30
Wikström, P.-O. and Treiber, K. (2008) *Offending behaviour programmes: Cognitive behavioural and multisystemic therapies*, Youth Justice Board Source Document
Wilcox, A. (2004) *National evaluation of the youth justice board's restorative justice projects*, London: YJB
Wilding, B. (2007) *Lack of ASBOs is a good thing*, Wales Online, 4 October
Williamson, B. and Cairns, L. (2005) *Working in partnership with young people: from practice to theory*, Durham: Investing in Children and Research in Practice
Williamson, H. (2011) European youth policy, *Youth Exploration*, 3, 89–92
Winterdyk, J. (2005) *Issues and perspectives on young offenders in Canada* (3rd edn), Toronto: Harcourt Brace
Wood, M. (2004) *Perceptions and experiences of antisocial behaviour*, London: Home Office

Yates, J. (2012) What prospects youth justice? Children in trouble in the age of austerity, *Journal of Social Policy and Administration*, 46, 4, 432, 447

YJB Cymru (2012) *A blueprint for promoting effective practice and improving youth justice performance in Wales*, London/Swansea: Youth Justice Board

YOT Managers Cymru (2013) www.yotmanagerscymru.org.uk/

Young, J. (1999) *The exclusive society: Social exclusion, crime and difference in late modernity*, London; Thousand Oaks: Sage Publications,

Youth Justice Board (2003a) *Assessment, Planning Interventions and Supervision*, London: YJB

Youth Justice Board (2003b) *Offending Behaviour Programmes*, London: YJB

Youth Justice Board (2004) *Prolific and Other Priority Offenders Strategy*, London: YJB

Youth Justice Board (2006) *YIP Management Guidance*, London: YJB

Youth Justice Board (2008a) *Engaging young people who offend*, London: YJB

Youth Justice Board (2008b) *Developing restorative justice: An action plan*, London: YJB

Youth Justice Board (2009) *Youth justice: The scaled approach. A framework for assessment and interventions. Post-consultation version two*, London: YJB

Youth Justice Board (2010) *Process evaluation of the pilot of a risk-based approach to interventions*, London: YJB

Youth Justice Board (2011) *Assessment and planning interventions: review and redesign project. Statement of intent – proposed framework*, London: YJB

Youth Justice Board (2012) *Key performance indicators*, London: YJB

Youth Justice Board (2013) *Assessment and planning interventions framework* – AssetPlus, model document, London: YJB

Youth Justice Board and Children and Young People Now (2009) *The scaled approach: Putting young people on the road to success*, London: CYP Now

Zernova, M. (2007) *Restorative justice: Ideals and realities*, Farnham: Ashgate

Index

F

G

Z

Lightning Source UK Ltd.
Milton Keynes UK
UKHW022022231121
394442UK00006B/356